THE WRITER'S SELECTIONS

Shaping Our Lives

Second Edition

Kathleen T. McWhorter

Niagara County Community College

HOUGHTON MIFFLIN COMPANY   Boston   New York

Senior Sponsoring Editor: Mary Jo Southern
Senior Associate Editor: Ellen Darion
Project Editor: Tamela Ambush
Senior Production/Design Coordinator: Jennifer Meyer Dare
Senior Manufacturing Coordinator: Priscilla Bailey
Senior Marketing Manager: Nancy Lyman

COVER DESIGN: Harold Burch, Harold Burch Design, New York City
COVER IMAGE: *Presence Byzantium IV*, 1989, by Richard Pousette-Dart

PHOTO CREDITS: **Chapter 1:** www.corbis.com/Warren Morgan; **Chapter 2:** Tsar
Fedorsky © 1999; **Chapter 3:** Reuters/Corbis-Bettmann; **Chapter 4:** James L.
Stanfield/*National Geographic Magazine;* **Chapter 5:** Lester Sloan/The Gamma Liaison
Network; **Chapter 6:** Corbis/Richard Pasley; **Chapter 7:** Edward Keating/*The New York
Times.*

Printed in the U.S.A.

Library of Congress Catalog Card Number: 99-71950

ISBN: 0-395-95842-3

123456789-CRS-03 02 01 00 99

As part of Houghton Mifflin's ongoing commitment to the environment, this text has
been printed on recycled paper.

Table of Contents

4.   Cultures That Shape Our Lives   121

7.   Technology That Shapes Our Lives   214

Brainstorming About Technology   215

Preface

The Writer's Selections: Shaping Our Lives is a thematic reader developed to meet the specific needs of beginning writers. Using readings as springboards for student writing is a well-recognized and established approach to the teaching of writing, but the readings in most anthologies are inappropriate for developing writers in terms of length, difficulty, and subject matter. Furthermore, beginning writers often lack sophisticated reading skills, and can find these readings troublesome and frustrating. We have all heard comments such as, "You mean I have to read all this just to write a one-page paper?" or "I just got lost trying to read it, so how could I write about it?" Instructors who use readers often find themselves spending more class time explaining the reading and less time teaching writing skills than they would like. *The Writer's Selections: Shaping Our Lives* addresses these concerns by offering brief, accessible, engaging readings and providing structured apparatus that focuses and directs students in order to stimulate writing.

Thematic Organization

Reading exposes us to ideas that can, as the book's subtitle suggests, shape or change our lives. The seven chapters in this text explore some major factors that shape our lives: decisions, other people, events, cultures, media, work, and technology. Each is a category relevant to students' daily experience — a category about which they can think and write. As students read about how people's lives have been shaped by these factors, they may become more fully aware of the impact of such factors on their own lives.

The Reading Selections

The 49 reading selections, chosen with the needs, interests, and learning characteristics of beginning writers in mind, offer instructors choices, but do not leave students with the complaint that most of the book was left unassigned. The readings have the following characteristics:

- **Short.** The readings range in length from very brief, three to four paragraphs, to a maximum of two to three pages. Students will regard them as realistic, "do-able" assignments.

- **Readable.** The readings are within the skill range of most beginning writers; they are thought-provoking but lack burdensome vocabulary or complicated writing style. An occasional longer, more challenging reading is included for instructors to assign to prepare students for readings typically assigned in freshmen composition courses.
- **Engaging.** The readings will spark interest and stimulate thought. Many are personal narratives to which students can relate immediately; others are issue-oriented on topics such as media bias, euthanasia, false advertising, the effects of music, part-time jobs, and inventions of the future. The readings are timely, sometimes humorous, and within the realm of the students' experience.
- **Representative of a Wide Range of Sources.** There is a wide sampling of writers, including Asian, Hispanic, Native American and black writers chosen from a range of periodicals, newspapers, and books. Both textbook writing and student writing are well-represented, with one textbook reading and one student essay included in each chapter.

The Apparatus

The Writer's Selections: Shaping Our Lives is a collection of essays, but it is also an instructional tool. Its apparatus is intended to guide students through the reading, prompt their thinking, and prepare them to write about the reading.

Writing and Reading Process Introduction

Because beginning writers need instruction in how to read and write more effectively, the book opens with an overview of the reading and writing processes. This section guides students through each process, offering numerous skills and strategies for becoming better writers and readers. Preceding this introduction are two four-color inserts that present the writing and reading processes in a visually appealing format.

Chapter Features

Each chapter opens with an introduction that briefly explores the chapter theme and guides students through preliminary "Brainstorming" that makes the theme real and personal. Each chapter concludes with a "Making Connections" section containing writing assignments that link two or more of the readings in the chapter. These assignments encourage students to synthesize ideas and to use sources to support their ideas.

Features Accompanying Each Reading

- **Headnote.** A brief introduction precedes the reading; it focuses the students' attention, identifies the source, and establishes a context for the reading.
- **Reading Strategy.** This section offers practical advice on how to approach each essay. It suggests a particular reading or review technique that will improve the student's comprehension and recall of each essay.
- **Vocabulary Preview.** A list of challenging words used in the reading together with their meanings is given before the reading. Since students preview the words and their meanings before reading, their comprehension of the essay will be strengthened.
- **Finding Meaning.** These questions guide the students in grasping the literal content of each essay. Answering these questions enables students to assess their understanding. Students either confirm that they understand the key points or realize that they have not read as carefully as necessary, in which case a closer reading is encouraged.
- **Understanding Technique.** This section offers questions designed to guide students in analyzing the writer's methodology. For example, students may be asked to evaluate a writer's thesis statement, assess the effectiveness of a title, introduction, or conclusion, or study how the writer uses topic sentences or transitional words and phrases.
- **Thinking Critically.** These questions engage students by provoking thought, sparking lively discussion, and fostering critical analysis. They may be used as collaborative activities or as brainstorming sessions to generate ideas about the reading.
- **Writing About the Reading.** Journal Writing assignments encourage students to explore their ideas and write about them in a journal format. Paragraph-length assignments offer writers the opportunity to explore a focused topic. Essay-length assignments give students experience in narrowing a topic and developing a short essay. Assignments often provide prompts that offer advice on how to approach the assignment or what to include.
- **A Creative Activity.** This activity is intended to stimulate interest and creativity by offering light, spontaneous writing assignments that, alternately, may be used as collaborative learning activities.

Changes to the Second Edition

- **New chapter, "Work That Shapes Our Lives."** Essays in this chapter reflect upon a variety of work experiences and issues including problems in the workplace, the meaning of work, the first jobs of famous people, and part-time employment.
- **New "Reading Strategies" apparatus.** Each essay is preceded by a section that suggests a specific reading or review strategy that will make the essay more accessible to students and improve their comprehension and recall. These strategies will prove useful to the student in other academic contexts, as well. Students may be asked to highlight descriptive language, draw a time line, write annotations, or identify topic sentences, for example.
- **New "Understanding Technique" apparatus.** Questions have been added following each essay that focus the student's attention on the writer's methodology. Students may be asked to analyze a particular part of the essay or determine why particular information is included in the essay, for instance.
- **Fifteen new readings.** New topics include work experiences at Disney, same-sex marriages, family responsibilities, and what it's like to shop for clothes when you cannot see.
- **Cross references.** Cross references have been added in the introductory writing and reading chapters. These references refer students to the Reading and Writing Success Strategies (4-color inserts) and make the strategies more accessible.

Ancillary Materials

The Writer's Guide. *The Writer's Guide* is a brief handbook that may be used in conjunction with *The Writer's Selections*. The two books may be ordered together for a discounted cost. *The Writer's Guide*, organized around questions that student writers frequently ask, provides a concise, easy-to-use reference for the five-step writing process as well as a practical review of grammar and mechanics.

Instructor's Resource Manual. This manual provides practical suggestions for teaching writing along with individual discussions of each reading in the book.

Expressways, Second Edition. Available in DOS, Windows, and Macintosh versions, **Expressways,** Second Edition software, is an interactive tutorial program that allows students to complete a range of writing activities and exercises at their own pace.

Dictionary Deal. The *American Heritage College Dictionary* may be shrink-wrapped with the text at a substantial savings.

Acknowledgments

I appreciate the excellent ideas, suggestions and advice of my colleagues who served as reviewers:

> Kirk Adams, *Tarrant County Junior College*, TX
> Teh-Min Brown, *Las Positas College*, CA
> Mark Connelly, *Milwaukee Area Technical College*, WI
> Bette Daudu, *Montgomery College—Takoma Park Campus*, MD
> Judith Hanley, *Wilbur Wright College*, IL
> Judy Hathcock, *Amarillo College*, TX
> Linda S. Houston, *Ohio State Agricultural Technical Institute*, OH
> Ann Judd, *Seward County Community College*, KS
> Daniel Lowe, *Community College of Allegheny County*, PA
> Julia Nichols, *Okaloosa Community College*, FL
> Michael A. Orlando, *Bergen Community College*, NJ
> Don Ross, *Lamar University—Port Arthur*, TX
> Audrey J. Roth, *Miami-Dade Community College*, FL
> Linda Tappmeyer, *Southwest Baptist University*, MO
> Robert W. Walker, *Daytona Beach Community College*, FL
> Mary Beth Wilk, *Des Moines Area Community College*, IA
> Deanna Yameen, *Quincy College*, MA

The entire staff at Houghton Mifflin deserves praise and credit for their assistance. In particular I wish to thank Mary Jo Southern for her support of the project and Ellen Darion for her guidance. I also wish to thank Beverly Ponzi for her assistance in typing and manuscript management. Finally, I thank my students who have helped me to select appropriate, meaningful readings.

THE WRITER'S SELECTIONS

Shaping Our Lives

Second Edition

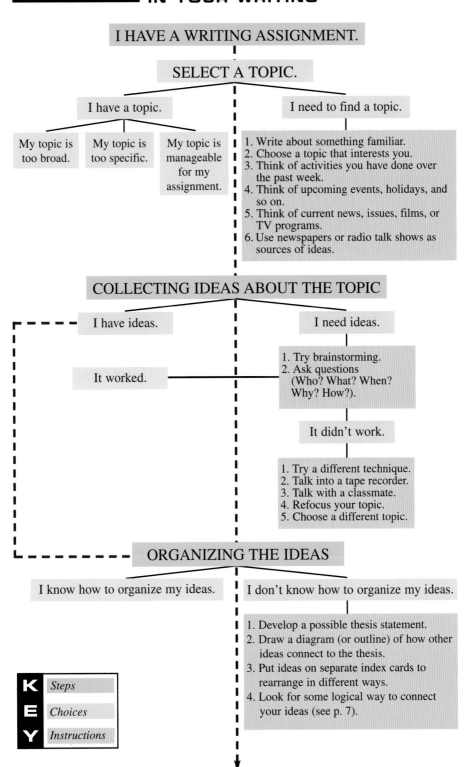

WRITING SUCCESS
Strategy #1

WORKING THROUGH PROBLEMS IN YOUR WRITING

I HAVE A WRITING ASSIGNMENT.

SELECT A TOPIC.

I have a topic.

- My topic is too broad.
- My topic is too specific.
- My topic is manageable for my assignment.

I need to find a topic.

1. Write about something familiar.
2. Choose a topic that interests you.
3. Think of activities you have done over the past week.
4. Think of upcoming events, holidays, and so on.
5. Think of current news, issues, films, or TV programs.
6. Use newspapers or radio talk shows as sources of ideas.

COLLECTING IDEAS ABOUT THE TOPIC

I have ideas.

It worked.

I need ideas.

1. Try brainstorming.
2. Ask questions (Who? What? When? Why? How?).

It didn't work.

1. Try a different technique.
2. Talk into a tape recorder.
3. Talk with a classmate.
4. Refocus your topic.
5. Choose a different topic.

ORGANIZING THE IDEAS

I know how to organize my ideas.

I don't know how to organize my ideas.

1. Develop a possible thesis statement.
2. Draw a diagram (or outline) of how other ideas connect to the thesis.
3. Put ideas on separate index cards to rearrange in different ways.
4. Look for some logical way to connect your ideas (see p. 7).

KEY
- Steps
- Choices
- Instructions

WRITING A FIRST DRAFT

I wrote a draft and I like it.

I'm having trouble getting started.

1. Don't try to write the paper in order from beginning to end; write any part to get started.
2. Just write ideas in sentence form; worry about organizing them later.
3. Write fast and keep writing; don't worry about anything except continuing to write.
4. Dictate into a tape recorder.

I don't like my draft.

1. Let it sit a day; come back when your mind is fresh.
2. Analyze each part (see p. 10-12): determine which parts are weak.
3. If the draft doesn't seem to say much, collect more ideas about your topic.
4. Refocus your topic; it may be either too broad or too narrow.

REVISING THE DRAFT

I know what to revise.

I don't know what to revise.

1. Let it sit a day; return with a fresh mind.
2. Use a revision checklist (see inside back cover).

PROOFREADING

I know how to find my errors.

I'm not sure I will find all my errors.

Spelling Errors

Punctuation Errors

Grammar Errors

1. Use the spelling checker, if using a computer.
2. Read your paper backward, from the last sentence to the first.

Read your paper several times, each time checking for a different type of error.

Read your paper aloud, listening for pauses; punctuation is usually needed.

K	Steps
E	Choices
Y	Instructions

FOLLOW AN ORGANIZING PLAN FOR YOUR ESSAY

To make your essay easy to read and understand, you should follow an organizing plan. An essay has specific parts and each part serves specific purposes for both the reader and the writer.

ESSAY

Note: There is no set number of paragraphs that an essay should contain. This discussion shows six paragraphs, but in actual essays, the number will vary greatly.

PARTS TO INCLUDE

WHAT EACH PART SHOULD DO

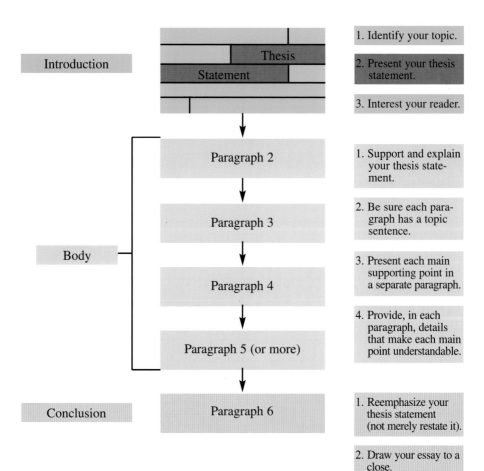

Introduction — Thesis Statement

1. Identify your topic.

2. Present your thesis statement.

3. Interest your reader.

Body — Paragraph 2, Paragraph 3, Paragraph 4, Paragraph 5 (or more)

1. Support and explain your thesis state-ment.

2. Be sure each para-graph has a topic sentence.

3. Present each main supporting point in a separate paragraph.

4. Provide, in each paragraph, details that make each main point understandable.

Conclusion — Paragraph 6

1. Reemphasize your thesis statement (not merely restate it).

2. Draw your essay to a close.

Note: Throughout the essay, transitional words, phrases, and sentences work to lead the reader from idea to idea.

SPEND TIME ORGANIZING EACH PARAGRAPH

Before you write each paragraph of your essay, plan out what you will say and the order in which you will say it.

PARAGRAPH

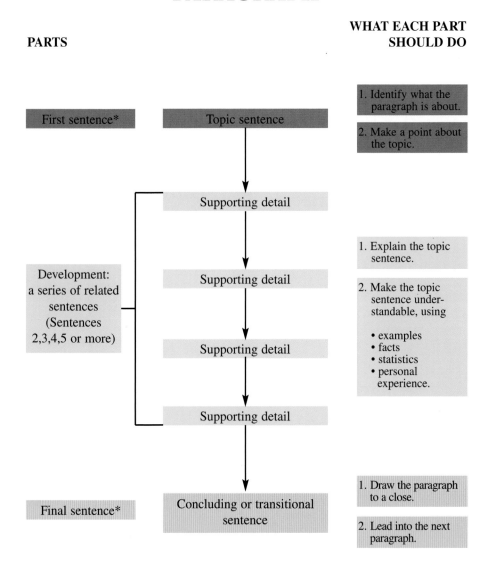

PARTS

WHAT EACH PART SHOULD DO

First sentence*

Topic sentence

1. Identify what the paragraph is about.

2. Make a point about the topic.

Supporting detail

Development: a series of related sentences (Sentences 2,3,4,5 or more)

Supporting detail

Supporting detail

Supporting detail

1. Explain the topic sentence.

2. Make the topic sentence under-standable, using

• examples
• facts
• statistics
• personal experience.

Final sentence*

Concluding or transitional sentence

1. Draw the paragraph to a close.

2. Lead into the next paragraph.

Note: The topic sentence is often placed first, but may appear elsewhere in the paragraph. For emphasis, writers sometimes even place it last in the paragraph.

USE PREVIEWING TO GET STARTED

Previewing is a quick way of finding out what a reading will be about BEFORE you read it. Try previewing the brief reading at the right using the steps listed below.

How to Preview

1. Read the title.

2. Read the introductory note.

3. Check the author's name.

4. Read the introductory paragraph.

5. Read the dark print headings (if any).

6. For readings without headings, read the first sentence of a few paragraphs per page.

7. Glance at any photographs or drawings.

8. Read the last paragraph.

Why Preview?

Previewing has a number of benefits:

1. It gives you a mental outline of the reading BEFORE you read it.

2. Reading will be easier because you have a mental outline: your comprehension will improve.

3. You will be able to remember more of what you read.

4. You will find it easier to concentrate.

Friends All of Us
Pablo Neruda

A Nobel Prize-winning poet's backyard lesson in brotherhood

One time, investigating in the backyard of our house in Temuco [Chile] the tiny objects and minuscule beings of my world, I came upon a hole in one of the boards of the fence. I looked through the hole and saw a landscape like that behind our house, uncared for, and wild. I moved back a few steps, because I sensed vaguely that something was about to happen. All of a sudden a hand appeared — a tiny hand of a boy about my own age. By the time I came close again, the hand was gone, and in its place there was a marvelous white sheep.

The sheep's wool was faded. Its wheels had escaped. All of this only made it more authentic. I had never seen such a wonderful sheep. I looked back through the hole but the boy had disappeared. I went into the house and brought out a treasure of my own: a pinecone, opened, full of odor and resin, which I adored. I set it down in the same spot and went off with the sheep.

I never saw either the hand or the boy again. And I have never again seen a sheep like that either. The toy I lost finally in a fire. But even now, in 1954, almost 50 years old, whenever I pass a toy shop, I look furtively into the window, but it's no use. They don't make sheep like that any more.

I have been a lucky man. To feel the intimacy of brothers is a marvelous thing in life. To feel the love of people whom we love is a fire that feeds our life. But to feel the affection that comes from those whom we do not know, from those unknown to us, who are watching over our sleep and solitude, over our dangers and our weaknesses — that is something still greater and more beautiful because it widens out the boundaries of our being, and unites all living things.

That exchange brought home to me for the first time a precious idea: that all of humanity is somehow together. That experience came to me again much later; this time it stood out strikingly against a background of trouble and persecution.

It won't surprise you then that I attempted to give something resiny, earthlike, and fragrant in exchange for human brotherhood. Just as I once left the pinecone by the fence, I have since left my words on the door of so many people who were unknown to me, people in prison, or hunted, or alone.

That is the great lesson I learned in my childhood, in the backyard of a lonely house. Maybe it was nothing but a game two boys played who didn't know each other and wanted to pass to the other some good things of life. Yet maybe this small and mysterious exchange of gifts remained inside me also, deep and indestructible, giving my poetry light.

KNOW WHAT TO LOOK FOR AS YOU READ

If you know what to look for as you read, you'll find reading is easier, goes faster, and requires less rereading. Use the list below to guide you in reading the essays in this book.

What to Look For

1. THE MEANING OF THE TITLE.

In some essays, the title announces the topic of the essay and may reveal the author's viewpoint toward it. In others, the meaning of the title becomes clear only after you have read the essay (as with the sample essay on the right).

2. THE INTRODUCTION.

The opening paragraph of an essay should be interesting, give background information, and announce the subject of the essay.

3. THE AUTHOR'S MAIN POINT.

This is often called the *thesis statement*. It is the one big idea that the entire essay explains. Often it appears in the first paragraph, but in the sample essay at the right, it does not.

4. SUPPORT AND EXPLANATION.

The essay should explain, give reasons, or offer support for the author's main point.

5. THE CONCLUSION.

The last paragraph should bring the essay to a close. Often, it will restate the author's main point. It may also suggest directions for further thought.

Friends All of Us

Pablo Neruda

A Nobel Prize-winning poet's backyard lesson in brotherhood

One time, investigating in the backyard of our house in Temuco [Chile] the tiny objects and minuscule beings of my world, I came upon a hole in one of the boards of the fence. I looked through the hole and saw a landscape like that behind our house, uncared for, and wild. I moved back a few steps, because I sensed vaguely that something was about to happen. All of a sudden a hand appeared — a tiny hand of a boy about my own age. By the time I came close again, the hand was gone, and in its place there was a marvelous white sheep.

The sheep's wool was faded. Its wheels had escaped. All of this only made it more authentic. I had never seen such a wonderful sheep. I looked back through the hole but the boy had disappeared. I went into the house and brought out a treasure of my own: a pinecone, opened, full of odor and resin, which I adored. I set it down in the same spot and went off with the sheep.

I never saw either the hand or the boy again. And I have never again seen a sheep like that either. The toy I lost finally in a fire. But even now, in 1954, almost 50 years old, whenever I pass a toy shop, I look furtively into the window, but it's no use. They don't make sheep like that any more.

I have been a lucky man. To feel the intimacy of brothers is a marvelous thing in life. To feel the love of people whom we love is a fire that feeds our life. But to feel the affection that comes from those whom we do not know, from those unknown to us, who are watching over our sleep and solitude, over our dangers and our weaknesses — that is something still greater and more beautiful because it widens out the boundaries of our being, and unites all living things.

That exchange brought home to me for the first time a precious idea: that all of humanity is somehow together. That experience came to me again much later; this time it stood out strikingly against a background of trouble and persecution.

It won't surprise you then that I attempted to give something resiny, earthlike, and fragrant in exchange for human brotherhood. Just as I once left the pinecone by the fence, I have since left my words on the door of so many people who were unknown to me, people in prison, or hunted, or alone.

That is the great lesson I learned in my childhood, in the backyard of a lonely house. Maybe it was nothing but a game two boys played who didn't know each other and wanted to pass to the other some good things of life. Yet maybe this small and mysterious exchange of gifts remained inside me also, deep and indestructible, giving my poetry light.

ANNOTATE:
READ WITH A PEN IN HAND

What is Annotation?

Annotating is a way of keeping track of your impressions, ideas, reactions, and questions AS YOU READ. It is also a way of marking key phrases, sentences, or paragraphs to return to. When you are ready to discuss and/or write about the reading, you will find your annotations helpful. Study the sample annotations on this page to see how it is done.

How to Annotate

Here is a partial list of the things you might want to annotate:

1. questions that come to mind as you read

2. key events that you may want to refer to again

3. particularly meaningful expressions or descriptions

4. important ideas you may want to find again

5. sections where you need further information

6. sections where the author reveals his or her feelings or reasons for writing

7. striking examples

8. key supporting information— dates, statistics, etc.

9. your personal reactions (agreement, anger, amazement, shock, surprise, humor)

10. ideas you disagree with

Timesaving Tip: Devise a code system. Bracket key ideas, underline key events, circle unusual expressions, etc. Consider using color to distinguish types of annotations.

Friends All of Us
Pablo Neruda

A Nobel Prize-winning poet's backyard lesson in brotherhood

One time, investigating in the backyard of our house in Temuco [Chile] the tiny objects and minuscule beings of my world, I came upon a hole in one of the boards of the fence. I looked through the hole and saw a landscape like that behind our house, uncared for, and wild. I moved back a few steps, because I sensed vaguely that something was about to happen. All of a sudden a hand appeared — a tiny hand of a boy about my own age. By the time I came close again, the hand was gone, and in its place there was a marvelous white sheep.

The sheep's wool was faded. Its wheels had escaped. All of this only made it more authentic. I had never seen such a wonderful sheep. I looked back through the hole but the boy had disappeared. I went into the house and brought out a treasure of my own: a pinecone, opened, full of odor and resin, which I adored. I set it down in the same spot and went off with the sheep.

I never saw either the hand or the boy again. And I have never again seen a sheep like that either. The toy I lost finally in a fire. But even now, in 1954, almost 50 years old, whenever I pass a toy shop, I look furtively into the window, but it's no use. They don't make sheep like that any more.

I have been a lucky man. To feel the intimacy of brothers is a marvelous thing in life. To feel the love of people whom we love is a fire that feeds our life. But to feel the affection that comes from those whom we do not know, from those unknown to us, who are watching over our sleep and solitude, over our dangers and our weaknesses — that is something still greater and more beautiful because it widens out the boundaries of our being, and unites all living things.

That exchange brought home to me for the first time a precious idea: that all of humanity is somehow together. That experience came to me again much later; this time it stood out strikingly against a background of trouble and persecution.

It won't surprise you then that I attempted to give something resiny, earthlike, and fragrant in exchange for human brotherhood. Just as I once left the pinecone by the fence, I have since left my words on the door of so many people who were unknown to me, people in prison, or hunted, or alone.

That is the great lesson I learned in my childhood, in the backyard of a lonely house. Maybe it was nothing but a game two boys played who didn't know each other and wanted to pass to the other some good things of life. Yet maybe this small and mysterious exchange of gifts remained inside me also, deep and indestructible, giving my poetry light.

Handwritten annotations:
How did he know?
Why? What has happened in his life?
How can he feel affection for people he doesn't know?
What happened?
Thesis explains why he writes poetry.

ASK CRITICAL THINKING QUESTIONS

To get the full meaning out of the essay and to make writing about the reading easier, ask yourself questions during and after reading that will help you think critically and analyze the reading. Here are some useful questions along with sample answers applied to the "Friends All of Us" reading.

Critical Reading Questions and Answers

1. **Q.** What types of evidence or reasons does the author use to explain or support the thesis statement? Was adequate support provided?

   A. Neruda uses an event (the exchange of toys), personal experience, and personal reactions to support his thesis.

2. **Q.** Did the author present a one-sided (biased) view of the topic or were both sides of the issue examined?

   A. Neruda's view was one-sided; he was presenting his personal viewpoint.

3. **Q.** What big issues (big questions about life) does this essay deal with? Do you agree or disagree with the author's viewpoint toward these issues?

   A. The essay deals with human relationships, brotherhood, and the common bond among people.

4. **Q.** Why did the author write the essay?

   A. Neruda wrote to explain how an event helped him understand human relationships and to explain how he sees poetry as a gift to others.

5. **Q.** What key message about "Shaping Our Lives," the theme of this book, does Neruda convey in this essay?

   A. Neruda shows how simple events —the exchange of toys—can have an impact on one's life.

6. **Q.** What further information, if any, did you need?

   A. More information is needed about the persecution and trouble Neruda experienced.

Friends All of Us
Pablo Neruda

*A Nobel Prize-winning poet's
backyard lesson in brotherhood*

One time, investigating in the backyard of our house in Temuco [Chile] the tiny objects and minuscule beings of my world, I came upon a hole in one of the boards of the fence. I looked through the hole and saw a landscape like that behind our house, uncared for, and wild. I moved back a few steps, because I sensed vaguely that something was about to happen. All of a sudden a hand appeared — a tiny hand of a boy about my own age. By the time I came close again, the hand was gone, and in its place there was a marvelous white sheep.

The sheep's wool was faded. Its wheels had escaped. All of this only made it more authentic. I had never seen such a wonderful sheep. I looked back through the hole but the boy had disappeared. I went into the house and brought out a treasure of my own: a pinecone, opened, full of odor and resin, which I adored. I set it down in the same spot and went off with the sheep.

I never saw either the hand or the boy again. And I have never again seen a sheep like that either. The toy I lost finally in a fire. But even now, in 1954, almost 50 years old, whenever I pass a toy shop, I look furtively into the window, but it's no use. They don't make sheep like that any more.

I have been a lucky man. To feel the intimacy of brothers is a marvelous thing in life. To feel the love of people whom we love is a fire that feeds our life. But to feel the affection that comes from those whom we do not know, from those unknown to us, who are watching over our sleep and solitude, over our dangers and our weaknesses — that is something still greater and more beautiful because it widens out the boundaries of our being, and unites all living things.

That exchange brought home to me for the first time a precious idea: that all of humanity is somehow together. That experience came to me again much later; this time it stood out strikingly against a background of trouble and persecution.

It won't surprise you then that I attempted to give something resiny, earthlike, and fragrant in exchange for human brotherhood. Just as I once left the pinecone by the fence, I have since left my words on the door of so many people who were unknown to me, people in prison, or hunted, or alone.

That is the great lesson I learned in my childhood, in the backyard of a lonely house. Maybe it was nothing but a game two boys played who didn't know each other and wanted to pass to the other some good things of life. Yet maybe this small and mysterious exchange of gifts remained inside me also, deep and indestructible, giving my poetry light.

Shaping Your Writing and Reading Skills:

An Introduction to This Book

Many people, events, and ideas influence our lives. This collection of readings explores seven major factors that influence our lives: decisions, events, work, cultures, others, media, and technology. You will read about how other people's lives have been shaped by these factors. By learning how these factors affect others, you will begin to realize more fully how they shape the course of your own life.

As you read these selections about factors that shape our lives, you will be shaping your own reading and writing skills. You will read a variety of articles and essays, some by professional writers and others by student writers from different colleges across the country. You will discover new ideas and new ways of looking at things. As you read, you will encounter a wide range of writing styles, ways of approaching a topic, and methods of organizing ideas. These will give you ideas for your own writing and will also make you a versatile reader who can adapt to a wide range of reading materials.

Following each reading, you will work with different writing tasks that include journal writing as well as paragraph, essay, and creative activity assignments. These assignments will give you an opportunity to explore your ideas about the topic of the reading and to explore how your life is shaped by decisions, events, work, cultures, others, media, and technology. As you complete these writing tasks, you will have the opportunity to plan, organize, write, and revise your ideas. The following section explains and gives examples of each of these steps. This text also contains two useful reference sections, "Success Strategies for Writers" and "Success Strategies for Readers" on pages xvii-xxiv. Refer to these often as you work through the reading and writing tasks.

1

THE WRITING PROCESS

Writing is a means of expressing your ideas. Throughout this book you will be asked to write essays in which you discuss your ideas about a reading or ideas suggested by it. This introduction will help you get started by showing you the steps that most writers follow to produce a well-written essay. The five steps are

1. Generating ideas
2. Organizing ideas
3. Writing a first draft
4. Revising and rewriting
5. Proofreading

If you use each of these steps, writing will become easier for you. You will avoid the frustration of staring at a blank sheet of paper. Instead, you will feel the satisfaction of putting your ideas into words and making headway toward producing a good essay. For more help, see Writing Success Strategy 1.

As you work through this chapter and complete the questions that follow each reading, if you meet unfamiliar terms about the writing process, check the Glossary on p. 251.

Generating Ideas

The first step before writing is to generate ideas about your topic. You can use four techniques to do this:

1. Freewriting
2. Brainstorming
3. Branching
4. Questioning

These four techniques can help you overcome the common problem of feeling that you have nothing to say. They can unlock ideas you already have and help you discover new ones. Each of these techniques provides a different way to generate ideas. Feel free to choose from among them, using whichever technique seems most effective for the task at hand.

Freewriting

Freewriting involves writing nonstop for a limited period of time, usually three to five minutes. Write whatever comes into your mind, whether it is about the topic or not. If nothing comes to mind, you can just write, "I'm not thinking of anything." As you write, don't be concerned with grammar, punctuation, or spelling, or with writing in complete sentences. Words and phrases are fine. Focus on recording your thoughts as they come to you. The most important thing is to keep writing without stopping. Write fast; don't think about whether your writing

> Playing the lottery is a get rich quick dream.
> Many people play it, but hardly anyone wins. Most
> people think they have a chance to win. They do
> have a chance, but it is a very small chance. So
> why do people continue to play? Some people are
> lucky and they win small amounts often and this
> keeps them going. My grandfather is like that.
> He wins a couple of dollars every month—
> sometimes more. But he has never won anything
> big. I wonder how much money a state makes from
> each lottery draw. I think lotteries take advantage
> of poor people. They really don't have the money
> to waste on a lottery, but the advertising draws
> them in. In New York state the slogan "All it
> takes is a dollar and a dream" is very misleading.
> Some people are addicted to playing, I don't think
> they could stop playing if they wanted to. At
> least the money earned from state-run lotteries
> should directly help those who play.

is worthwhile or makes sense. After you finish, reread what you have written. Underline everything that you might be able to use in your paper. Above is a sample of freewriting on the topic of playing the lottery.

Freewriting is a creative way to begin translating ideas and feelings into words, without being concerned about their value or worrying about correctness. You'll be pleasantly surprised by the number of usable ideas this technique uncovers. Of course, some of your ideas will be too broad; others might be too personal; still others may stray from the topic. In the freewriting above, there are several usable sets of ideas: addiction to lotteries, reasons people play, misleading advertising, and use of revenues from lotteries.

Brainstorming

Brainstorming is a way of developing ideas by making a list of everything you can think of about the topic. You might list feelings, ideas, facts, examples, or problems. There is no need to write in sentences; instead, list words and phrases. Don't try to organize your ideas, just list them as you think of them. Give yourself a time limit. You'll find that ideas come faster that way. You can brainstorm alone or with friends. You'll discover many more ideas with your friends, because their ideas will help trigger more of your own. When you've finished, reread your list and mark usable ideas. Here is an example of ideas generated during a brainstorming session on the topic of stress.

Sample Brainstorming

pressure
things not under control
feel like you're losing it
little things bother you
how to get rid of or control
daily hassles add up
need to relax
need to learn to manage my time
feeling put upon

headaches, neck aches
feel tired and rushed
can ruin your day
avoid problems
everybody experiences it
stressed-out people are crabby
big problems make it worse
avoid stressful situations
keep a balanced outlook

Stress is too broad a topic for a short essay, but there are several groups of usable ideas here: symptoms of stress, causes of stress, and ways to control stress. Any of these topics would make a good paper.

Branching

Branching is a visual way of generating ideas. To begin, write your topic in the middle of a full sheet of paper. Draw a circle around it.

BRANCHING DIAGRAM I

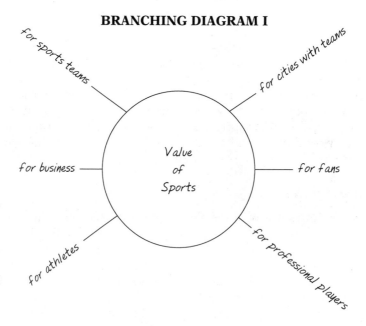

Next, think of related ideas and write them near your center circle. Connect each to the central circle with a line. Call these ideas the primary branches. Your topic is like a tree trunk, and your ideas are like primary limbs that branch out from it. On page 4 is an example of a branching diagram that one student drew on the topic of the value of sports.

You can connect other related ideas to the main branches with smaller, or secondary, branches. In the next example, the student looked at his first branching diagram and decided to focus on one of the narrower topics (the value of sports for athletes) he had put on a primary branch.

BRANCHING DIAGRAM II

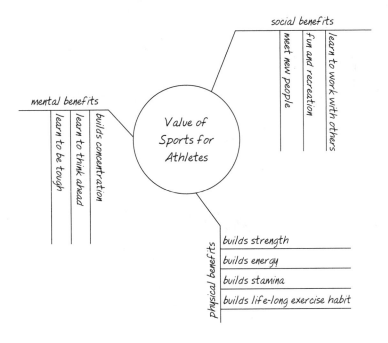

The student used "value of sports for athletes" as the trunk; then he created primary branches: mental benefits, social benefits, and physical benefits. Then he drew secondary branches onto each of the primary ones, and he could have kept going. If you use this technique, you can branch from your branches until you run off the paper. But there's no need to develop secondary branches for every main branch. Choosing one branch that interests you or that you're familiar with and ignoring all the other possibilities is fine. When you have finished branching, use a different color pen to mark those branches that seem usable for your paper.

Questioning

Another way to generate ideas about a given topic is to ask questions. The questions *what? why? where? when? how?* and *who?* are an effective way to explore any topic. As with freewriting and brainstorming, write any question that comes to mind. Don't worry if it seems silly, and don't stop to evaluate whether it is really related to the topic. If you can think of answers, include them as well, but don't limit yourself to questions for which you know the answers. When you have finished, reread what you have written and underline questions or answers that you might be able to use in writing your paper. Here are the questions one student wrote on the topic of television talk shows:

Sample Questions

Why do people watch them?

Does it make them feel better to see others with problems?

Do viewers get hooked on talk shows?

Why aren't they doing more important things, like working?

Do the shows help them forget their own problems?

How are participants chosen?

Are they paid?

Why do they participate?

What do the participants' families think of them?

Why are these shows so popular?

How do they affect those who watch?

When to Use Which Technique

Now that you have tried freewriting, brainstorming, branching, and questioning, you are probably wondering when to use each technique. In general, there are no rules to follow. The best advice is to use the technique that you find most comfortable. Try to use each more than twice before deciding which you prefer. You may find that for certain topics, one technique works better than the others. For example, suppose you decided to write an essay about your mother's sense of humor. While it might be difficult to think of questions, freewriting might help you remember important, humorous events in your life together. In a different situation, however, questioning might be the most effective technique. Suppose you are studying religious institutions in your sociology class, and your instructor has assigned a paper that requires you to explain your personal religious beliefs. Asking questions about your beliefs is likely to produce useful ideas that you can include in your paper.

Sorting Usable Ideas

Freewriting, brainstorming, branching, and questioning each produce a wide range of usable ideas, but you shouldn't feel as if you need to write about all of them. You can sort through them to decide which ones you can put together to produce your paper. Sometimes you may find that you would like to narrow your topic and develop just one idea in your paper, as did the student who made the branching diagram on the value of sports.

Organizing Ideas

Once you have used freewriting, brainstorming, branching, or questioning to generate ideas about your topic, the next step is to decide how to organize these ideas. Ideas in an essay should progress logically from one to another. Group or arrange your ideas in a way that makes them clear and understandable. See Writing Success Strategy 2.

Suppose you used brainstorming to generate ideas on the topic of television talk shows, as was done on page 6. Then you decided to focus on the narrower topic of reasons why people watch talk shows. From a second brainstorming, you identified the following ideas for possible use in your essay:

shows can be informative
forget your own problems
can't stop watching
offer a place to belong, feel part of something
shows fill empty time
people like to hear about other people

learn how other people solved their problems
get "hooked"
like to watch people be exploited by host
like to watch audience reactions

In rereading your list, suppose you decide to organize your ideas by arranging them from most to least obvious or well known. The next step is to rewrite your list, listing your ideas in the order in which you will discuss them in your paper. Then reread your new list and cross off ideas that you don't like, or ideas that are too similar to another idea. For example, "get 'hooked'" is similar to "can't stop watching," so cross it out. Here is a revised list of ideas, arranged from most to least obvious:

1. people like to hear about other people
2. like to watch audience reactions
3. learn how other people solved their problems
4. shows can be informative
5. forget your own problems
6. like to watch people be exploited by host
7. offer a place to belong, feel part of something
8. can't stop watching

Your ideas will not always sort out as neatly as these, but trying to organize your ideas will help you develop a well-structured essay. Sometimes new ideas will grow out of your efforts to rework and rearrange other ideas.

Writing a First Draft

Drafting is a way of trying out ideas to see if and how they work. When drafting, before you settle on what your final essay will say, you can experiment with expressing your ideas one way, then expressing them differently. In your first draft you might use examples to explain your idea; if that does not work, you might switch to using reasons.

A first draft expresses your ideas in sentence form. Work from your organized list of ideas, focusing on expressing and developing each one more fully. Don't be concerned with grammar, spelling, or punctuation at this stage; instead, concentrate on what you are saying. See Writing Success Strategies 2 and 3.

TIPS for Writing a First Draft

1. After you have thought carefully about the ideas in your list, try to write one sentence that expresses your overall main point. Think of this as a working thesis statement.
2. Concentrate on developing and explaining your working thesis statement.
3. Write down more fully developed ideas from your list in the order in which you organized them.
4. If you are not sure whether you should include an idea from your list, include it. You can always delete it later. Add new ideas as you think of them.
5. Do not get bogged down in finding the best wording for an idea. Just write the idea as you think of it. You will have time to fix it later as you revise.
6. Think of a first draft as a chance to experiment with different ideas and methods of organization. While you are

working, if you think of a better way to organize or express your ideas, make changes or start over.

7. As your draft develops, feel free to change your focus or even your topic. If you decide to change your draft, use freewriting, brainstorming, branching, or questioning to develop new ideas.

8. Be prepared to change things around later. What you write as your last sentence might turn out to be a good beginning.

9. If your draft is not working, don't hesitate to throw it out and start over. Most writers have many false starts before they produce a draft with which they are satisfied.

10. If you think you need more ideas, go back to the generating ideas step. It is always all right to go back and forth among the steps in the writing process.

11. When you finish your first draft, you should feel as if you have the beginnings of an essay you will be happy with.

Here is a sample early draft of an essay on why people watch talk shows.

First Draft

It seems like every time I turn on my television, some kind of talk show is on. A few years ago, they were on mornings or late evenings, but now talk shows are on at all hours of the day. Why do people watch them? They watch them for a number of reasons, some good, some not so good.

The most obvious reason is that people find talk shows relaxing and entertaining. They also like to hear about other people. They like to get involved with other people, their problems, the details of their lives. And certainly talk show participants do tell you everything about their lives. Part of this involvement with other people comes from watching the audience and listening to their reactions and questions. Watching a talk show gives people ideas of how to solve their own problems and to get a sense of where a particular situation is headed if it is not corrected.

Talk shows can be informative. Viewers learn sources of help with personal problems. They may learn something about what to do or not to do to improve a personal relationship.

Talk shows help the viewer forget his or her own problems. By getting involved with someone else's problems, viewers tend to forget their own. Also, the problems on the show are so terrible that the viewer's own problems seem small by comparison.

Talk shows appeal to the instinct that many of us have for enjoying watching other people. We like to watch the participants, but we also like to watch the host exploiting, embarrassing, or taking advantage of the participants.

People like to feel as if they are part of something. Some friends of mine are on a first-name basis with several talk show hosts and talk as if they are personal friends with them.

Finally, some people watch talk shows because they can't help themselves—they're addicted. Before I started back to school I was a talk show addict. I would watch talk shows all morning and a good part of the afternoon. Then I would wonder what happened to my day and why I didn't get anything done. Although talk shows do have benefits, and there are plenty of good reasons people watch them, I feel they are dangerous!

Revising and Rewriting

Revision is a process that involves evaluating a draft and changing it to make it more effective. When you finish a first draft, you are more or less satisfied with it. Then, when you reread it later, you see you have more work to do.

Before you submit a paper, you may need to write two, three, or even four drafts. Revising often involves much more than changing a word or rearranging a few sentences. (See the Revision Checklist on the inside of the back cover.) Revising requires that you *rethink* your ideas. It might mean changing, deleting, or rearranging some of them and adding to them. Revision is not concerned with correcting spelling and punctuation errors, or with making sentences grammatical. Make these changes later when you are satisfied with your ideas. Here is a later draft of the first draft shown on pp. 9 and 10.

Later Draft

It seems as if every time one turns on the television, some kind of talk show is on. A few years ago, they were on mornings or late evenings, but now talk shows are on at all hours of the day. Why do people watch them? They watch them to relax, to watch others, and to feel part of something.

The most obvious reason that people watch talk shows is that they find talk shows relaxing and entertaining. The shows provide a welcome relief from daily hassles. By getting involved with someone else's problems, viewers tend to forget their own. Also, the problems on the show are so terrible that the viewer's own problems seem small by comparison. Who could worry about being able to make a car payment when a man on the show has just discovered that his wife is also married to his brother?

Talk shows are also popular because they appeal to our instinct to enjoy watching other people. This instinct is sometimes called voyeurism. People like to watch and hear about other people. They like to hear about their problems and the details of the lives of others. Certainly talk show participants do tell you everything about their lives. Viewers like to watch the participants, but they also enjoy watching the host exploiting, embarrassing, or taking advantage of them. Viewers enjoy watching the audience react and question the participants.

Finally, people watch talk shows because they like to feel as if they are part of something. Some friends of mine are on a first-name basis with several talk show hosts and talk as if they were personal friends with them. They become personally involved with the participants and act as if they are part of the audience.

There is one last reason why people watch talk shows—because they can't help themselves. They are addicted. Before I started back to school, I was a talk show addict. I would watch talk shows all morning and a good part of the afternoon. Then I would wonder what happened to my day and why I didn't get anything done. Although talk shows do have benefits, and there are plenty of good reasons people watch them, they are dangerous!

In making the above revision, the writer decided that the first draft seemed like a list with many very short paragraphs, and so he decided to group the ideas into three main categories: the need to relax, the need to watch, and the need to feel part of something. Then he reorganized the essay and reworked several paragraphs. The author also removed the idea that talk shows provide information, since it did not seem to fit into any of his new categories.

TIPS for Revising and Rewriting

1. Try to let your first draft sit a while before you begin revising it. If possible, wait until the next day, but even a few hours away from the draft will be helpful.
2. Reread the sentence that expresses your main point. It must be clear, direct, and complete. Experiment with ways to improve it.
3. Reread each of your other sentences. Does each relate directly to your main point? If not, cross it out or rewrite it to clarify its connection to the main point. If all of your sentences relate to a main point that is different from the one you've written, rewrite the sentence that expresses the main point.
4. Make sure your essay has a beginning and an end.

5. Read your draft again to see whether your sentences connect to one another. If necessary, add words or sentences to connect your ideas.
6. Delete or combine sentences that say the same thing.
7. Replace words that are vague or unclear with more descriptive words.
8. If you get stuck at any of these stages and cannot see what changes are needed, ask a friend to read your essay and mark ideas that are unclear or need more explanation.
9. After you have made one set of revisions, wait a few hours and then repeat all of these steps.
10. When you have finished revising, you should feel quite satisfied both with what you have said and with the way you have said it.

Proofreading

Proofreading is checking for errors, a final polishing of your work. Don't be concerned with proofreading until all your rethinking of ideas and other revisions are done. Check for each of these types of errors:

- Run-on sentences
- Sentence fragments
- Spelling
- Punctuation
- Grammar
- Capitalization

TIPS for Proofreading

1. Review your essay once for each type of error. First, read it for run-on sentences and sentence fragments. Then read it four more times, each time paying attention to only one thing: grammar, spelling, punctuation, and so forth.
2. To spot spelling errors, read your essay from last sentence to first sentence and from last word to first word. The flow of ideas will not matter, and so you can focus on spotting errors.
3. Read each sentence aloud, slowly and deliberately. This will help you catch missing words, endings you have left off verbs, or missing plurals.

4. Check for errors again as you rewrite or type your essay in final form. Don't do this when you are tired; you might introduce new mistakes. Then proofread your final paper one last time.
5. Use the grammar-and-spell check on your computer. These programs may not catch all your errors, but they may find some you have overlooked.

THE READING PROCESS

Reading is a means of understanding and responding to an author's message. In this book you will read a wide variety of essays, each written by a different author. As you read each essay, first focus on what the author says and then, once you've understood the message, think about and react to the ideas the essay presents. This introduction will help you to read essays by offering some practical advice on how to get involved, understand the author's message, read and think critically, remember what you have read, and get ready to write.

Getting Involved with the Reading

If you are interested in and involved with an essay, it will be easier to read, as well as easier to react to and write about. Use the following suggestions to get involved with each essay you are assigned.

Choose the right time and place to read. Be sure to read at a time when you can concentrate—when you are not tired, weary from working on other assignments, hungry, or feeling stressed. Choose a place that is quiet and free of distractions—one in which nothing will compete for your attention.

Preview the essay. Use the steps listed in Reading Success Strategy 1, "Use Previewing to Get Started," to become familiar with what the essay is about before you read it. Refer to this color insert frequently until you are familiar with the previewing process. Previewing will enable you to read the essay more easily because you will know what to expect and how the essay is organized.

Connect the topic of the essay with your own experience. Try to discover what you already know about the topic of the essay. At first, you may think you know little or nothing about it, but for most of the essays in this book, you do have some knowledge of or experience with the topic. For example, suppose an essay is about managing stress. At first, you may not think you know much about it, but all of us have experienced stress and have learned how to deal with it. What do you do when you are under pressure? How do you react? What do you do to cope with or escape the pressure? These questions are probably bringing ideas to mind. Here are two ways to jump-start your memory on a given topic:

- Ask as many questions as you can about the topic. Suppose your topic is radio talk show hosts. You could ask questions such as, Why are they popular? What kinds of personalities do they have? Who is the most popular? Why do they sometimes insult people? Why do people agree to talk to them? Who chooses the topics they discuss? Questions such as these will get you interested in the reading and help you maintain interest as you read.
- Brainstorm a list of everything you know about the topic. Suppose the topic is the treatment of AIDS. Make a list of the things you know. You might list people you know who were treated, information you have read about experimental drugs, and so forth.

Read the discussion questions or writing assignments before reading the essay.   If you know what you will be expected to discuss and write about after reading, you will find it easier to keep your mind on the reading.

Getting the Author's Message

Before you can discuss or write about a reading, you have to be sure you have understood what the author was saying. At times, this is easy. But sometimes, depending on the author, the style of writing, and the topic, it is not so easy. Here are some suggestions to use to be sure you are getting the author's message. (See also Reading Success Strategy 2.)

Understand Essay and Paragraph Organization

Once you are familiar with the way essays and paragraphs within essays are organized, you will find them easier to understand. Begin by studying the charts in Writing Success Strategies 2 and 3. These charts describe how you should organize essays and paragraphs as you write; however, they also explain how other writers organize essays and paragraphs as they write. You are probably beginning to see that as you improve your skills in writing essays and paragraphs, you will also find that your skill in reading them increases. As you read, be sure to identify

- The **thesis statement**
- The **topic sentence** of each paragraph and how it supports the thesis statement
- The key supporting **details** the author provides

Many students find it helpful to underline or highlight these parts as they find them.

Reading Success Strategy 2, "Know What to Look for As You Read," identifies and illustrates the key parts of the essay. Refer to this reference insert often as you read. It will focus your attention on what is important to know and remember.

Use Questions to Guide Your Reading

Be sure you can answer the following questions about each essay you read. These questions together produce a condensed summary of the content of the essay.

Who (or what) is the essay about?	When did the action occur?
	Where did the action occur?
What happened? (What action took place?)	Why did the action occur?
	How did the action occur?

These questions focus your attention on the literal, or factual, meaning of the essay. You will also want to ask critical questions that help you respond to, react to, and evaluate the essay. Refer to Reading Success Strategy 4 for a list of useful questions.

Read with a Pen or Highlighter in Hand

To write about a reading, you will need to refer to it frequently; however, you should not have to reread the entire essay each time you want to locate a key point. (Rereading an essay *is* useful at times, and sometimes it is necessary if you are to understand the essay fully, but you should not have to reread to find particular information.) To avoid unnecessary rereading, underline or highlight important parts of the essay, parts you would like to reread, key statements, parts about which you have questions, and parts you think you may want to refer to as you write.

In addition to marking or highlighting key parts, you should also make marginal notes. These are called annotations. Think of annotations as a way of recording your thoughts as you read and as a means of "talking back" to the author. Reading Success Strategy 3, "Annotate: Read with a Pen in Hand," describes and illustrates how to annotate. Refer to this reference insert often to remind yourself of the kinds of annotations that are useful to make.

Deal with Difficult Vocabulary

Before each reading, a list of vocabulary words is given, along with a brief definition of each word as it is used in the reading. Be sure to look through this list *before* you read, checking the meaning of each word that is unfamiliar. Highlight or place an asterisk (*) next to each unfamiliar word. While reading, you may need to refer back to the list, since no one expects you to remember a definition after reading it only once.

In addition to the words listed, you may find other unfamiliar words in the essay. If you come across an unfamiliar word while reading, finish reading the sentence it is in. Often, you will be able to figure out enough about the word from the way it is used in the sentence to continue reading without losing meaning. Since you will have a pen in your hand, mark or circle the word so that you can check its exact meaning later. If you cannot figure out what the word means from the way it is used, then you will need to work on it further. First try pronouncing it aloud; often hearing the word will help you find out its meaning. If you still do not know it, take the time to look it up in a dictionary. (Keep one nearby for convenient reference.) Once you find the meaning, circle the word and write its definition or a synonym in the margin—you may want to refer to it again as you discuss or write about the reading.

Reading and Thinking Critically

To write about an essay, you must understand the author's message, but you must also react to and evaluate that message. You must be able to do more than summarize what the author said. You must analyze, interpret, judge, and respond to the ideas presented. Reading Success Strategy 4 lists six useful questions and illustrates how to find clues to their answers in the reading. Refer to this reference insert often to get in the habit of reading and thinking critically.

Annotating, as described above, will also help you read and think critically. By "talking back" to the author, you will find yourself adopting a challenging, questioning attitude that promotes critical thinking.

Remembering What You Read

Reading an essay once does not guarantee that you will remember it; in fact, the odds are that you will not remember it in detail unless you take certain steps after you read it. Use the following techniques to increase your recall of material you have read.

Underline or highlight and annotate as you read.   As noted above, underlining and highlighting are useful ways to locate information without rereading; annotating is an effective way to record your ideas and reactions to the reading. Each of these techniques, however, also will help you remember what you read. To underline or highlight or annotate, you have to *think* about what you are reading. The thinking process aids recall.

Review the reading as soon as you finish.   While it is tempting to close the book and reward yourself for finishing an assignment, doing so is a mistake. Instead, spend three or four minutes reviewing what you have just read. These few minutes will pay high dividends in the amount you will be able to remember later. Review the reading by following the same steps you used to preview the reading (see p. xxi). This postreading will fix ideas in your mind, clarify others, and show you how ideas are connected.

Write a summary.   Many students find it helpful to write a summary of an essay right after they finish reading it. Writing the summary is another way to review key points and prevent memory loss. Additionally, your summary will be useful later as a means of refreshing your memory without rereading and as a handy reference during class discussions.

Getting Ready to Write

You can take many steps to make writing about an essay easier. Several of these you have learned already. Underlining, highlighting, annotating, and summarizing prepare you to write about what you have read. Each identifies important ideas that may be used as starting points for writing. Here are a few additional tips.

Write an outline or draw a diagram.   As you write, the organization will become clearer and you will be reviewing the content.

Keep a notebook or journal.   Use it to record your ideas, reactions, feelings, and responses to the reading.

Discuss the reading with classmates.   You may discover new ideas or find that your own ideas become clearer once you express them in conversation.

Chapter 1

Decisions That Shape Our Lives

EACH DAY we make hundreds of decisions. We decide what time to get up, what to wear, where to sit on the bus or train or in a classroom, which assignment to read first, what to eat for dinner, and so forth. Many of these decisions are not very important in the long term. What you choose for dinner tonight will have little impact on your life two years from now, for example.

Other decisions have a more immediate and direct impact on your life. A decision to attend college, to marry, to take a certain job, to have children, to move, or to change careers clearly has long-term effects. Suppose, for instance, that the father of three small children decides to return to school so that he can get a more interesting and better-paying job. Since his family still needs his current income, he attends school at night so that he can keep working during the day. This decision means that he will be able to spend much less time with his family now, but that they will all have a better life a bit later. When we are faced with major decisions, we usually go through a process of weighing our options, looking at the pros and cons, and trying to evaluate the best course of action. The alternative is acting impulsively, which is another kind of decision that shapes people's lives, for better or worse.

The readings in this chapter will give you perspectives on some decisions that other people have made and how their lives have been shaped accordingly. You will read about personal choices involving family, such as a woman who travels to China and must choose which infant to adopt ("The Chosen One"); a woman who must decide whether to leave her fiancé ("Saying Good-bye to Eric"); and a student's decision to leave her family in Honduras to attend school in the United States ("The Gift of Sacrifice"). You will read about a career decision in "Christopher Keiser: In-Line Skating Instructor," and a decision about what constitutes normal behavior ("I'm OK; You're a Bit Odd"). You will also consider two moral or ethical decisions: mercy killing ("Euthanasia: A Moral Dilemma") and marriages between partners of the same sex ("Evan's Two Moms").

Brainstorming About Decisions

Class Activity: The following circumstances are situations that require choices. Choose one situation, analyze it, and make a decision. Then write a description of what you think would happen.

Situation 1: If you could acquire one new skill or talent by simply asking, what would you ask for?

Situation 2: If a drug that made it possible for you to sleep only one night per week became available, would you decide to take it?

Situation 3: If you could exchange places for a day with anyone in history, dead or alive, famous or infamous, whom would you choose to be?

The Chosen One

▶ Laura Cunningham

In this reading, the author describes one of the most important decisions in her life—which baby to adopt. This essay originally appeared in the "Hers" column of The New York Times Magazine.

Reading Strategy

This is a personal essay in which the author expresses her feelings, doubts, and fears about adoption. As you read, highlight statements that reveal Cunningham's attitude toward the adoption process and the decision she made.

Vocabulary Preview

articulate (5) put into words
simpatico (6) compatible; holding similar attitudes and
                        beliefs
hydraulic (7) forceful
unprecedented (7) unlike anything before
ambiguous (8) unclear, having more than one meaning
emissary (8) an agent representing someone else
paraphernalia (10) equipment; all the objects or items used
                        in a place or with an object
staccato (16) abrupt sounds
fetid (19) having an offensive odor
luminous (22) bright

A year ago, I boarded a flight to Shanghai during a gale force wind.   1
The plane shivered and taxied back to the hangar twice before takeoff.
It is testimony to my anxiety about the purpose of my journey that I
felt no fear of flying. I carried with me an empty infant car bed (aptly
named the Dream Ride), a three-week supply of diapers, wipes, pediatric antibiotics, bottles and disposable nipples. I was on my way to
adopt one of the tens of thousands of baby girls abandoned in China
each year.

Today as I write, my 1-year-old daughter sleeps in a crib in the next   2
room. She lies in the position of trust—on her back, her arms widespread, her face tip-tilted as if for the next kiss.

A happy ending, so far, for my darling Chinese daughter, and for   3
me. But the journey to Shanghai has somehow not ended. Many

nights, I wake at 3 A.M.—yanked from my dream, my heart hammering alarms. At that silent, moonlit time, I remember my choice.

I am embarrassed now to recall the doubt that accompanied me to China. The orphanage had sent a fax (yes, in the new China, orphanages send faxes): "We have a baby for you. We would have taken her picture but it was too cold."   4

My concern, if I can articulate the chill gut slide of panic as a "concern," was that somehow I would walk into the orphanage and fail to respond to the baby; that somehow she would not feel like "the right one." I would have to go ahead with the adoption out of momentum, some grim sense of decency, but without the hoped-for love at first sight.   5

The baby, it seemed from the fax, was already chosen. And while I claimed to love all babies, in my secret, cowering heart I had to admit that I was more drawn to some babies than to others. It wasn't beauty or even intelligence that I required of a baby, but some sign of being, well, simpatico.   6

I could not see her until the orphanage opened Monday morning. I had arrived in Shanghai on Saturday night. The interval was the high tide of my fear—suspense seemed hydraulic; blood rushed through me at unprecedented speed.   7

Until Monday I had only the ambiguous answers of Ms. Zhang, the orphanage's emissary who had greeted me at the airport. When I asked: "How old is the baby? How big?" Ms. Zhang answered only with another question: "What size baby clothes have you brought with you?"   8

Her response raised some possibility of control, or at least influence. Maybe the baby was *not* yet chosen. In my sneaking secret chicken heart, I could still pick the best and the brightest star of abandoned baby girlhood in Shanghai.   9

Passing the time until I could meet "my baby," I met another baby at the hotel, already adopted by a single man. (China permits adoptions by foreigners, whether married or unmarried. Its adoption policy is unusual in that citizens, as well as foreigners, must be at least 35 years old to adopt.) She struck me, however, as not meant to be my baby. She did seem just right for her new father, an American psychologist, who carried with him a sitcom's supply of baby paraphernalia.   10

Next I went to the nearest tourist attraction, the Temple of the Jade Buddha, where there was said to be a Buddha to whom mothers pray for a good baby.   11

The Buddha glowed in the dim temple. It wasn't jet lag that sent me reeling to my knees before the Buddha. Half-Jewish, half-Southern Baptist, all doubt, I knelt in truest prayer. *Let the baby be one I can truly love.*   12

At 9 sharp the next morning I waited in the orphanage, wearing my   13
winter coat indoors (now I understood the fax). Even in midwinter
there was no heat. Vapor rose from the thermoses of hot tea carried by
the female employees. The translator announced that the baby was being carried in from the nursery building.

"You will have a choice," she said.   14

I looked out the window as she pointed across a courtyard filled   15
with dead bamboo and gray laundry. The window itself was grimy, but
through it I saw two women in blue smocks, running toward me. Each
held a bundle. There were *two* babies.

They were swaddled in comforters, their heads completely draped   16
in towels. The first baby was unveiled. There was a staccato of Chinese,
translated as: "Pick this one. She is more beautiful. She is more intelligent." Baby No. 1 was the nurses' favorite, a 2-month-old of unsur-
passed good looks and robust health. She smiled.

But I couldn't take my eyes from the second baby, who was   17
revealed almost as an afterthought. She was thin, piteous, a green-
complexioned elf, with low-set ears that stuck out. She wheezed. In a
pocket of my coat, I held a vial of antibiotics, carried on good advice
from a friend.

I had no choice. The second baby was sick. I had medicine impos-   18
sible to obtain here. I accepted the tiny green baby, gasping and ooz-
ing, into my arms. I noticed she also had a bald spot, from lying
unmoved in her crib.

Shame over my earlier indecision blew from the room like a fetid   19
draft of disease and poverty.

Was it love at first sight? I knew in that instant that we were at the   20
start of our life together.

Love overtakes you at odd moments. I was trying to collect a urine   21
sample, required for a medical test. I held her, her little purple fanny
over a rice bowl, in my arms all night. I drew the blankets around us
both as a tent to keep away the cold. We waited, silently, all night, until she took a literal "tinkle." Her eyes met mine, on the other side of
the world, and I knew Little-Miss-Ears-Stick-Out, With-Tears-in-Her-
Eyes was mine, all right.

Within 24 hours, the medicine had taken effect: she turned ivory   22
pink; her eyes cleared. She was beyond my dreams, exquisite, a luminous old soul with contemporary wit. I gazed at her and saw the fate-
fulness of every mother's choice. It is not the beautiful baby who is
chosen, but the chosen baby who becomes beautiful.

To enter a house filled with unwanted babies is to pass through a   23
door that you can never shut. At 3 A.M., I see the others—the aisles of
green cribs holding bundled babies. I try to close my eyes to them, but
they refuse to disappear. They are lying there. They are cold; they are

damp. I see one baby girl especially. She had an odd genetic defect: the skin of her body was coal black, but her face had no color. she looked as if she were wearing the white theatrical mask of tragedy.

Last Christmas, I was able to choose the green, sick baby over the laughing, healthy one. Would I have had the courage to take one of the others? Would someone? I wake up and see the small faces. They are lying there waiting, waiting to be chosen.

24

Examining the Reading

Finding Meaning

1. Why was the author on her way to China?
2. What was the author's greatest concern before she met the baby?
3. Why did she choose one baby over the other?
4. Describe the baby's state of health by the time the author left Shanghai.
5. Describe the conditions in the orphanage.

Understanding Technique

1. Cunningham uses sensory details (details that appeal to the senses: sight, sound, taste, smell, and touch) in her writing. Underline several places where the sensory details are particularly powerful.
2. Highlight the transitions Cunningham uses to move from one event to the next.

Thinking Critically

1. If you were in the author's place and had a choice of two babies to adopt, which one would you choose? Why?
2. The Chinese government has a policy that adoptive parents must be at least 35 years old. Do you think this is a good policy? Why or why not?
3. Why do you think the orphanage gave the author a choice of two babies to adopt?
4. What did the author mean when she said, "It is not the beautiful baby who is chosen, but the chosen baby who becomes beautiful"?

Writing About the Reading

A Journal Entry

Write a journal entry explaining how you feel before planned important events, such as job interviews or public presentations.

A Paragraph

1. Write a paragraph describing whether or under what conditions you might consider adopting a child.
2. Cunningham seemed to have little difficulty making her decision. She seemed to know intuitively which baby to choose. Write a paragraph describing a similar situation in which you seemed to know the right decision to make.

An Essay

1. The author suggests that all mothers think their own children are beautiful. From your experience as a child, as a parent, or as both, write an essay agreeing or disagreeing that parents see beauty (physical or otherwise) in their children and tend to overlook their children's faults. Support your position with examples from your experience.
2. Cunningham felt doubtful and anxious as she awaited the important moment when she would see her baby. Write an essay describing an event about which you felt anxious or nervous. Explain why you were anxious and how the event turned out.

A Creative Activity

Suppose the author decided to write a letter to the other baby, explaining why she had not chosen her. What do you think she would have said? Write a first draft of the letter.

Christopher Keiser:
In-Line Skating Instructor

▶ **Eric Zicklin**

The choice of a career is an important life decision. In this reading you will see why Christopher Keiser, an in-line skating instructor, is satisfied with his career decision. This article was first published in Rolling Stone *magazine.*

Reading Strategy

This reading explains why Keiser is satisfied with his career choice. As you read, annotate or highlight sections that suggest reasons for his satisfaction.

Vocabulary Preview

ultimately (3) eventually
quadrupled (3) increased to four times as great
fetching (3) earning; commanding a salary of
lucrative (6) well-paying
evangelical (10) enthusiastic; ardent
rush (10) surge of quick and intense excitement

*C*hristopher Keiser is about the happiest person he knows. "I've met   1
so many lawyers and accountants who say, 'Man, you've got the greatest job.' And I say, 'Yeah, I do.' "

Keiser's job is to teach those lawyers and accountants how to avoid   2
physical disaster when they step into their in-line roller skates and attempt the street's most dangerous sport. As an instructor at the Roller-
blade Inc.–sponsored Blade School, in Los Angeles, Keiser, 25, has
found a way to make money doing exactly what he loves to do—skating.

There are about 1,500 in-line instructors nationwide, but that   3
number is ultimately expected to hit 20,000. The fastest-growing sport

Source: Excerpt from "Mod Jobs: Strange and Twisted Paths to Contentment and Prosperity" by Eric Zicklin from *Rolling Stone*, October 20, 1994. By Straight Arrow Publishers Company, L. P. 1994. All rights reserved. Reprinted by permission.

of the '90s, in-line skating has created an industry that has quadrupled during the past five years and is now worth an estimated $400 million a year. The sport has more participants than alpine skiing; blading also has a startling injury rate, so people like Keiser are in demand, fetching $12–$35 per hour for lessons.

Like most people in their 20s, Keiser has struggled through brain-numbing jobs behind store counters. Unlike most he has also worked on the crews of touring yachts, and he even juggled on the streets to pay for his two years at Northern Colorado University. "I wasn't too happy," he says of those times.   4

Now, though, Keiser acknowledges that he sometimes laughs at his good fortune. "I live 10 blocks from the beach," he says. "I just bought a new road bike, and my patio is bigger than my entire first apartment. Something's definitely going right."   5

With his teaching experience and encyclopedic knowledge of in-line products, Keiser is qualified to take a step up the corporate ladder. "I just declined an extremely lucrative offer from another company to be a sales rep," he says, "which made me realize that I'm pretty marketable in this business. That was an eye-opener. I mean, I could really have a future here."   6

So could many other people. According to the Bureau of Labor Statistics' *Occupational Outlook Quarterly,* recreation-related jobs are expected to grow "faster than average in response to population growth, increased interest in health and fitness and rising demand for organized recreational activities." Dr. Victor R. Lindquist, former dean of placement at Northwestern University and the executive director of Career Management Research Institute, in Oak Brook, Ill., agrees. "There is a tremendous market of people who are looking for new ways to take care of their bodies."   7

Although Keiser races professionally, consistently placing in the top 5 percent, his athleticism did not win him his position at Blade School. Teaching skills—rather than blinding speed or airborne stunts—separate competent skaters from employable instructors. "You have to love to skate, and you have to want to teach," Keiser says of his job's most important requirements. "A couple of our instructors actually learned how to skate right here at Blade School. So you don't have to be a superstar."   8

The school's instructors learn how to teach through training programs sponsored by the International In-line Skating Association, in Atlanta. A weekend of intensive clinics (and a $275 fee) can turn anyone with skating proficiency into a certified instructor.   9

On the subject of instructing, Keiser is downright evangelical. "It's the most incredible feeling to watch the beginners learn," he says. "They're always so shocked that they're actually skating. Then they're   10

hooked on the sport, and that's such a rush. I mean, I'm turning people on to good stuff here. It's like taking someone to your favorite restaurant and watching them discover how great it is. I do that with 20 people every day."

Keiser's excitement hasn't been lost on the people around him. His father recently told him how impressed he was with his son's enthusiasm for work. "He told me for the first time that he was proud of me," the younger Keiser says. "He's pretty miserable with his job, and he said he was proud that I'm taking care of myself and enjoying it at the same time. He was amazed by that, and I said, 'I am, too.'" 11

Examining the Reading

Finding Meaning

1. How is the author able to make money while being involved in his favorite sport?
2. According to the reading, in the next ten years there will be a good market for jobs related to recreation. Why?
3. According to the author, what is the most important quality in Keiser's job?
4. How can a skater become a certified instructor?

5. In the author's experience, what is the reaction of people who are just beginning to skate?

Understanding Technique

1. Identify several sections in which dialogue is used effectively to express meaning.
2. How does the last paragraph, or conclusion, draw the essay to a close?

Thinking Critically

1. Why do you think in-line skating has grown so quickly as a sport?
2. Do you think any professional skater could do Keiser's job? Why or why not?
3. What do you think Keiser likes best about his job?
4. Can you think of any disadvantages to Keiser's job? What are they?
5. Why do you think Keiser decided not to accept the position of sales representative?

Writing About the Reading

A Journal Entry

Write a journal entry on in-line skating. If you have tried it, describe your experience. If you haven't, would you like to? Why or why not?

A Paragraph

1. Think of your favorite teacher from childhood and describe the qualities that made him or her a good teacher.
2. An important part of teaching is decision making. Write a paragraph explaining the types of decisions that you have observed teachers making.

An Essay

1. Most of us have to make the important decision of choosing a career. Keiser is clearly satisfied with his choice. Based on the reading and your personal experience, write an essay explaining what factors make a job satisfying.
2. Suppose you were asked to teach a subject, sport, or activity of your choice. Write an essay on what you would teach to whom. Be sure to include whether you think you would make a good teacher.

A Creative Activity

Suppose Keiser eventually accepts a position as sales representative. Two years later he is promoted to regional sales manager; now he teaches other sales representatives how to sell. Write a paragraph explaining whether you think Keiser is happy in his new position and why.

I'm OK; You're a Bit Odd

▶ **Paul Chance**

Are you normal? Are all of your friends normal? What standards would you use to decide? This reading explores the issue of how to define normal behavior. It was originally published in Psychology Today.

Reading Strategy

Although written from a humorous viewpoint, this essay does present three different models for defining mental health. As you read, identify each model and try to describe its characteristics and limitations.

Vocabulary Preview

amorous (1) loving; sexual
emulate (2) imitate; attempt to be like
subjective (3) personal
apt (5) likely
sadist (8) one who enjoys hurting others
masochist (8) one who enjoys being hurt
psychopath (8) person exhibiting aggressive or criminal
                   tendencies
deviate (12) differ; vary
paragon (13) ideal; perfect model
cultivate (13) develop
benchmark (14) standard
gauge (14) measure; judge

The new groom was happy with his bride, and everything, he ex-   1
plained, was fine. There was just this one peculiarity his wife had. During lovemaking she insisted that he wear his motorcycle helmet. He found it uncomfortable, and he felt just a tad foolish. Is it normal to

want someone to wear a helmet during amorous activities? Does a quirk of this sort keep one off the rolls of the mentally fit? The answer depends on how you define mental fitness. There are several ways of going about it.

One model calls to mind the Platonic ideal.[1] Somewhere in the heavens there exists a person who is the perfect specimen of psychological health. (Or maybe there are two of them: the perfect man may be different from the perfect woman. At least, one would hope so.) We all fall short of this ideal, of course, but it provides a model that we can emulate. Unfortunately, the Platonic answer merely begs the question, since somebody has to describe what the ideal is like. And how do we do that?

The everyday way of defining mental health is more subjective: if I do it, it's healthy; if I don't do it, it's sick. Is it crazy to spend Saturdays jumping out of airplanes or canoeing down rapids? Not to skydivers and white-water canoers. Is it sick to hear voices when no one is there? Not if you're the one who hears the voices—and you welcome their company.

This commonsense way of defining mental health sets ourselves up as the standard against which to make comparisons. There's nothing wrong with this, except that it's just possible that some of us—not me, you understand—are a bit odd ourselves. And you can't measure accurately with a bent ruler.

The psychodynamic model of mental health suggests that psychological fitness is a kind of balancing act. There are, according to this view, impulses in all of us that society cannot tolerate. The healthy person is not the one who always keeps these impulses under lock and key but the one who lets them out once in a while when nobody's looking. If you run around the house smashing delicate things with a hammer, for example, someone's apt to object. But if you hammer a nail into a board, and seem to have a good excuse for it, nobody minds. So the healthy person with violent impulses builds a deck behind the house.

The chief problem with the psychodynamic model is that it doesn't define the standard by which balance is to be measured. Building a deck may be an acceptable outlet for violent impulses, but what if every time a person feels like slugging someone he adds on to the deck until his entire backyard is covered in redwood? He's directing his impulses constructively, but his family might find him easier to live with if he just broke something once in a while.

2

3

4

5

6

---

[1]Plato (427?–347 B.C.), the Greek philosopher, asserted that ideal forms exist apart from the imperfect world. [Editor's note.]

Behaviorists offer a different solution. They focus on behavior, nat-   7
urally, and decide whether behavior is healthy on the basis of its consequences. If the results are good, the behavior is good. In this view,
there is nothing nuts about building a two-acre redwood deck so long
as the person enjoys it and it doesn't get him or her into trouble. Normal behavior, then, is whatever works.

The behavioral approach appears to offer an objective and rational   8
way of defining mental health. Alas, appearances are deceiving. We
may agree that a person enjoys an activity, but is that enough? A sadist
and a masochist may work out a mutually rewarding relationship, but
does that make them healthy? A psychopath may flimflam oldsters out
of their life savings and do it with such charm that they love him for it,
but should the rest of us emulate the psychopath?

An alternative is to let society decide. What is healthy then be-   9
comes what society finds acceptable; what is unhealthy is whatever
society dislikes. Thus, aggression is abnormal among the gentle Tasa-
day of the Philippines but normal among the fierce Yanomamo of
Venezuela.

The societal model has a lot of appeal, but it troubles some mental-   10
health workers. There is something about fixing mental health to a mail-
ing address that they find unsettling. They think that there ought to be
some sort of universal standard toward which we might all strive. Besides, does it really make sense to say that murder and cannibalism are
OK just because some society has approved them? And if it is, then why
not apply the same standards to communities within a society? Murder
is a popular activity among Baltimore youth. Shall we say that, in that
city, murder is healthy?

A similar problem exists with the statistical model of mental   11
health. In this case, being mentally healthy means falling close to average. Take the frequency of sexual activity among married couples, for
example. Let's say that, on average, married people your age have in-
tercourse about twice a week. That's the norm. If you indulge more or
less often than that, you're abnormal—with or without a helmet.

There's some logic to this view. The further people deviate from the   12
average, the more likely they are to seem strange. You may think, for
instance, that limiting sex to two times a week is a bit prudish, but almost everyone is likely to think that once an hour is excessive. Again,
however, there are problems.

Does it really make sense to hold up the average person as the   13
paragon of mental health? This logic would have everyone cultivate
a few phobias just because they happen to be commonplace; even
the best students would strive to earn Cs; and all couples in the
country would be frustrated by their inability to have exactly 1.8
children.

We can all agree that there are a lot of weirdos around, but there   14
seems no way for us to agree about who's weird. And so there's no way
for us to agree about what mental health is. That's unfortunate, because it gives us no clear goal toward which to strive and no stable
benchmark against which to gauge our progress. Even so, I'm damned
if I'm gonna wear a helmet to bed.

Examining the Reading

Finding Meaning

1. What one question does the entire reading attempt to answer?
2. Summarize each model or method that the author describes.
3. Summarize the problems or limitations of each method.

Understanding Technique

How does Chance make transitions from one model of mental health
to another? Reread the essay and note transitional words and phrases.

Thinking Critically

1. Make lists of behaviors that most class members agree are normal
   and abnormal.
2. Make a list of behaviors that class members hold different opinions on.
3. Give an example of the statistical model of mental fitness.
4. How do you react to someone who, according to your standards,
   does odd or strange things?

Writing About the Reading

A Journal Entry

Write an entry listing behaviors that you feel are abnormal. Is it likely
that everyone would agree with you? Have you ever discussed or argued about these behaviors with anyone?

A Paragraph

1. Write a paragraph evaluating whether a person wearing a tiger
   mask to a Detroit Tigers football game is or is not normal. Use the
   statistical model to help in your evaluation.

2. Write a paragraph evaluating whether eating three packages of Oreo cookies during an afternoon of study is normal. Use the behavioral approach to help in making your decision.

An Essay

1. Write an essay describing a behavior that you feel is abnormal. Use one or more of the methods used in the reading to explain why it is abnormal.
2. Write an essay on dyeing one's hair green and purple and explain how this act can be considered normal. Call on several methods from the reading to support your answer.

A Creative Activity

Suppose the author had decided to wear a motorcycle helmet to bed. Write a paragraph explaining what you think his partner would say.

Saying Good-bye to Eric

> ▶ **Jennifer S. Dickman**

In this essay, published in Nursing *magazine, Jennifer S. Dickman describes how a personal tragedy motivated her to become a nurse.*

Reading Strategy

Eric's accident and what happened afterwards certainly took a terrible emotional toll on the author. Review the essay and underline those sections where the author expresses her feelings about the events connected to this tragedy.

Vocabulary Preview

intubated (5) had tubes inserted to assist bodily functions
ventilation (5) breathing
evacuate (5) to remove the contents of
hematoma (5) a blood-filled swelling of the brain
debride (5) surgically remove unhealthy tissue
temporal lobe (5) section of the brain containing the sensory
　　　　　　　　area associated with hearing
frontal lobe (5) section of the brain responsible for higher
　　　　　　　thought
intraventricular catheter (5) a tube inserted into a ventricle,
　　　　　　　　　　　or small cavity in the brain
intracranial (5) within the skull
neurology (6) dealing with disorders of the brain and nervous
　　　　　system
irony (7) strange twist; joke or a turnaround of events
secretions (8) fluids
weaned (9) gradually removed from

As Eric rode off on his motorcycle that crisp November day, he 　1 turned and gave me a smile and a wave. I never dreamed that would be the last expression I'd ever see on my fiancé's face.

A few hours later, I was driving to the regional trauma center, my 　2 hands trembling on the steering wheel, my eyes blurred with tears. Eric's bike had skidded out of control on wet pavement and he'd been thrown into a field.

Please let him be okay, I prayed. *We're in the middle of planning our wedding.*   3

When I arrived at the trauma center, my worst fears were immediately confirmed. He'd suffered a serious brain injury.   4

Caring for Eric

Eric had been intubated in the ED and required assisted ventilation. He was initially admitted to the neurology ICU—later that day he underwent surgery to evacuate a hematoma and to debride damaged parts of his temporal and frontal lobes. During surgery, an intraventricular catheter was inserted to continuously monitor his intracranial pressure.   5

I stumbled through those first few hours—and then days—in a fog of shock and disbelief. I never left the hospital, choosing to sleep in the visitor's lounge. When Eric was finally moved to a private room in the neurology unit, I slept on a cot next to him.   6

Grief prevented me from seeing the irony in my situation. I'd taken a semester off from nursing school because I wasn't sure if I wanted to be a nurse—I didn't know if I was up to it. And now I was devoting all of my time to caring for Eric.   7

I bathed him, turned him, did his catheter care, and learned to give his tube feedings. I read to him, talked to him, and played all of his favorite music. I even convinced his doctors to let me give herbal tea through his feeding tube cause I'd read that certain herbs help decrease lung secretions.   8

After 4 months, Eric's condition improved slightly. He began blinking his eyes, making small hand and foot movements, and trying to breathe on his own. I was thrilled, even though deep down I knew that these weren't signs of recovery. When Eric was finally weaned from the ventilator and began breathing on his own, I felt like shouting for joy. that's when his doctor took me aside.   9

"You'd better get on with your life, Jennifer," he said gently but firmly. "Eric's reached a plateau, and he'll be this way as long as he lives."   10

Confronting Reality

At first, I refused to believe him. But then, with the help of my family and friends, I took an honest look at the situation. For 6 months, I'd given up everything to devote my energy to Eric. I'd lost a lot of weight and was mentally and physically exhausted. I knew the time had come to accept his condition and start living my own life—which, I decided, included returning to nursing school.   11

A few weeks after I'd reached my decision, Eric was transferred to a long-term-care facility. Before he left I said a final good-bye.   12

I still feel the pain of losing Eric—and I'm sure I always will. But I also remember how caring for him helped clear up any confusion over my career choice. Although I couldn't bring Eric back, his tragedy brought me back to nursing. 13

Examining the Reading

Finding Meaning

1. How did Eric's accident occur?
2. Describe the injuries he suffered.
3. How did the author provide care for Eric?
4. What effect did caring for Eric have on Dickman's life and health?
5. What did the author decide to do after six months of caring for Eric?

Understanding Technique

1. What techniques does Dickman use to make her story real and compelling?
2. Why do you think she included in paragraph 5 the technical details of Eric's medical condition?

Thinking Critically

1. How did Eric's accident affect Dickman at first?
2. What did the author mean by "Grief prevented me from seeing the irony in my situation"? What was this irony?
3. Why did the doctor tell the author that she should get on with her life just when Eric seemed to be improving?
4. Was there a chance that Eric might have recovered completely from his accident?
5. Do you think there was a connection between the author's inability to nurse her fiancé back to health and her decision to return to nursing school? Explain.

Writing About the Reading

A Journal Entry

Write a journal entry about a difficult decision that you were forced to make.

A Paragraph

1. Someone might say that if Dickman had truly loved Eric, she would have continued to care for him for the rest of his life. Write a paragraph defending or rejecting this idea.
2. Write a paragraph on what you imagine would be the hardest part of being a nurse and why.

An Essay

1. The author had some difficulty deciding whether or not to become a nurse, but this experience helped her make that decision. Write an essay describing an experience in your life that helped you discover your career goals.
2. Sometimes it takes a tragic event to remind us of our blessings or to awaken us to a new, important direction for our lives. Write an essay about how such an experience made you a better person.

A Creative Activity

Imagine that Eric would have survived with only minimal brain damage. How do you imagine this might have changed the ending for the author? Rewrite the ending as though this were the case.

Evan's Two Moms

▸ Anna Quindlen

Anna Quindlen, a Pulitzer Prize–winning syndicated columnist for The New York Times *and many other newspapers, presents her position on same-sex marriages in the following essay. It was taken from her 1993 book:* Thinking Out Loud: On the Personal, the Political, the Public, and the Private.

Reading Strategy

The author of this essay has a definite opinion on the idea of same-sex marriages, which is expressed in various parts of the essay. After you have read the essay, review it and underline those phrases or sentences that most clearly express the author's position on same-sex marriages.

Vocabulary Preview

bulwark (1) strong support or protection; defense
quadriplegic (2) a person who is paralyzed in both arms and both legs
rads (5) radicals; those who wanted to bring about sweeping changes in society
linchpin (5) most important part; unifying feature
tenets (7) beliefs; convictions
ironically (7) by a strange twist; just the opposite
secular (7) nonreligious
amorphous (9) unclear or vague; open to many meanings
thwart (10) block; prevent
guise (10) form; way; manner

*E*van has two moms. This is no big thing. Evan has always had two   1
moms—in his school file, on his emergency forms, with his friends. "Ooooh, Evan, you're lucky," they sometimes say. "You have two

moms." It sounds like a sitcom, but until last week it was emotional truth without legal bulwark. That was when a judge in New York approved the adoption of a six-year-old boy by his biological mother's lesbian partner. Evan. Evan's mom. Evan's other mom. A kid, a psychologist, a pediatrician. A family.

The matter of Evan's two moms is one in a series of [recent] events . . . that lead to certain conclusions. A Minnesota appeals court granted guardianship of a woman left a quadriplegic in a car accident to her lesbian lover, the culmination of a seven-year battle in which the injured woman's parents did everything possible to negate the partnership between the two. A lawyer in Georgia had her job offer withdrawn after the state attorney general found out that she and her lesbian lover were planning a marriage ceremony; she's brought suit. The computer company Lotus announced that the gay partners of employees would be eligible for the same benefits as spouses. 2

Add to these public events the private struggles, the couples who go from lawyer to lawyer to approximate legal protections their straight counterparts take for granted, the AIDS survivors who find themselves shut out of their partners' dying days by biological family members and shut out of their apartments by leases with a single name on the dotted line, and one solution is obvious. 3

Gay marriage is a radical notion for straight people and a conservative notion for gay ones. After years of being sledgehammered by society, some gay men and lesbian women are deeply suspicious of participating in an institution that seems to have "straight world" written all over it. 4

But the rads of twenty years ago, straight and gay alike, have other things on their minds today. Family is one, and the linchpin of family has commonly been a loving commitment between two adults. When same-sex couples set out to make that commitment, they discover that they are at a disadvantage: No joint tax returns. No health insurance coverage for an uninsured partner. No survivor's benefits from Social Security. None of the automatic rights, privileges, and responsibilities society attaches to a marriage contract. In Madison, Wisconsin, a couple who applied at the Y with their kids for a family membership were turned down because both were women. It's one of those small things that can make you feel small. 5

Some took marriage statutes that refer to "two persons" at their word and applied for a license. The results were court decisions that quoted the Bible and embraced circular argument: marriage is by definition the union of a man and a woman because that is how we've defined it. 6

No religion should be forced to marry anyone in violation of its tenets, although ironically it is now only in religious ceremonies that 7 gay people can marry, performed by clergy who find the blessing of two who love each other no sin. But there is no secular reason that we should take a patchwork approach of corporate, governmental, and legal steps to guarantee what can be done simply, economically, conclusively, and inclusively with the words "I do."

"Fran and I chose to get married for the same reasons that any two 8 people do," said the lawyer who was fired in Georgia. "We fell in love; we wanted to spend our lives together." Pretty simple.

Consider the case of *Loving* v. *Virgina,* aptly named. At the time, 9 sixteen states had laws that barred interracial marriage, relying on natural law, that amorphous grab bag for justifying prejudice. Sounding a little like God throwing Adam and Eve out of paradise, the trial judge suspended the one-year sentence of Richard Loving, who was white, and his wife, Mildred, who was black, provided they got out of the State of Virginia.

In 1967 the Supreme Court found such laws to be unconstitu- 10 tional. Only twenty-five years ago and it was a crime for a black woman to marry a white man. Perhaps twenty-five years from now we will find it just as incredible that two people of the same sex were not entitled to legally commit themselves to each other. Love and commitment are rare enough; it seems absurd to thwart them in any guise.

Examining the Reading

Finding Meaning

1. What legal and economic disadvantages are faced by gay couples?
2. Why does Quindlen conclude that same-sex marriage would be a solution to many of these problems?
3. Why does the author think some gay people are suspicious of marriage?
4. Why did some court decisions reject same-sex marriages?
5. How does the author think that the controversy over same-sex marriages will be resolved?

Understanding Technique

1. What is Quindlen's thesis?
2. What type of evidence does she offer to support it?

Thinking Critically

1. What does Quindlen believe is the most important reason for gay couples to marry legally?

2. What is a "circular argument," as described in paragraph 6?
3. Why does the author think it is ironic that gay couples can be married only in religious ceremonies?
4. Why do you think the *Loving* v. *Virginia* case was included in this essay?

Writing About the Reading

A Journal Entry

The author describes the experience of a lesbian couple being turned down for family membership by the Y as, "one of those small things that can make you feel small." Write a journal entry about an incident in your lfie that might seem small to others but had a tremendous impact on the way you felt about yourself.

A Paragraph

Write a paragraph giving your definition of what makes up a family.

An Essay

1. Do you think same-sex couples should be allowed to marry? Write an essay explaining and supporting your viewpoint.
2. Think of another social isue that was considered controversial in the past but is acceptable today. Write an essay explaining how public opinion has changed and what you think these changes tell us about society.

A Creative Activity

Describe a law or a school or family rule that you think is unfair. How should it be changed and what can you do to change it?

Euthanasia:
A Moral Dilemma

▶ **Saul Kassin**
Textbook Excerpt

When, if ever, is it right to take the life of another person? This excerpt, taken from a textbook titled Psychology, *explores the issue of mercy killing.*

Reading Strategy

Mercy killing is a controversial issue in our society. As you read, make marginal annotations to record your own thinking on the issue and your reactions to the two cases of mercy killing described here.

Vocabulary Preview

confronted (1) faced
conspiracy (1) agreement by people to carry out an illegal act
retaliate (1) get back at; get even with
osteoporosis (2) a painful bone disease
corroborated (2) supported; agreed with
complied (3) cooperated; carried out
acquitted (3) cleared of legal charges
profound (4) very deep; far-reaching
precedence (4) priority; importance
condone (4) forgive; overlook

*J*uries have long been confronted with moral dilemmas. Before the   1
Civil War, northern juries regularly failed to convict people charged with aiding escaped slaves. During the turbulent Vietnam era, many juries refused to convict antiwar activists on political conspiracy charges. Today, cases involving battered women who retaliate against their abusive husbands and crime victims who kill their assailants in self-defense also present moral dilemmas to the jury. In cases of this nature, the jury has the power to vote its conscience, even if it means overruling or "nullifying" the law.

Two poignant stories illustrate different kinds of moral reasoning in action. The first involved the death of Emily Gilbert, a seventy-three-year-old woman who was suffering from Alzheimer's disease and a crippling case of osteoporosis. After years of agony, she pleaded with her husband Roswell to terminate her life. She was in such a state, Gilbert told his attorney, that "hospitals wouldn't take her, private nursing homes wouldn't take her. . . . In a state hospital, they'd have to strap her down. She'd be dehumanized." So one day, as Emily sat on a sofa looking out a window in their tenth-floor condominium, he shot her twice in the back of her head. Tried for murder, Gilbert pleaded not guilty. Several witnesses, including many friends of the elderly couple, corroborated the claim that Emily had begged for her own death. Nevertheless, ten women and two men in Fort Lauderdale, Florida, convicted Gilbert of first-degree murder punishable by life imprisonment. One of the jurors said later, "We had no choice. The law does not allow for sympathy."

The second case involved George Zygmanik, who was the tormented victim of a car accident that left him paralyzed from the neck down. From his hospital bed, Zygmanik cried to his younger brother Lester, "I want you to promise to kill me. I want you to swear to God." So one night, Lester complied with the request. He entered his brother's hospital room, shot him in the head with a 20-gauge sawed-off shotgun, dropped the gun by the bed, and turned himself in. He confessed to the killing immediately, and described it as an act of love for his brother. Zygmanik was charged with first-degree murder, which, in his home state of New Jersey, carries a mandatory life prison sentence. During the trial, he testified that on the night of the killing, "I asked him if he was in pain. At this time, he couldn't speak at all. He just nodded that he was. He nodded yes. So I says, 'I am here to end your pain—is that all right with you?' And he nodded yes. And the next thing I knew, I shot him." The jury acquitted him.

The conflict in these events is profound: the law strictly prohibits *euthanasia,* or mercy killing, yet both Emily Gilbert and George Zygmanik desperately wanted to die. What should their loved ones have done, and how should society react? For killing his wife of fifty-one years, Roswell Gilbert was found guilty of murder and sent to prison until he was released in 1990, five years later. The reason for the jury's verdict? As we saw earlier, one juror—expressing a conventional level of morality—explained that "the law does not allow for sympathy." Yet Lester Zygmanik was found *not* guilty for very similar actions. Again, the reason? Exhibiting another level of morality, his jury felt that compassion for a loved one takes precedence over the letter of the law. Is it morally superior to condone rather than punish mercy killing? No, [some people are] quick to point out that moral development is measured not by *what* the decision is but by *how* it is reasoned. [A different] jury could have convicted Gilbert, had it based its verdict not on the law but on the ethic that "human life should never be sacrificed."

Examining the Reading

Finding Meaning

1. When is a jury permitted to stray from "the letter of the law" to arrive at a verdict in a murder trial?
2. How did Gilbert's friends try to help him in court?
3. Why did George Zygmanik's brother kill him?
4. How did the moral thinking of each jury lead to the two different verdicts?
5. According to the article, is a jury that does not convict a mercy killer better morally than one that convicts? Why?

Understanding Technique

1. Evaluate the introduction. How does it lead to the subject of the essay?
2. Kassin uses two specific cases of mercy killing to illustrate the issues involved. Explain why this is an effective technique.

Thinking Critically

1. Do you think Gilbert should have been found guilty? Why or why not?
2. Do you think Zygmanik should have been charged with first-degree murder? Justify your answer.
3. Currently the law prohibits euthanasia. Do you believe this law should be changed? Explain your answer.
4. Some people believe that a medical doctor should be able to assist in the suicide of a terminally ill patient. Do you agree or disagree?
5. How did the victim in each of the two cases play a significant role in the juries' final decision?

Writing About the Reading

A Journal Entry

Write an entry on how this reading makes you feel about the issue of euthanasia.

A Paragraph

1. Write a paragraph on how you would have voted had you been a juror in the Gilbert case. Discuss why you believe your point of view is morally correct.
2. Write a paragraph explaining how the law allows the juror's conscience to enter into a decision of guilty or not guilty.

An Essay

1. Imagine that someone you love is terminally ill and asks you to assist in his or her suicide. Write an essay explaining whether and how you would help this person. Include the steps you would take to arrive at such a decision.
2. Imagine that you have become paralyzed from the neck down. Would you request that someone end your life? Write an essay explaining what factors would influence your decision.

A Creative Activity

Suppose George Zygmanik's brother had not turned himself in after shooting his brother. Write a paragraph explaining whether or not you think the jury's verdict would have been different.

The Gift of Sacrifice

▸ Blanca Matute
Student Essay

In this essay a young woman describes a childhood decision to leave her parents and move to the United States. Matute wrote this essay while a student at college.

*W*hen we make decisions, we have to live with the consequences. 1
Hopefully, we like the decisions and are grateful that we made them, but in some cases, we regret the decision. Unfortunately, we cannot go back in time and change our original choice, even though the decision we made put us in a difficult or challenging position. Eight years ago, I learned that when a person makes a decision, he or she must stick with the choice and persevere.

When I was ten years old, I made a decision that greatly affected 2
my life. I had to decide whether to move to the United States to continue my education or stay in Honduras with my family. The idea of studying in the United States sounded like a wonderful opportunity, but it meant growing up without my mother's constant presence and guidance. I decided to leave my mother in Honduras with the rest of my family to journey to New York to pursue a better education. My family supported this decision because they knew it was a good opportunity for me. They were also sad because I would be away for many years.

I came to the United States because I believed it was going to make 3
a difference in my life. At first I found it difficult to understand how my family expected me to get a good education without my mother's support. In the beginning, I regretted my decision to come to this country. Adjusting to the different languages, the diverse cultures, and the crowded surroundings was an enormous challenge. With the help of the family I lived with, my sisters and their mother, I worked hard to adjust to my new life. I still, however, missed my mother.

As time passed, I was often sad because I had not seen my mother 4
for many years. I doubted my decision and questioned my mother's motives for encouraging me to come to the United States. At times, I felt as if my life was over because I thought that she had just wanted to get rid of me. Eventually, I learned that I had made the right decision

and that my mother had supported it because she loved me. I realized that our separation had been just as difficult for her as it had been for me. Because of her love for me, she was willing to let me go so that I could have better opportunities in life. Ultimately, she taught me an important lesson in life, the gift of sacrifice.

As I became accustomed to my new life, many wonderful things   5
began to happen; I learned a new language; I made new friends; I started to do well in school. Because of my academic achievement, I represented my junior high school at various assemblies in New York State. For example, I traveled to upstate New York as a school representative to receive an award for my school's having the best bilingual program in the public schools' twelfth district.

In 1990, I was awarded a scholarship to Aquinas High School for   6
high achievement in junior high school, and I was selected to participate in the Student/Sponsor Partnership Program. This program sponsors academically gifted students through high school. At Aquinas I met teachers who really cared about their students' education. A new world opened up to me. I joined the Spanish Club, the Math Club, the String Ensemble, where I learned to play the viola, and the Concert Band, where I played the clarinet. I became class president in my senior year.

Each time I wrote my mother to tell her how well I was doing, she   7
wrote back expressing her pride in me and my accomplishments. Even in my second year at Aquinas, when my grades were not as good as they could have been, my mother was still proud of me. With the help of a special teacher at Aquinas and hard work, I was able to bring my grades back up again. Now, I look back on all I have learned and what I have accomplished since I left Honduras and my mother eight years ago. It seems impossible that I ever regretted my decision to come to the United States.

I have learned that making a decision can sometimes lead to happiness and sometimes to sadness; in my case it led to both. At first I regretted coming to this country, but now I see that I made the right decision. It gave me not only a chance for a good education, but also a good opportunity to succeed in life. Even though I still miss my mother, I know that she is happy and proud to know of my college plans. I look to the future with awe and excitement.   8

Examining the Essay

1. How did Matute organize her ideas?
2. In which paragraph(s) do you think more detail is needed?
3. Evaluate the author's use of descriptive language—words that help you visualize and imagine people, places, or objects.

Writing an Essay

1. In "The Gift of Sacrifice," Matute describes the sacrifice that her mother made for her. Write an essay evaluating a sacrifice you made or one that was made for you. Was it worth it?
2. In leaving Honduras, Matute faced numerous challenges and difficult situations, including learning a new language, meeting new friends, and so forth. Write an essay discussing a difficult situation you faced and how you handled it.

 Making Connections —————————

1. Both Matute in "The Gift of Sacrifice" and Dickman in "Saying Good-bye to Eric" make a decision and experience its consequences. Write an essay comparing the type of decisions they made and the importance and possible outcomes of these decisions.

2. Both Quindlen in "Evan's Two Moms" Kassin in "Euthanasia: A Moral Dilemma" discuss moral issues. Compare how each author approaches the issue and the types of evidence each presents.

3. Cunningham in "The Chosen One," Dickman in "Saying Good-bye to Eric," and Matute in "The Gift of Sacrifice" face difficult decisions. Compare how each author made her decision. Was it primarily rational or emotional? Was it well thought out or impulsive, and is one approach better than the other? Why or why not?

Chapter 2

Events That Shape
Our Lives

MANY DAILY EVENTS—conversations, meals, classes, purchases, interactions with friends—seem important at the time but are not particularly memorable in the long term. Occasionally, however, a single event will make a difference and leave a lasting impression. It may be a landmark event, such as meeting your future spouse, getting a job, playing in a big game, celebrating a big birthday in a notable way, or receiving an important prize or award. Or perhaps something happened to your health that led you to make a change in your habits or behavior.

Other times, it may be a much smaller, more ordinary, and seemingly less significant event that has a dramatic or meaningful effect on the direction of your life or contributes to making you who you are. For example, the first time you picked up a guitar or heard a piano, you may have realized that you wanted to be a musician. One friend's frank comment might have caused you to reexamine your priorities and decide to pursue a more practical way to make a living. But another friend might have encouraged you to work hard at your music, and you could go on to have a successful recording career. Watching children play on a playground might help you realize that having a child must be an important part of your future plans.

The selections in this chapter describe how events, both large and small, both chance and planned, can have a shaping effect on people's lives. Each reading will help give you a perspective on the importance of events in the human experience. You will read about encounters with birth ("A Letter to My Daughter" and "Under the Overpass") and death, both in war ("Desert Storm and Desert Shield") and in a neighborhood park ("To Mr. Winslow"). You'll also read about how an academic award shaped a young girl's attitude toward the world ("The Scholarship Jacket") and how a date chosen for a marriage ceremony connects the bridegroom to his past ("Breaking Glass"). In addition, you'll read about a major historical event in our legal system ("Sandra Day O'Connor: First Woman Supreme Court Justice").

Brainstorming About Events

Class Activities:

1. Working in groups of three or four, make a list of events that are *supposed* to be memorable (graduations, birthdays, etc.).
2. Prepare a second list, including only events that made a difference in your life.
3. Compare the two lists. How frequently does the same event appear on both lists?
4. Discuss conclusions that can be drawn.

The Scholarship Jacket

‣ Marta Salinas

This fictional story describes a young girl's experience in which she struggles to receive an award she has earned. The essay was reprinted from Cuentos Chicanos: A Short Story Anthology.

Reading Strategy

When reading short stories such as this one, try to identify the following elements:

- Setting—Where and when does the story takes place?
- Characters—Who are the important people involved in the story?
- Point of view—Through whose eyes is the story being told?
- Plot—What major events occur?
- Theme—What is the meaning of the story? What is its message?

Vocabulary Preview

agile (2) coordinated
eavesdrop (4) listen in
rooted (4) held uncontrollably
filtered (7) passed through
fidgeted (8) moved about nervously
muster (12) gather
mesquite (15) a sugary plant with bean pods
gaunt (25) extremely thin
vile (29) foul; repulsive
adrenaline (31) a chemical secreted by the body causing a
    great surge of energy

The small Texas school that I attended carried out a tradition every   1
year during the eighth grade graduation; a beautiful gold and green
jacket, the school colors, was awarded to the class valedictorian, the
student who had maintained the highest grades for eight years. The
scholarship jacket had a big gold S on the left front side and the win-
ner's name was written in gold letters on the pocket.

My oldest sister Rosie had won the jacket a few years back and I   2
fully expected to win also. I was fourteen and in the eighth grade. I had

been a straight A student since the first grade, and the last year I had looked forward to owning that jacket. My father was a farm laborer who couldn't earn enough money to feed eight children, so when I was six I was given to my grandparents to raise. We couldn't participate in sports at school because there were registration fees, uniform costs, and trips out of town; so even though we were quite agile and athletic, there would never be a sports school jacket for us. This one, the scholarship jacket, was our only chance.

In May, close to graduation, spring fever struck, and no one paid 3 any attention in class; instead we stared out the windows and at each other, wanting to speed up the last few weeks of school. I despaired every time I looked in the mirror. Pencil thin, not a curve anywhere, I was called "Beanpole" and "String Bean" and I knew that's what I looked like. A flat chest, no hips, and a brain, that's what I had. That really isn't much for a fourteen-year-old to work with, I thought, as I absentmindedly wandered from my history class to the gym. Another hour of sweating in basketball and displaying my toothpick legs was coming up. Then I remembered my P.E. shorts were still in a bag under my desk where I'd forgotten them. I had to walk all the way back and get them. Coach Thompson was a real bear if anyone wasn't dressed for P.E. She had said I was a good forward and once she even tried to talk Grandma into letting me join the team. Grandma, of course, said no.

I was almost back at my classroom's door when I heard angry 4 voices and arguing. I stopped. I didn't mean to eavesdrop; I just hesitated, not knowing what to do. I needed those shorts and I was going to be late, but I didn't want to interrupt an argument between my teachers. I recognized the voices: Mr. Schmidt, my history teacher, and Mr. Boone, my math teacher. They seemed to be arguing about me. I couldn't believe it. I still remember the shock that rooted me flat against the wall as if I were trying to blend in with the graffiti written there.

"I refuse to do it! I don't care who her father is, her grades don't 5 even begin to compare to Marta's. I won't lie or falsify records. Marta has a straight A plus average and you know it." That was Mr. Schmidt and he sounded very angry. Mr. Boone's voice sounded calm and quiet.

"Look, Joann's father is not only on the Board, he owns the only 6 store in town; we could say it was a close tie and—"

The pounding in my ears drowned out the rest of the words, only a 7 word here and there filtered through. ". . . Marta is Mexican. . . . resign. . . . won't do it. . . ." Mr. Schmidt came rushing out, and luckily for me went down the opposite way toward the auditorium, so he didn't see me. Shaking, I waited a few minutes and then went in and grabbed my bag and fled from the room. Mr. Boone looked up when I came in but didn't say anything. To this day I don't remember if I got in trouble in P.E. for being late or how I made it through the rest of the afternoon. I went home very sad and cried into my pillow that night so Grandmother wouldn't hear me. It seemed a cruel coincidence that I had overheard that conversation.

The next day when the principal called me into his office, I knew   8
what it would be about. He looked uncomfortable and unhappy. I decided I wasn't going to make it any easier for him so I looked him straight in the eye. He looked away and fidgeted with the papers on his desk.

"Marta," he said, "there's been a change in policy this year regard-   9
ing the scholarship jacket. As you know, it has always been free." He cleared his throat and continued. "This year the Board decided to charge fifteen dollars—which still won't cover the complete cost of the jacket."

I stared at him in shock and a small sound of dismay escaped my   10
throat. I hadn't expected this. He still avoided looking in my eyes.

"So if you are unable to pay the fifteen dollars for the jacket, it will   11
be given to the next one in line."

Standing with all the dignity I could muster, I said, "I'll speak to my   12
grandfather about it, sir, and let you know tomorrow." I cried on the walk home from the bus stop. The dirt road was a quarter of a mile from the highway, so by the time I got home, my eyes were red and puffy.

"Where's Grandpa?" I asked Grandma, looking down at the floor so   13
she wouldn't ask me why I'd been crying. She was sewing on a quilt and didn't look up.

"I think he's out back working in the bean field."   14

I went outside and looked out at the fields. There he was. I could   15
see him walking between the rows, his body bent over the little plants, hoe in hand. I walked slowly out to him, trying to think how I could best ask him for the money. There was a cool breeze blowing and a sweet smell of mesquite in the air, but I didn't appreciate it. I kicked at a dirt clod. I wanted that jacket so much. It was more than just being a valedictorian and giving a little thank you speech for the jacket on graduation night. It represented eight years of hard work and expectation. I knew I had to be honest with Grandpa; it was my only chance. He saw me and looked up.

He waited for me to speak. I cleared my throat nervously and   16
clasped my hands behind my back so he wouldn't see them shaking. "Grandpa, I have a big favor to ask you," I said in Spanish, the only lan-

guage he knew. He still waited silently. I tried again. "Grandpa, this year the principal said the scholarship jacket is not going to be free. It's going to cost fifteen dollars and I have to take the money in tomorrow, otherwise it'll be given to someone else." The last words came out in an eager rush. Grandpa straightened up tiredly and leaned his chin on the hoe handle. He looked out over the field that was filled with the tiny green bean plants. I waited, desperately hoping he'd say I could have the money.

He turned to me and asked quietly, "What does a scholarship jacket mean?"　17

I answered quickly; maybe there was a chance. "It means you've earned it by having the highest grades for eight years and that's why they're giving it to you." Too late I realized the significance of my words. Grandpa knew that I understood it was not a matter of money. It wasn't that. He went back to hoeing the weeds that sprang up between the delicate little bean plants. It was a time consuming job; sometimes the small shoots were right next to each other. Finally he spoke again.　18

"Then if you pay for it, Marta, it's not a scholarship jacket, is it? Tell your principal I will not pay the fifteen dollars."　19

I walked back to the house and locked myself in the bathroom for a long time. I was angry with Grandfather even though I knew he was right, and I was angry with the Board, whoever they were. Why did they have to change the rules just when it was my turn to win the jacket?　20

It was a very sad and withdrawn girl who dragged into the principal's office the next day. This time he did look me in the eyes.　21

"What did your grandfather say?"　22

I sat very straight in my chair.　23

"He said to tell you he won't pay the fifteen dollars."　24

The principal muttered something I couldn't understand under his breath, and walked over to the window. He stood looking out at something outside. He looked bigger than usual when he stood up; he was a tall gaunt man with gray hair, and I watched the back of his head while I waited for him to speak.　25

"Why?" he finally asked. "Your grandfather has the money. Doesn't he own a small bean farm?"　26

I looked at him, forcing my eyes to stay dry. "He said if I had to pay for it, then it wouldn't be a scholarship jacket," I said and stood up to leave. "I guess you'll just have to give it to Joann." I hadn't meant to say that; it had just slipped out. I was almost to the door when he stopped me.　27

"Marta —wait."   28

I turned and looked at him, waiting. What did he want now? I   29
could feel my heart pounding. Something bitter and vile tasting was
coming up in my mouth; I was afraid I was going to be sick. I didn't
need any sympathy speeches. He sighed loudly and went back to his
big desk. He looked at me, biting his lip, as if thinking.

"Okay, damn it. We'll make an exception in your case. I'll tell the   30
Board, you'll get your jacket."

I could hardly believe it. I spoke in a trembling rush. "Oh, thank   31
you, sir!" Suddenly I felt great. I didn't know about adrenaline in those
days, but I knew something was pumping through me, making me feel
as tall as the sky. I wanted to yell, jump, run the mile, do something. I
ran out so I could cry in the hall where there was no one to see me. At
the end of the day, Mr. Schmidt winked at me and said, "I hear you're
getting a scholarship jacket this year."

His face looked as happy and innocent as a baby's, but I knew bet-   32
ter. Without answering I gave him a quick hug and ran to the bus. I
cried on the walk home again, but this time because I was so happy. I
couldn't wait to tell Grandpa and ran straight to the field. I joined him
in the row where he was working and without saying anything I
crouched down and started pulling up the weeds with my hands.
Grandpa worked alongside me for a few minutes, but he didn't ask
what had happened. After I had a little pile of weeds between the rows,
I stood up and faced him.

"The principal said he's making an exception for me, Grandpa, and   33
I'm getting the jacket after all. That's after I told him what you said."

Grandpa didn't say anything, he just gave me a pat on the shoulder   34
and a smile. He pulled out the crumpled red handkerchief that he always carried in his back pocket and wiped the sweat off his forehead.

"Better go see if your grandmother needs any help with supper."   35

I gave him a big grin. He didn't fool me. I skipped and ran back to   36
the house whistling some silly tune.

Examining the Reading

Finding Meaning

1. Why didn't the author participate in school sports, although she
   was athletic?
2. What were Marta's two teachers arguing about?
3. Why did Marta's grandfather refuse to give her the money for the
   scholarship jacket?
4. What kind of a person was Marta's grandfather?

5. Why did Marta's math teacher, Mr. Boone, want the scholarship jacket to go to another student?

Understanding Technique

1. Discuss Salinas's use of dialogue. What purpose does it serve in the story?
2. What is the theme of the story?

Thinking Critically

1. Why do you think the Board decided to charge for the scholarship jacket?
2. Why do you think the principal changed his mind about charging Marta for the jacket?
3. Discuss the character differences between Marta's teachers.
4. After Marta told her grandfather she was getting the scholarship jacket, what did she mean when she said his reaction "didn't fool me"?

Writing About the Reading

A Journal Entry

Write a journal entry exploring your attitudes about winning games, prizes, or awards. Is this important to you? Why or why not?

A Paragraph

1. The author implied that Mr. Schmidt, her history teacher, was willing to quit his job if Marta did not receive the scholarship jacket that was rightfully hers. Suppose you were Mr. Schmidt: would you have been willing to quit your job over the issue of fairness? Write a paragraph stating and defending your decision.
2. Suppose you were in a position to win a game or contest and then realized that someone else was about to win it unfairly. Write a paragraph describing how you would handle the situation.

An Essay

1. The author became so anxious while talking to her principal that she was afraid she was going to become sick. Write an essay describing a situation in your life that caused you the same level of anxiety and explain how you resolved it.

2. The awarding of the scholarship jacket is a memorable event illustrating a choice between right and wrong that the author recalls from her childhood. Write an essay recalling such an event from your childhood, and explain how it affected you and whether it ended happily or not.

A Creative Activity

Suppose the principal had decided not to make an exception for Marta. How might she have felt? What, if anything, might she say to Joann? What might her grandfather say? Rewrite the ending of the story, answering the above questions.

Under the Overpass

) Michael Datcher

In this essay a young man describes how a single event has changed the course of his life and shattered his dreams. This essay was first published in Image *magazine.*

Reading Strategy

Writers often give additional meanings to ordinary objects. For example, in the song lyric in the third paragraph of this essay, the word *storm* refers to a weather event, but also a stormy or troubled state of mind or condition.

Vocabulary Preview

overpass (1) bridge
repugnance (3) distastefulness
salvage (4) save; restore; find and fix up
legacies (4) inheritances; histories
eclipsing (4) overshadowing
feat (5) accomplishment
vantage point (5) perspective; viewpoint
entrepreneurs (5) creators of businesses
ironic (7) opposite in meaning
in lieu of (8) in place of; instead of

You have just walked under the overpass (a place where you can get just below the funk) and, down here, we have picket fence fantasies too. We dream of wives and kids and playing catch in the park. We long for Father-Son picnics where we fall over the sack race finish line first. I never knew my father so my fatherhood fantasies started early. I would be the dream father for my son so he wouldn't have to fantasize about his. I would wait for my soul mate and let nature take its course. This was my dream.

An old black woman once told me, "A girl becomes a woman when her dreams die." The same may be said for a black man. Before I could meet my soul mate a girl masquerading as a woman made me her dream. Despite the pills (I never saw swallowed) in her purse and the latex lining my wallet, she said, "I'm having your baby." What I heard: "Your dream is dead."

Dreams die hard, here, under the overpass because they are often   3
all we have. Dreams allow us to look at the despair of our days and repugnance of our nights and somehow keep on going. Dreams allow us
to sing, "The storm is passin' o-vah," even when there is no relief in
sight. I guess we call this faith. Faith in some higher being, a Creator,
that seems to have a hate/love relationship with His black creations ev-
idenced by the great pain He has allowed us to endure and the same
pain that he has allowed us to overcome. This is the faith that I will
need to draw upon as I enter fatherhood with no soul mate, no picket
fence.

In times such as these, raising a black child has become a political   4
act: an act of self defense. Our children will be on the front lines trying
to salvage the few inroads that we will have managed to provide for
them. Their road will be a difficult one. We have to prepare our children to confront a world that will not appreciate their beauty, will not
understand their minor chord lives. The black father's role in this preparation will be critical. History is rich with the heroic parental deeds of
our underpass sisters, mothers and matriarchs. Where is the memory
of the heroic black male father? Black fathers need to create their own
memories, leave their own legacies. The absentee black father has begun to define the image of all black fathers, eclipsing the images of the
fathers who read their children bedtime stories after bringing home
the bacon. Overshadowing all the fathers who learned how to cornrow
their daughter's hair. If there were more black fathers providing and
reading and cornrowing, the absentee father image would begin to
ring false. Black fathers must begin to step forward—especially in raising black sons.

My mother managed to raise me with no soul mate, no picket fence.   5
Given our neighborhood, this feat is a testimony to her strength and
love. She is another black heroic mother. Yet, with all of her heroism
she could never teach me how to be a man because that was one thing
that she was not. She could never show me how to vibe with the brothers on the block. She could never be an example of how a man should
treat a woman. . . . Kids learn by observation. They are tiny mirrors
trying to make their way in the world. My mother could tell me how to
be a man but she couldn't show me. So I took my cue from young
males in the neighborhood who, from my vantage point, looked like
men. The blind leading the blind. Our fathers need to be there to raise
our sons. We cannot lay such a great responsibility on "urban entrepreneurs" and tired ass niggas.

There is too much at stake. We are in danger of losing a whole gen-   6
eration of young black boys to drug addiction, prison, AIDS, and homi-
cide. The oft noted statistics are staggering. Since children learn
through imitation, our black fathers have got to be there to walk with

their sons. To live lives that are worthy of imitation. To teach by loving themselves first, so that their sons can observe then follow. It is self-love that will be the savior of our young boys. Self-love that will be the savior of our community.

It is ironic that with all of the complex social ills that are plaguing 7 us here, under the overpass, a love for ourselves is what we need most. Education, balanced diets, drug prevention, jobs. These are the remedies for improving our life chances, but self-love is the motivation. Medicine without a desire to take it and get well is meaningless medicine. Love then is the greatest gift that our black fathers have to offer. Let us not get caught up in allowing the wider societal structure define the kinds of fathers we need to be. We have different priorities. We are trying to prevent the loss of a whole generation of black boys. We are trying to stop the destruction of our legacy. This is one battle that we cannot lose.

This is one battle that I cannot lose. By the time you reach this last 8 paragraph, I will be fighting to deal with the loss of my dream while struggling to be the father that I never knew. In lieu of my dream, I will be holding on to faith that the storm will pass o-vah, here, under the overpass.

Examining the Reading

Finding Meaning

1. What is a "picket fence" fantasy?
2. According to the essay, when does a girl become a woman?
3. What was the author's dream?
4. Why does the author feel he has lost his dream?
5. What is the author's main point in writing the essay?

Understanding Technique

1. Evaluate Datcher's paragraph structure.
2. How does the title contribute to the meaning of the essay?

Thinking Critically

1. What does the author mean when he says that "raising a black child has become a political act" (paragraph 4)? Do you agree? Why or why not?
2. Why is it especially important for black fathers to play a major role in raising their sons?
3. What does the author mean when he states that "black fathers must begin to step forward" (paragraph 4)?

4. Discuss your feelings about the author. Do you feel sympathy? Do you respect him for accepting responsibility?

Writing About the Reading

A Journal Entry

Write an entry discussing a dream you have or one you once had that did not come true.

A Paragraph

1. Write a paragraph explaining one important characteristic of a good father. Include specific examples or experiences from your childhood, your observations, or your experience as a father.
2. Write a paragraph describing a dream that came true.

An Essay

1. The author suggests that children reach adulthood when their dreams die and they are forced to face and accept reality, often in the form of a difficult situation. Write an essay describing a situation that forced you to "grow up."
2. Write an essay describing how a single event shaped or changed the course of your life. What were your options when this happened? Why did you do what you did, and would you do the same thing if you had the choice now?

A Creative Activity

Suppose the author's girlfriend finds out that her pregnancy tests were wrong and that she is not pregnant after all. Write a new ending to the story, indicating how you think the author feels and what he might do to realize his dream.

A Letter to My Daughter

▶ **Siu Wai Anderson**

This letter, written by a mother to her infant daughter, discusses issues of cross-cultural adoptions. It was first published in an anthology of writings by women of color: Making Face, Making Soul.

Reading Strategy

Anderson uses a personal letter to describe her ancestry and express her feelings toward her daughter. As you read, think about why Anderson uses the letter format. What advantages does it give her as a writer?

Vocabulary Preview

auspicious (1) favorable
travail (1) painful work; childbirth
demographical (3) conforming to the average of the population
proverbial (3) as in a popular saying or proverb
legacy (3) inheritance
agonizing (4) extremely painful
ancestral (5) having to do with forebears
hail (7) welcome
deprivation (7) doing without necessities
lavishing (10) giving abundantly

August 1989, Boston

Dear Maya Shao-ming,

You were born at Mt. Auburn Hospital in Cambridge on June 6, 1989, 1
an auspicious date, and for me, the end of a long, long travail. Because you insisted on being breech, with your head always close to my heart, you came into the world by C-section into a chilly O.R. at the opposite end of the labor and delivery suite where, exhausted yet exuberant, I pushed out your brother in a birthing room nearly four years ago.

    I couldn't believe my ears when your father exclaimed, "A girl!" All 2
I could do was cry the tears of a long-awaited dream come true. You are so beautiful, with your big dark eyes and silky black hair. Your skin is more creamy than golden, reflecting your particular "happa haole"

blend. But your long elegant fingers are those of a Chinese scholar, prized for high intelligence and sensitivity.

You are more than just a second child, more than just a girl to   3
match our boy, to fit the demographical nuclear family with the proverbial 2.5 children. No, ten years ago I wrote a song for an unborn dream: a dark-haired, dark-eyed child who would be my flesh-and-blood link to humanity. I had no other until your brother came. He was my first Unborn Song. But you, little daughter, are the link to our female line, the legacy of another woman's pain and sacrifice thirty-one years ago.

Let me tell you about your Chinese grandmother. Somewhere in   4
Hong Kong, in the late fifties, a young waitress found herself pregnant by a cook, probably a co-worker at her restaurant. She carried the baby to term, suffered to give it birth, and kept the little girl for the first three months of her life. I like to think that my mother—your grandmother—loved me and fought to raise me on her own, but that the daily struggle was too hard. Worn down by the demands of the new baby and perhaps the constant threat of starvation, she made the agonizing decision to give away her girl so that both of us might have a chance for a better life.

More likely, I was dumped at the orphanage steps or forcibly re-   5
moved from a home of abuse and neglect by a social welfare worker. I will probably never know the truth. Having a baby in her unmarried state would have brought shame on the family in China, so she probably kept my existence a secret. Once I was out of her life, it was as if I had never been born. And so you and your brother and I are the missing leaves on an ancestral tree.

Do they ever wonder if we exist?   6

I was brought to the U.S. before I was two, and adopted by the An-   7
glo parents who hail you as their latest beautiful grandchild. Raised by a minister's family in postwar American prosperity and nourished on three square meals a day, I grew like a wild weed and soaked up all the opportunities they had to offer—books, music, education, church life and community activities. Amidst a family of blue-eyed blonds, though, I stood out like a sore thumb. Whether from jealousy or fear of someone who looked so different, my older brothers sometimes tormented me with racist name-calling, teased me about my poor eyesight and unsightly skin, or made fun of my clumsy walk. Moody and impatient, gifted and temperamental, burdened by fears and nightmares that none of us realized stemmed from my early years of deprivation, I was not an easy child to love. My adoptive mother and I clashed countless times over the years, but gradually came to see one another as real human beings with faults and talents, and as women of strength in our own right. Now we love each other very much, though the scars and memories of our early battles will never quite fade. Lack-

ing a mirror image in the mother who raised me, I had to seek my identity as a woman on my own. The Asian American community has helped me reclaim my dual identity and enlightened my view of the struggles we face as minorities in a white-dominated culture. They have applauded my music and praised my writings.

But part of me will always be missing: my beginnings, my personal history, all the subtle details that give a person her origin. I don't know how I was born, whether it was vaginally or by Cesarean. I don't know when, or where exactly, how much I weighed, or whose ears heard my first cry of life. Was I put to my mother's breast and tenderly rocked, or was I simply weighed, cleaned, swaddled and carted off to a sterile nursery, noted in the hospital records as "newborn female"? 8

Someone took the time to give me a lucky name, and write the appropriate characters in neat brush strokes in the Hong Kong city register. "Siu" means "little." My kind of "wai" means "clever" or "wise." Therefore, my baby name was "Clever little one." Who chose those words? Who cared enough to note my arrival in the world? 9

I lost my Chinese name for eighteen years. It was Americanized for convenience to "Sue." But like an ill-fitting coat, it made me twitch and fret and squirm. I hated the name. But even more, I hated being Chinese. It took many years to become proud of my Asian heritage and work up the courage to take back my birthname. That plus a smattering of classroom Cantonese, are all the Chinese culture I have to offer you, little one. Not white, certainly, but not really Asian, I straddle the two worlds and try to blaze your trails for you. Your name, "Shaoming," is very much like mine—"Shao" is the Mandarin form of "Siu," meaning "little." And "ming" is "bright," as in a shining sun or moon. Whose lives will you brighten, little Maya? Your past is more complete than mine, and each day I cradle you in your babyhood, lavishing upon you the tender care I lacked for my first two years. When I console you, I comfort the lost baby inside me who still cries out for her mother. No wonder so many adoptees desperately long to have children of their own. 10

Sweet Maya, it doesn't matter what you "become" later on. You have already fulfilled my wildest dreams. 11

I love you,

Mommy

Examining the Reading

Finding Meaning

1. What does the author know about her biological mother?
2. Why did the author's brothers tease her and call her names?

3. Explain Siu Wai's reaction to being called Sue.
4. How does the author feel about her Asian identity?
5. What did the author most want to tell her daughter?

Understanding Technique

1. What type of details does Anderson include to make her essay lively and interesting?
2. Although she describes events, Anderson does not follow a strict chronological sequence. Why doesn't she and what effect does this have?

Thinking Critically

1. As a Chinese female raised by American parents and not knowing her biological mother, the author faces numerous problems in growing up. What kinds of problems do you think these were?
2. It seems to be especially important to the author that she be an excellent mother to her infant daughter. Why do you think this is?
3. What does the author mean at the end of the story when she writes to her daughter, "It doesn't matter what you 'become' later on. You have already fulfilled my wildest dreams"?
4. Suppose the author had given birth to a second son instead of a daughter. Would she have written a letter? If so, how would it differ from the letter to Maya?

Writing About the Reading

A Journal Entry

Write an entry discussing your reactions to this letter. How did it make you feel? What questions did it raise?

A Paragraph

1. If you could see a videotape of one day of your childhood, what day would you choose? Write a paragraph explaining your choice.
2. If you could communicate briefly with only one deceased relative or friend, whom would you choose? Write a paragraph explaining your choice and what you would want to say.

An Essay

1. Write a letter to someone close to you explaining a difficult part of your childhood.

2. Suppose you have just learned that the parents who raised you were not your biological parents. Next week you will meet your biological parents. Write an essay identifying the three most important questions you want to ask them. Explain why each is important. If you are adopted, explain whether you know or want to know your birth parents.

A Creative Activity

Suppose Maya is now 15 years old and has decided to write a letter to her biological grandmother (Siu Wai's biological mother). What do you think she will say? Write the opening paragraph of the letter.

To Mr. Winslow

▶ **Ian Frazier**

*The death of Mr. Winslow was a tragic event that affected the
lives of many. This essay, first published in* The New Yorker
*magazine, describes how community members memorialized his
death.*

Reading Strategy

This essay is a good example of the use of descriptive language.
Frazier conveys his ideas by presenting numerous details that
show you the scene of Mr. Winslow's death and help you to understand the community's response to it. As you read, highlight
particularly striking and descriptive words and phrases that
help capture the author's meaning.

Vocabulary Preview

cobbled (1) paved with rounded stones
discarded (2) thrown away
carafe (2) bottle
avenge (2) punish; take revenge for
accumulation (3) gathering of items
sprigs (3) twigs; small branches
converge (6) come together, meet

*O*n June 1st, in the afternoon, four teen-agers approached a forty-   1
two-year-old drama teacher named Allyn Winslow on Quaker Hill, in
Brooklyn's Prospect Park, and tried to steal his new mountain bike.
When he resisted and rode away, they shot him four times with a .22-
calibre pistol. He rode down the hill to the cobbled path leading to the
Picnic House, fell off his bike, and died. The TV news that evening
showed the bike on the grass, and his body, covered by a sheet, next to
it. I recognized the spot where he lay. I take my daughter to the pond
nearby to throw bread to the ducks. She and I had sat there, or near
there.

I walked by the spot the next day. It was marked by a wad of dis-   2
carded surgical tape and an inside-out surgical glove. The day after,
when I went by there I saw a Timberland shoebox with a bouquet of

flowers in it, and a glass wine carafe with more flowers. In the shoebox was a piece of lined paper on which someone had written in blue ink: "To the biker Mr. Winslow, May you be in a better place with angels on a cloud." These words echoed in the media as reporters quoted and misquoted them. Men and women were carrying microphones and TV cameras in the vicinity, and if you weren't careful they would interview you. About a week later, an American flag had been stuck into the ground next to the shoebox. There was a bunch of papers in a clear-plastic envelope, and the one on top said, "AVENGE THIS ACT OF COWARDICE." In and around the shoebox were notes addressed to Mr. Winslow and his wife and their two children; a blue-and-white striped ribbon; a ceramic pipe; a bike rider's reflector badge in the image of a peace sign; a red-and-white bandanna; a flyer from the Guardian Angels organization; and an announcement of an upcoming service to be held in his memory.

The following week, the accumulation around the shoebox had grown. The flowers in it and in the wine carafe were fresh—roses, peonies, yellow freesias. Someone had arranged many pinecones and sprigs of oak leaves in a circle on the perimeter. In the ground by the flag was a cross made of wood, bound with red ribbon and draped with a string of purple glass beads, and, near the cross, a photocopy of a newspaper photograph of Allyn Winslow. A Dover edition of Shakespeare's "Complete Sonnets" rested on a pedestal made of a cross-section of a branch from a London Plane tree. There were also several anti-N.R.A. stickers, a blue candle in a plastic cup, and a five of spades from a pack of Bicycle playing cards. Chunks of paving stones held down a poster showing the number of people killed in 1990 by handguns in various countries: thirteen in Sweden, ninety-one in Switzerland, eighty-seven in Japan, sixty-eight in Canada, ten thousand five hundred and sixty-seven in the United States. A girl visiting the park on a class picnic asked another girl, "Is he buried here?"

A week or two later, many of the items had vanished. Someone had burned the flag, but the charred flagpole remained. The cross, broken off at the base, lay on the ground. The plastic cup with the candle was cracked. The grass around the spot was worn down in a circle and littered with dried flower stems. The carafe had a big chip out of the top. The shoebox had begun to sag. The papers were gone, except for a rain-stained sign saying, "To Honor, To Mourn Allyn Winslow," and a pamphlet, "Verses of Comfort, Assurance and Salvation."

By mid-July, the shoebox was in pieces. There were a few rocks, two small forked branches stuck in the ground, the ashes of a small fire, and a "You gotta have Park!" button. By mid-August, the tramped-down grass had begun to grow back. I noticed a piece of red-and-white string and a scrap from the shoebox. By September, so little of the memorial remained that the spot was hard to find. A closer look revealed the burned patch, some red and white string now faded to pink, and flower stems so scattered and broken you'd have to know what they were to recognize them.

Just now—a bright, chilly fall day—I went by the place again.   6 Color in the park's trees had reached its peak. In a grove of buckskin-brown oaks, yellow shot up the fountain of a ginkgo tree. A flock of pigeons rose all at once and glided to a new part of the Long Meadow, circling once before landing, like a dog before it lies down. A police car slipped around the corner of the Picnic House, a one-man police scooter rode down the path, a police helicopter flew by just above the trees. At first, I could find no trace of the memorial at all: grass and clover have reclaimed the bared dirt. I got down on one knee, muddying my pants. Finally, I found a wooden stake broken off about half an inch above the ground; the base of the memorial cross, probably—the only sign of the unmeasured sorrows that converge here.

Examining the Reading

Finding Meaning

1. Why was the memorial site located in a park?
2. Give some examples of how other people who used the park expressed their feelings about Mr. Winslow's death.
3. Why did people choose items such as Shakespeare's "Complete Sonnets" and anti-N.R.A. stickers for the memorial?
4. How did the media handle the tragedy of Mr. Winslow's death?

Understanding Technique

1. Describe the essay's organization.
2. Evaluate the essay's title. What is Frazier's thesis? Is it stated or implied (suggested)?

Thinking Critically

1. What impact did this event seem to have on the community and on the author?
2. What is the main message that the author is trying to get across to the reader?
3. Judging from his tone, how do you think the author felt about the media? Why?
4. One of the papers in the clear-plastic envelope said, "Avenge this act of cowardice." What do you think the writer was suggesting?

5. Do you think Mr. Winslow's family was comforted by the memorial in the park? Why?
6. What conclusion(s) can you draw from the number of handgun deaths in the United States compared to the number in other countries? Why do we have so many handgun deaths?

Writing About the Reading

A Journal Entry

Write an entry about how you would like to be remembered after you die.

A Paragraph

1. Write a paragraph on how this type of event alters the lives of everyone involved.
2. Write a paragraph about how this tragedy might have been prevented.

An Essay

1. Imagine that you were one of Mr. Winslow's students. Write an essay discussing what you might say to his family to comfort them in their tragedy.
2. If someone you knew well died the way Mr. Winslow did, what would you do to honor him or her?

A Creative Activity

Suppose you were the person who wrote the message, "Avenge this act of cowardice" that was placed at Winslow's memorial. Continue this story by telling what you would do to avenge this killing and what would result from your actions.

Breaking Glass

▶ Jonathan Rosen

This essay, which was originally published in The New York Times Magazine *in 1996, explains what a Jewish wedding custom came to mean to the author. He also describes how his wedding anniversary has become linked with his father's past.*

Reading Strategy

The writer of this essay switches back and forth in time. After you read the essay, construct a time line, a list, or diagram of the events in the order in which they occurred.

Vocabulary Preview

pulverizing (2) crushing
symbolic (2) standing for or representing something else
euphoniously euphemistic (3) more pleasant sounding than the truth
ran amok (3) savagely attacked everyone in their path
eerie (5) weird; strange
perverse (5) odd; offbeat
pogrom (6) organized violence against an identified group
obliterating (6) wiping out
commemoration (6) act of honoring the memory of an event
grandiose (8) extremely ambitious and impressive
naïve (8) simple minded

*T*he morning of my wedding, my father gave me a piece of unexpected advice. "When you step on the glass," he said, "why don't you imagine that all the doubts and fears of childhood are inside and that you're smashing them too?"

He was referring to one of the more mysterious customs at a Jewish wedding, in which the bridegroom stamps on a glass, marking the end of the ceremony. I liked my father's suggestion, though I was so afraid that the wineglass, wrapped in a white handkerchief, would shoot out unbroken (as I had once seen happen) that I forgot everything in my pulverizing zeal. But I was touched by his words, particularly because breaking the glass had already assumed a symbolic place in my mind—though one connected not to my own childhood but to his.

I was married on November 10, the anniversary of Kristallnacht. The German name, which means "the night of broken glass," is too euphoniously euphemistic to describe accurately what really happened in 1938, beginning on the night of November 9 and running into the next day. Mobs, urged on by the Nazi Government, ran amok throughout Germany and Austria, murdering, looting, smashing Jewish shop windows and burning synagogues. Thirty thousand Jews were arrested—including my grandfather, my father's father.   3

My father was 14, and Kristallnacht shattered his world. One month later he left Vienna on a children's transport, finding refuge first in Scotland and later in the United States. He never saw his parents again. Strange then, that I chose the anniversary of this terrible day for my wedding five years ago.   4

I cannot claim this was strictly by design. I'd wanted to get married in winter and my wife-to-be had inched the date forward until we settled on November 10. It was my father who pointed out the eerie accident. He did not ask me to change the date, but we easily could have. We had planned a small wedding in my parents' house. But after initial discomfort the coincidence had a distinct, if perverse, appeal.   5

More than 50 years had passed since the pogrom of 1938. The world could not be counted on to remember forever—hadn't I myself forgotten the date? Here was a way to graft my father's story onto my own. Soon the year 2000, with its obliterating zeros, would roll the terrible events of the twentieth century deeper into the past. My wedding would at least guarantee a kind of private commemoration. I would lash a piece of history to my back and carry it with me into the future.   6

But by mingling Kristallnacht with my own wedding, was I preserving it or erasing it further? Perhaps I did not wish to mark the date so much as unmark it—a typical childhood fantasy. I wanted to make whole my father's broken past, to offer up my own wedding as the joyful answer to tragic times.   7

Both impulses, of course, are equally grandiose and impossibly naïve. My own life can never contain or summarize the suffering of earlier generations, any more than it can answer or redeem those losses. My father understood this when he spoke to me on the morning of my wedding. For all he knew of the world, he could still have for me a father's wish—that I would banish the fears of childhood, even though the fears of *his* childhood were fully founded in real events. Every generation is born innocent, and if that is bad for history, it is nevertheless necessary for life.   8

And yet how can I stop trying to connect myself in some way to the   9
past? Which brings me back to my wedding and the ritual of the broken glass, which forms the final moment of the traditional Jewish ceremony. There are several explanations for this practice. The one I like
is that it is a reminder of the destruction of the temple in Jerusalem—
an event that happened some 1,900 years ago—and in a larger sense, a
reminder that the world itself is broken and imperfect. Smashing the
glass recalls this fact and introduces a fleeting note of sadness into an
otherwise festive occasion.

It is in this spirit that I celebrate my wedding anniversary today. I   10
think about my grandparents who were murdered and their son—my
father—who escaped to America and married my mother. I think
about my own lucky American life and joyful marriage and how little,
and how much, separates the past from the present, sorrow from celebration. I hear my father's kind advice, the cheerful cries of friends and
family and the distant echo of breaking glass.

Examining the Reading

Finding Meaning

1. What happened in Germany and Austria, on November 9–10, 1938?
2. What happened to Jonathan Rosen's father and grandparents after
   Kristallnacht?

3. Why does the bridegroom break a glass at traditional Jewish weddings?
4. What did the author's father want him to think about when he broke the glass?
5. Why didn't the author change his wedding date?

Understanding Technique

1. Discuss the effect of using dialogue to open this essay.
2. Evaluate how Rosen's use of questions helps to develop the essay.

Thinking Critically

1. Why did the author want to remember such a sad event at a happy occasion?
2. What are the different meanings of "breaking glass" in this essay?
3. What does the author think will happen to memories of twentieth century events, after the year 2000, "with its obliterating zeros"?
4. What does the author mean by "every generation is born innocent, and if that is bad for history, it is nevertheless necessary for life"?

Writing About the Reading

A Journal Entry

Write about an event in your life or your family's history that you would like people to remember.

A Paragraph

1. If you were the author, would you have chosen a different wedding date? Why or why not?
2. Why is it important for people to remember what happened during the Holocaust?

An Essay

1. Write an essay about how your childhood was different from your parents'. In what ways do you think yours was better; in what ways was theirs better?

2. Write an essay about some of your family's traditions and what they mean to you.

A Creative Activity

What do you think the author will tell his children about their grandparents' and great-grandparents' experiences?

Sandra Day O'Connor: First Woman Supreme Court Justice

▶ **Carol Berkin, Christopher L. Miller, Robert W. Cherny, and James L. Gormly**
Textbook Excerpt

This selection explores how an important event—the appointment of the first woman to the Supreme Court—occurred and its immediate and long-range effects. This excerpt is taken from a history text, Making America: A History of the United States.

Reading Strategy

Highlight the sections of the text that answer this question: How has O'Connor's position on the court changed over the years?

Vocabulary Preview

confirmed (1) approved by Congress
platform (2) what a candidate promises to do if elected
sanctity (2) sacredness; holiness
commission (4) military rank
activist (7) favoring vigorous action
swing vote (7) deciding vote
mandate (8) require; force on others
overarching (9) of primary importance or meaning
ideology (9) set of ideas or beliefs

On July 7, 1981, President Ronald Reagan announced that his 1
choice to replace Supreme Court justice Potter Stewart was "a person for all seasons": Sandra Day O'Connor. The 102nd justice appointed to the Court, she was the first woman nominated and the first confirmed.

Reagan's choice drew conflicting responses. Many within the con- 2
servative wing of the Republican party bitterly objected to O'Connor.

They reminded the president that she favored abortion rights and the Equal Rights Amendment. They pointed out that he had run on a platform promising that judges appointed by the Reagan administration would "respect family values and the sanctity of human life." Some liberals applauded Reagan for nominating a woman, but were nonetheless suspicious of any Reagan appointee. After all, O'Connor believed in judicial restraint, the idea that the Court should defer to Congress, the president, and public consensus to resolve controversial social and political questions.

The nomination was quickly approved by the Senate Judiciary 3 Committee and confirmed by the Senate. On September 26, 1981, Sandra Day O'Connor became associate justice of the Supreme Court.

The daughter of an Arizona rancher, Sandra Day attended Stan- 4 ford University, receiving a B.A. in economics and in 1952 a law degree. She graduated third in her law class, behind fellow Arizonian William Rehnquist, who by 1981 was also an associate justice of the Supreme Court. In 1952 she married John O'Connor. Despite high graduating rank and a Stanford law degree, Sandra Day O'Connor had difficulty finding a job as an attorney with a private law firm. A company in Los Angeles offered her a legal secretary's position, which she declined. Unable to land a job with a private firm, she worked as a county deputy attorney in northern California while her husband finished his law degree at Stanford. After he had graduated and received his commission in the army, she resigned from her job and joined him in Frankfurt, Germany, where she worked as a civilian lawyer for the army.

In 1957 the O'Connors returned to the United States and settled in 5 the Phoenix area. Two years later, following the birth of the first of three sons, Sandra Day O'Connor opened her own law firm with a friend. In 1960, when her second son was born, she stopped working to become a full-time mother. Doing volunteer work, she became active in Republican politics and served on a statewide committee on marriage and the family in 1965. That year, recognizing her skills as an organizer and a lawyer, the governor appointed her an assistant attorney general for Arizona. "I wanted a family and . . . I wanted to work," she recalled.

During her first five years on the Court, O'Connor most often voted 6 with the conservative bloc but frequently issued an independent opinion. In her opinions, she chose to emphasize two recurring themes: her belief that states are equal partners with the national government within the federal system and that courts should not play an active role in shaping social and political values.

With the arrival of other justices appointed by Reagan and by 7 George Bush, the Court in 1990 became more activist in the name of conservatism and rewrote several earlier liberal decisions. Conservatives hoped that the Court, with its conservative agenda, would move forward to reverse positions on abortion, separation of church and state, free speech, and affirmative action. As the Court became increasingly activist, Justice O'Connor's position shifted slightly away from the conservative bloc and toward the center. During the 1990–1991 session, she frequently was the swing vote in 5-to-4 decisions. One observer of the Court commented, "As O'Connor goes, so goes the Court."

By the end of the 1991–1992 session, she was regarded as a leading   8
member of a centrist bloc, which also included justices Anthony Kennedy and David Souter. In perhaps the most controversial decision of the Court's calendar, *Planned Parenthood of Southeastern Pennsylvania* v. *Casey* (1992), she co-authored the majority decision, which reaffirmed the right of women to seek an abortion, while criticizing the constitutional argument in the *Roe* v. *Wade* decision. Writing for the majority, O'Connor explained her choice, "Some of us as individuals find abortion offensive to our most basic principles of morality, but that cannot control our decision. Our obligation is to define the liberty of all, not to mandate our own moral code."

As the Supreme Court enters a new era under the Clinton adminis-   9
tration and with the appointment of the second woman justice—Ruth Bader Ginsburg—many observers expect the O'Connor center will be strengthened. But the same observers have difficulty predicting how O'Connor herself will vote, except to say that because of her open-minded conservative approach and lack of an overarching ideology that could predetermine her decision, she will continue to guide her choices in judging each case based on its own merits.

Examining the Reading

Finding Meaning

1. How did Ronald Reagan describe Sandra Day O'Connor?
2. Why did Reagan's choice for the Supreme Court draw "conflicting responses"?
3. What two themes run through Justice O'Connor's legal opinions?
4. How did she become involved in Republican politics?
5. What was O'Connor's first job?

Understanding Technique

1. Describe the organization of this textbook excerpt.
2. Find the topic sentence in each paragraph. Once you've located each topic sentence, think about its location. Why do you think the

authors placed it where they did? Would it have been equally effective if it were placed elsewhere in the paragraph? Why or why not?

Thinking Critically

1. Do you think O'Connor has been a good judge? Why or why not?
2. Why do you think Ronald Reagan appointed O'Connor to the Supreme Court?
3. What is meant by the statement, "As O'Connor goes, so goes the Court"?
4. Do you think O'Connor's decisions shaped the public's political opinion of Ronald Reagan? If so, how?
5. The reading stated that "During her first five years on the Court, O'Connor most often voted with the conservative bloc but frequently issued an independent opinion." What does this mean?
6. While explaining her decision in *Roe* v. *Wade*, O'Connor stated that "Our obligation is to define the liberty of all, not to mandate our own moral code." What did she mean by this statement?
7. Why do you think O'Connor initially had difficulty finding a job after finishing law school? What information in this article supports your opinion?

Writing About the Reading

A Journal Entry

Write an entry on a politician who has shaped your life in some way.

A Paragraph

1. Select one political issue and write a paragraph discussing the differences between the conservative point of view and the liberal point of view.
2. If you could change one law in this country, which would it be? Write a paragraph explaining what law you would change and why you would change it.

An Essay

1. O'Connor indicated that her personal views on abortion were different from her public views. Write an essay explaining this inconsistency.
2. The excerpt states that O'Connor believed the "courts should not play an active role in shaping social and political values." Do you agree or disagree with this statement? Write an essay explaining why you agree or disagree.

3. People in public offices often affect other people by the example they set through their actions. Select one person who has been in public office and write an essay on whether he or she provided a good or bad role model for others. Be sure to give reasons and examples to support your viewpoint.

A Creative Activity

Sometimes decisions that people make for other than career-related reasons alter the courses of their careers. If Sandra Day O'Connor had not stopped working to become a full-time mother, her career might have developed differently. Rewrite the ending of this excerpt to show what might have happened had she not put personal matters before her career in 1960.

Desert Storm and Shield

▸ **Scott Stopa**
Student Essay

Scott Stopa, a college student, wrote this essay explaining how a phone call from his platoon sergeant changed his life. His essay describes how his experiences in the Persian Gulf became a turning point in his life.

*T*here are many events that have been major turning points in my life. Some of these are my marriage, the birth of my children, my divorce, going back to school, and joining the Marine Corps. The biggest turning point in my life, however, was going off to war in the Persian Gulf (Operations Desert Shield and Desert Storm). It was November 1990 when the 8th Tank Battalion, of which I was a part, was activated. I was 20 years old and just out of boot camp. I had only been home for two weeks when we were sent overseas.

When Iraq invaded Kuwait, there was a lot of talk of the United States going to war, but of course I never thought in a million years that I would be sent off to war. I thought, no, I'd never be sent. After all, I'm only in the reserves. Boy, was I wrong. The news came by phone. I was living at my parents' house at the time. My mother answered the phone. It was my platoon sergeant. When my mother handed me the phone, I could see the tears in her eyes. Then he gave me the news. My heart dropped. I was speechless when I got off the phone. All I could do when I looked at my mother was tell her I'm sorry.

I remember that night like it was yesterday. I got in my car and drove, with nowhere special in mind. I ended up down by the falls, where I walked around and did a lot of thinking. What would we be in for, and how would I react if certain situations arose? At that point I made up my mind that no matter what, I was coming home. I was scared, and if anybody says they weren't, they're lying. This was going to be life as I never knew it, and it was.

Other than the ground war, the first month was probably the most difficult. A lot of thinking about home and being there for Christmas didn't make matters any better. After a while I got used to it. A situation like that makes you grow up quickly and appreciate the basic things in

1

2

3

4

life, like running water, hot showers, hot meals, a bed—just things like that. You don't realize how much you take these things for granted until you're forced to be without them. I can remember countless nights of walking guard duty in the pouring rain, being soaked all day, going to sleep wet and freezing, and being totally miserable because of these discomforts. But now I realize that it has made me a very strong person.

The night before the ground war started, our company was briefed   5
on what was expected and what exactly our mission was after we breached the minefield and got into Kuwait. During the briefing, they told us we were expected to take at least 70 percent casualties. You could have heard a pin drop. We knew it wasn't going to be easy because we were a tank battalion and we'd be right on the front line with the tanks. If ever at one instant I felt like I "grew up overnight," that was it, definitely.

The morning came, and we went in. We took incoming fire going   6
through the minefield. Fortunately, we made it through. The ground war only lasted three days, but it was the most intense three days of my life. Explosions, blown-up tanks and vehicles everywhere, fires, lots of smoke, planes and helicopters flying overhead—it was like a movie. But it was reality, definitely reality, and when I encountered sights of death, more and more I realized this is war. I guess you could say reality set in. Seeing things like that really makes you cherish your life a little more. Unfortunately, I lost a very good friend over there, but his memory will never be forgotten—Thomas Scholand, from Semper, Florida.

Although these experiences may all seem bad, nothing can ever   7
take away the feeling of pride, rolling through Kuwait City and seeing people lining the streets waving and calling out in appreciation of the fact that we had just liberated their country. Seeing the faces of the men, women, and especially the children was a feeling that no words can explain.

In summary, of all the events that unfolded for me as well as for   8
others who served in Operations Desert Shield and Desert Storm, this was a major turning point in my life. I learned a lot about myself and life in general. I now look at things in a positive perspective. I've grown up a lot overseas, and now I take nothing for granted anymore. Life's short; appreciate all it has to offer, and live it to the fullest. I will!

Examining the Essay

1. Evaluate Stopa's thesis statement.
2. Stopa uses details to make his experiences seem real and vivid. In which parts of the essay was his use of detail particularly effective?

Writing an Essay

1. Write an essay describing your response to receiving surprising or important news. Describe how you reacted and how the news affected you.
2. Stopa says he felt as if he grew up overnight. Write an essay discussing a situation in which you were forced to grow up or accept responsibility. Explain how the situation affected you.
3. Stopa's experiences made him value his life and appreciate basic things in life. Write an essay recounting an experience that helped you see life in a new or different way.

 ## Making Connections

1. The birth of a child certainly shapes the parents' lives. Compare Anderson's ("A Letter to My Daughter") attitude toward her daughter with Datcher's ("Under the Overpass") attitude toward his soon-to-be-born child.

2. Salinas's "The Scholarship Jacket," and "Sandra Day O'Connor" are concerned with achievement. Write an essay comparing the types of achievement discussed in these two readings and the effect these achievements had on Salinas's and O'Connor's lives.

Chapter 3

Work That Shapes
Our Lives

WORK IS A COMPLEX, important part of our lives. Jobs, of course, provide needed income to purchase life's necessities. Some jobs offer an outlet for creative expression or help develop skills such as problem-solving. Other jobs can simply be repetitive and dull. Even those jobs, however, can be a source of personal satisfaction, a means of demonstrating that we are competent, self-sufficient individuals. By contrast, work can also make leisure time valuable and meaningful. Work can open new doors, as well as lead to new friends, new experiences, and new realizations.

The readings in this chapter provide several different perspectives on work and the workplace. You will read about how the first job of four well-known people shaped their lives ("My First Job"). You will also discover how to use part-time jobs to prepare yourself for your career ("Working Students Need to Look for Career Experience"). Two readings demonstrate the meaning of work experiences and how they affected the lives of the authors ("The Family Farm" And *"Mojado* Like Me"). Problems of the workplace are addressed in the chapter's textbook excerpt ("Sexual Harassment"). A student offers a humorous perspective on his part-time job at a fish market ("A Seafood Survey").

Brainstorming About Work

Class Activity: Working in groups of three or four students, discuss and attempt to define the ideal or perfect job. Identify its characteristics and try to think of examples. Also try to take into account individual differences. Why may a job be ideal for one person and unappealing to another?

My First Job

> **Daniel Levine**

This article from Reader's Digest *describes the first job experiences of four highly successful people. They explain how the lessons they learned from low-paying jobs helped them achieve successful careers.*

Reading Strategy

As you read each person's story, look for the similarities or differences among their experiences. Take notes on each story as you read.

Vocabulary Preview

ethic (1) belief in the value of something
persistence (7) never giving up; determination
taskmaster (10) person who expects you to perform difficult
  work
methodical (15) organized; regular; dependable
actuarial (16) computing insurance risks and premiums
automatons (17) robots; people who act like machines
stringer (19) part-time newswriter
stereotypes (20) oversimplified, inaccurate ideas about
  others

The Auto Prepper: Jay Leno[1]

I acquired a very strong work ethic from my parents, both of whom   1
lived through the Great Depression. They couldn't understand people
who didn't work regularly. I once told my mom that Sylvester Stallone
was getting $12 million for ten weeks of work. "What's he going to do
the rest of the year?" she asked.

---

[1]Jay Leno is host of NBC's "The Tonight Show."

I took my parents' work ethic into my first job at Wilmington Ford   2
near my hometown of Andover, Mass., when I was 16. I worked until
five or six o'clock on school days and put in 12-hour days during the
summer as a prepper. This meant washing and polishing the new cars,
and making sure the paper floor mats were in place. Another responsibility was taking off the hubcaps at night, so they wouldn't get stolen,
and replacing them the next day. This was hard work because we had
about seven acres of cars.

One day, carrying an armful of hubcaps around a corner, I almost   3
bumped into our new general manager. Startled, I dropped them all.
He fired me on the spot.

I was too ashamed to tell my parents. Every day for about two   4
weeks, I stayed busy until evening. Then I would go home and say I
had a great day at work.

Desperate, I wrote a letter to Henry Ford II and told him what hap-   5
pened. I said that we were a loyal Ford family and that when I was old
enough, I was going to buy a Mustang. Eventually the owner of the
dealership called. "I don't know who you know in Detroit," he said,
"but if you want your job back, you got it."

Later, during college, I wanted to work at a Rolls-Royce dealership,   6
but the owner said there were no openings. So I started washing cars
there anyway. When the owner noticed me, I said I was working until
he hired me. He did.

It takes persistence to succeed. Attitude also matters. I have never   7
thought I was better than anyone else, but I have always believed I
couldn't be outworked.

The Cashier: Jill Barad[2]

I was ten when I first sat with my grandmother behind the register in   8
her Manhattan pharmacy. Before long, she let me sit there by myself. I
quickly learned the importance of treating customers politely and saying "thank you."

At first I was paid in candy. Later I received 50 cents an hour. I   9
worked every day after school, and during the summer and on weekends and holidays from 8 A.M. to 7 P.M. My father helped me set up a
bank account. Watching my money grow was more rewarding than
anything I could have bought.

---

[2]Jill E. Barad is chairman and CEO of Mattel, Inc., the world's largest toymaker.

Grandma, a tough taskmaster, never gave me favorable treatment. 10
She watched me like a hawk yet allowed me to handle high-pressure situations such as working during the lunch rush. Her trust taught me how to handle responsibility.

By the time I was 12, she thought I had done such a good job that 11
she promoted me to selling cosmetics. I developed the ability to look customers directly in the eye. Even though I was just a kid, women would ask me such things as "What color do you think I should wear?" I took a genuine interest in their questions and was able to translate what they wanted into makeup ideas. I ended up selling a record amount of cosmetics.

The job taught me a valuable lesson: that to be a successful sales- 12
person, you didn't need to be a rocket scientist—you needed to be a great listener. Today I still carry that lesson with me: I *listen* to customers. Except they are no longer women purchasing cosmetics from me; instead, they are kids who tell me which toys they would like to see designed and developed.

The Cotton Picker: Charley Pride[3]

Every summer, from the time I was five until I was 16, I worked in the 13
cotton fields of Sledge, Miss., where my father rented 40 acres. My daddy paid me $1.50 for every 50 pounds of cotton I picked. But when I was 14, he gave me one of the 600-pound bales of cotton I had helped produce that year. I sold it for $220. I was rich! I bought a Silvertone guitar from Sears, Roebuck and Co., and began teaching myself to play.

The family radio was often tuned to country music. There was only 14
one thing I loved more, and that was baseball. I used to sneak out of the house on Sundays to play. When I left home, I played in the old Negro leagues and then for a minor-league team in Helena, Mont. After singing and playing guitar over the PA system before one game, I received offers to perform in local nightclubs.

Methodical work got me where I am today. More than 50 years 15
ago, on the cotton farm, I learned about committing myself to a job and seeing it through. Now I own that farm, and I rent it to other cotton pickers who aren't so different from me.

---

[3]Country singer Charley Pride has sold an estimated 35 million albums, including 11 gold, and has won three Grammy Awards.

The Office Boy: Bob Levey[4]

After my freshman year at the University of Chicago, I landed a sum- 16
mer job with the Martin E. Segal Co., an actuarial and employee-ben-
efits firm in New York City. I was paid $45 a week, but I remember
being shocked to see that sum shrink to $39 after state and federal
taxes were deducted.

It was my job to push a grocery cart filled with file folders through 17
the building, emptying and refilling in/out boxes. Not wanting to dis-
turb people, I tried to work quickly and quietly. But many people initi-
ated conversations and asked about my interests, and offered to write
letters of recommendation. I learned that office workers are not the automatons they're sometimes made out to be, and that people will surprise you if you let them.

---

[4]Bob Levey has been a columnist for the *Washington Post* since 1967.

I even surprised myself. Before then, I was always late and never 18
worried about how I presented myself. That summer I had to get out of
bed five days a week, shave, shower and get to work by 9 A.M.

I had already decided on newspaper writing for a career. When I 19
returned to the university in the fall, I was named editor-in-chief of the
school paper and worked as a stringer for the Chicago *Sun-Times* and
New York Times.

Emptying and filing in/out boxes had nothing to do with breaking 20
news stories. It had everything to do with learning valuable life lessons
that have stayed with me ever since. As a reporter, I still look beyond
the stereotypes—and let people surprise me.

Examining the Reading

Finding Meaning

1. Why was Jay Leno fired from his first job, and how did he get re-hired?
2. How did Jay Leno get his job at the Rolls-Royce Company?
3. What did Jill E. Barad learn from her first job that helped her succeed in her future career?
4. How did Charley Pride's first job as a cotton picker get him started in his music career?
5. What did Bob Levey learn about human nature during his summer job as an office boy?

Understanding Technique

1. Does this essay have an introduction and conclusion? If so, identify them. If not, would the essay benefit from having an introduction and conclusion?
2. What is the writer's implied thesis?

Thinking Critically

1. Do you think that what Jay Leno did to get his job at Rolls-Royce is a realistic approach to today's workplace? Why or why not?
2. Jay Leno wrote that he "acquired a very strong work ethic" from his parents. After reading these four accounts, how would you define the term *work ethic*?
3. When Jill E. Barad worked as a cashier, she said she "developed the ability to look customers directly in the eye." Do you consider this a useful ability? Why?

4. Bob Levey says that even today he allows people to surprise him and that this helps him in his work. How do you think this quality helps him?

5. What is the most important life lesson each of these people learned from his or her first job?

Writing About the Reading

A Journal Entry

Write a journal entry about an important lesson you learned from a job you had.

A Paragraph

1. Write a paragraph describing your first job.
2. If you owned a business, what qualities would you expect your employees to have? Write a paragraph describing what you think are the most important characteristics of a good employee.

An Essay

1. Choose two of these accounts and describe the influence of the authors' families on their first jobs and on their later career success.
2. Some colleges require students to do internships in their field of study as part of their coursework. Write an essay stating your opinion about this type of requirement, and explain why you agree or disagree with it.

A Creative Activity

Choose one of these four people and write a letter to him or her asking for a summer job. Describe your qualifications and explain why he or she should hire you.

Working Students Need to Look for Career Experience

▸ **Sabra Chartrand**

The following article examines the benefits of a part-time job for college students and offers suggestions on how to find one. It appeared in a weekly column titled "Careers" found on the Job Market *page of* The New York Times *Web site.*

Reading Strategy

Before you read, divide your paper in two columns. Label one "Benefits of Part-Time Jobs;" label the other "How to Find Part-Time Jobs." Fill in both columns during or after reading.

Vocabulary Preview

internships (3) temporary jobs that can provide career experience, money, and college credit.
stipend (4) salary; regular pay
dominate (3) take over; control
mentors (4) experienced professionals who offer advice and guidance
complement (9) help; improve

*M*illions of young people are heading to university and college 1 campuses [soon], but they won't just be students for the next few years. Many also have jobs—for some, work they began over the summer, for others, jobs they will find through a campus bulletin board or placement center. For a vast majority, work is a financial necessity to help pay for tuition, supplies, and campus living. But a part-time job during college should be more than just a way to pay the bills and earn pocket money—it should also serve as a career planning tool.

The Bureau of Labor Statistics says that in 1996, over half of full- 2 time college students also worked, and 86 percent of part-time college students held jobs.

Not all of those are jobs worked for money. Some students accept 3 internships in order to gain work experience with a company or in a chosen field. In return for that kind of experience, many people agree to an internship that doesn't pay or provides only a minor stipend. Students who need to earn money often take whatever job is available. But since a part-time job can consume free time from school and dominate a student's priorities, a way should be found to make it part of the education experience. Internships are generally seen as a career tool. Students should approach the part-time job search the same way.

Part-time work can offer students the best of both worlds—a flexible schedule with the ability to earn money, find mentors, gain experience and references. Students have a chance to practice skills learned in the classroom, acquire real-world professional skills, keep up-to-date on workplace technology, and test the waters of specific careers and companies.   4

A part-time job can have unexpected results, too—experience on the job or advice from a mentor can help a student choose college courses and electives tailored for a future job. Some careers require specific technical skills, for example, and a student can improve his chances of eventually landing that job by getting the technical training in college.   5

With demand high for computer scientists, engineers, and software developers, some recruiters are approaching college students through internships, part-time employers, and even during their junior or early senior years through college placement centers.   6

Students have particular needs, like the ability to arrange their work hours around class schedules, to work flexible shifts with full days reserved for weekends, and to have the option of working full-time during holidays, between semesters, and in the summer. So they should look for job openings, employers, and recruiters that take those conditions into account.   7

One way of finding a part-time job is through a temporary staffing agency. Olsten Corporation (www.olsten.com), one of the largest of those firms, says it will find jobs for thousands of college students. . . . Temping may be a good way for a student to get experience at several companies in one year without having to commit to any of them. Many of Olsten's openings are in office, technical, and clerical jobs.   8

Other companies recruit students to fill traditional part-time jobs. Recruiting sites like www.collegexpress.com, encourage students to sign up early in college so they can plan their school-and-work schedules to complement each other. Others, like the College Connection page at www.careermosaic.com, offer links that jump to some of the more prominent sites with information about internships. At www.occ.com, the On Campus page links to a list of college placement centers, corporate recruiters, and job search services.   9

Many colleges have work-study programs like the one posted on www.stanford.edu that lists job openings for students receiving financial aid.   10

Other online job sites have part-time openings buried in their list- 11
ings of thousands of jobs. Use www.espan.com to plug in key words
like *part-time,* a city, and profession to find out whether there are any
openings beyond those listed on the college pages. And then there's always the direct approach—choose a specific company and go straight
to its Web page. The Boeing Company (www.boeing.com) for example,
allows interested students to do a key word search for jobs or to
browse all Boeing openings from its home page.

Elsewhere on the Web, www.jobtrack.com boasts connections to 12
600 colleges and universities, MBA programs, and alumni associa-
tions. Its site allows students to plug in their school's name and get
back listings of part-time jobs and internships in their area.

These programs offer no guarantee of a job after graduation. It is 13
difficult for many 18 and 19-year-olds to plan strategies for the working world when that need seems a few years down the road. But it's a
fact that most college students have to hold down a part-time job. So
they might as well make it work for them.

Examining the Reading

Finding Meaning

1. In addition to earning money, how can part-time employment be
   useful to college students?
2. According to the author, what are some "unexpected results" of a
   part-time job?
3. According to this article, what career fields currently have the most
   job openings?
4. What are the advantages of working for a temp agency?
5. Name three sources of job information mentioned in this article.

Understanding Technique

1. This reading appeared on an Internet site. Discuss how the reading
   differs from essays that appear in print sources.
2. Evaluate the author's use of transitions. Where are they used effectively? Where could transitions be added?

Thinking Critically

1. Why do you think it is important for college students to get work experience in their career fields?
2. Under what circumstances do you think an internship would be a
   better choice than a part-time job?

3. The author identifies finding a mentor as one of the benefits of working part-time. How do you think a mentor could help advance your career?
4. Where at your school can you find the career and job information described in this article?
5. Do you think internships should be required for college students? Why or why not?

Writing About the Reading

A Journal Entry

Write a journal entry describing one of your job-search experiences.

A Paragraph

1. Write a paragraph describing some of the ways college students can find part-time jobs, other than those described in the reading.
2. Write a paragraph describing a part-time job that helped you learn something you did not expect to learn from it.

An Essay

1. Think of a part-time job in your field of study for which you could apply. Write a cover letter to submit with your résumé. Describe your career goals, academic and work experiences, and personal characteristics that qualify you for the job.
2. Write an essay describing the ideal part-time job for you while attending college. Be sure to include a discussion of why this job would be the best option.

A Creative Activity

Imagine that you are required to participate in an internship for five hours a week each week during the semester. Where would you choose to do your internship and why?

The Family Farm

▶ David Mas Masumoto

For most people, there is a clear separation between home and the workplace. In this essay, the author, who lives and works on the family farm, describes what it is like when home and work are joined. This reading was taken from his book, Epitaph for a Peach: Four Seasons on My Family Farm.

Reading Strategy

As you read, highlight words and phrases that reveal Masumoto's attitudes toward his family farm. Using a different color, highlight the attitudes of others toward the farm.

Vocabulary Preview

cringed (1) backed off in fear; winced
ventured (3) went; took a chance
alienated (4) turned off; distanced emotionally
disdain (5) lack of respect and deep dislike
condescension (5) looking down upon another; snobbishness
ritual (9) usual habit; regular activity
reluctance (11) unwillingness; resistance

I grew up knowing my father's work. He was a peach and grape   1
farmer, and I saw him at work daily, sometimes working alongside
him. As a young child I knew some of the crises he faced. I cringed at
the sight of worms attacking ripe fruit. I too could feel the searing heat
of the summer sun as it blistered exposed fruit.

Now I farm the California land that my father and mother farmed,   2
the land where my grandparents labored as farm workers. My children
will know the work of their father, too. But where my father rarely
showed emotion, I show it all. My daughter has seen me yell at the sky
as September rain clouds approach my raisins or curse about lousy
fruit prices when no one wants my peaches. It is a family farm—my

parents, wife and children spend time in the fields—and our family is bound to the land. Our farm survives as both a home and a workplace.

When I was in college, I asked friends about their parents' work. I thought my questions would be a safe way of getting to know someone. But most of my friends never ventured beyond one-line answers: "My dad is an engineer" or "He works for a bank" or "He handles sheet metal for an air-conditioning company." 3

I would respond, "What kind of engineer?" or "Why'd he choose banking?" or "How's the sheet-metal business?" Such questions alienated some of my friends: family seemed to be a painful subject. After I told them my dad was a farmer, rarely did they ask a second question. I stopped interpreting their initial response, "Oh, really?" as one of positive surprise. 4

Returning home after college, I felt uncomfortable telling others, "I farm." I translated blank looks as disdain mixed with condescension. I could see images flashing through their minds of Old MacDonald and hayseeds who spend weekends watching corn grow. As my peers were securing their corporate jobs and advancing as professionals in law or medicine, I spent long hours talking with my dad, getting to know fifty acres of vines and twenty acres of peach trees, preparing to take over the farm. 5

I'd listened for hours before I noticed that Dad's stories of growing up on the farm seemed to revolve around the pronoun *they*. "They" meant my grandparents and the entire family of four sons and two daughters. I had to adjust my thinking. My image of work was singular in nature, one man in one job, not a family's combined effort to make a living. I learned the significance of work that is inseparable from home, when work is also the place you live and play and sleep. 6

Dad tells the story of hot, summer nights when he was a boy and the wooden platform that *Jiichan* (grandfather) built. Fresno's one-hundred-degree heat would beat down on the place where they lived, a shack with a tin roof that required hours to cool after sunset. They didn't have a cooler or fan (out in the country there was no electricity), but it didn't matter. 7

Jiichan made a low wooden platform from old barn wood. It rose about two feet off the ground with a flat area big enough for the whole family. In the evenings everyone would lie on the platform, side by side, almost touching. 8

After a long day together in the fields, and following a simple dinner and refreshing *ofuro* (Japanese bath), the family would gather and begin an evening ritual of talking, resting, and gazing upward at the night sky, waiting until their shack home had cooled down. The dirt yard was beneath them, the closest vineyards a few feet away. If a little 9 breeze came they could hear the grape leaves shifting and rustling, creating an illusion of coolness. It seemed to make everyone feel better.

Years later, my brother and I passed hot summer nights together, sometimes camping out in the fields. During a break between the summer fruits and the family packing-shed work, we pitched a tent made from an old bed sheet and tree rope. You would think after working all day with the peaches and grapes, we'd be weary of them. But we wanted to sleep "in the wilderness" and drew no lines between our fields of play and the fields of work. This wasn't just a farm, it was our home.

When I tell these stories to friends, their eyes widen and they smile. They tell me how fine it must be to raise children on a farm. I now realize that my college friends' reluctance to talk about family arose from a youthful notion that one could get away from them. We hoped to journey beyond that horizon; what we didn't know was that some of us were actually seeking what was right in front of us.

It's been a struggle to keep the farm, but I know now that I am not just competing with nature—I am creating, as my father did, something called home.

Examining the Reading

Finding Meaning

1. How did Masumoto's college friends react to his questions about their parents' jobs?
2. Why did the author decide to become a farmer after graduating from college?
3. The author states that "stories of growing up on the farm seemed to revolve around the pronoun *they.*" Who are "they"?
4. How did the author's friends react to his decision to become a farmer?
5. What do his friends today think about his life as a farmer?

Understanding Technique

1. How does Masumoto demonstrate his close connections to the family farm?
2. Why does Masumoto include the story of his grandfather? What does it contribute to the essay?

Thinking Critically

1. Why didn't Masumoto's college friends want to talk about their families?
2. Why did the platform the author's grandfather built mean so much to his family?
3. Why do you think Masumoto's friends now think differently about his occupation?
4. What does the author mean when he says "our family is bound to the land"?
5. Do you think the writer likes having no separation between work and home life? Why?

Writing About the Reading

A Journal Entry

Write a journal entry describing a family member's job. Explain why you would or wouldn't want to follow in this person's footsteps.

A Paragraph

1. Write a paragraph describing a situation in which you were treated with disdain or condescension.
2. Write a paragraph comparing your view of work with that of an older family member.

An Essay

1. The author's attitudes toward being a farmer changed as he grew older. Write an essay describing how your own attitudes or opinions about something changed as you matured.
2. Write an essay about an incident in your life when you discovered that what you were seeking was right in front of you.

A Creative Activity

If the author owned a restaurant, do you think each member of the family would be as involved in this business as they are in the farm? Why or why not? If yes, in what ways?

Disney's Head Trips

▸ Jane Keunz

Do you think it would be fun to work as a character at Disney World? This selection describes some difficulties faced by people who hold this kind of job. It was published as an article in South Atlantic Quarterly. *Jane Keunz is the author of* Inside the Mouse: Work and Play at Disney World.

Reading Strategy

As you read, highlight details that are particularly effective in creating an impression of Disney World.

Vocabulary Preview

realm (1) territory; world; place
perception (1) idea; way of thinking
cardinal (2) main; most important
illusion (2) fantasy; make-believe
dicey (4) risky; dangerous
regurgitation (5) vomit
exhibition (7) showing; display

When employees of Florida's Disney World arrive at the park each   1
day for work, they enter a realm with its own rules and its own language, one that borrows phrases from both the language of real estate and the language of theater. When they are within the boundaries of the park, they are "on property." This is not the same thing as "on-stage," which implies being in public view and being in contact with guests as an employee and representative of the Walt Disney Company. For Disney's employees, however, this is only a rough distinction; their perception is that anyplace they might go "on property" is always a workplace, a stage, whether or not they are actually at work. This is a place where workers, workplace, and labor are referred to as cast,

theater, and performance; a place where the entire staff shows up each day not in "uniform" but in "costume."

For the workers who walk around the park dressed as Mickey, Minnie, and the rest of the Disney "cast," the cardinal rule is never to be seen out of costume and particularly out of the head; in other words, never to let the costume be seen as a costume. Such a display would destroy the park's magic, the illusion that the characters are real. One Disney spokesperson I talked to refused for an hour to acknowledge even that there are actual human beings inside the character costumes: "That's one of the things I really can't talk about. Not because I work there but because it keeps it kind of sacred."

Inside the huge heads, the heat of a Florida afternoon builds. Some say it gets as high as 130 degrees. Characters are supposed to appear for no longer than twenty or twenty-five minutes at a time, but, even then, it is not unusual for characters to pass out onstage.

It's unclear exactly how many of the Disney characters faint on a given summer day, although everyone is sure that some do pass out. One man reports that during the summer a large part of his job is devoted to driving around retrieving characters where they fall. One day he picked up three at one stop: Donald, Mickey, and Goofy. "All of them had passed out within five minutes of each other. They were just lined up on the sidewalk." This took place in Epcot, which, unlike the Magic Kingdom with its system of underground tunnels, has a backstage area behind the various attractions to which the characters can escape if they have to. If they are in the Magic Kingdom, however, or on a parade float, they must simply ride it out or wait until they're recovered enough to walk unassisted, in costume, to a tunnel entrance. This can get a bit dicey, since passing out is sometimes preceded by throwing up inside the head, which cannot be removed until the character is out of public view.

> You're never to be seen in a costume without your head, ever. It was automatic dismissal. It's frightening because you can die on your own regurgitation when you can't keep [away from] it. I'll never forget Dumbo—it was coming out of the mouth during the parade. You have a little screen over the mouth. It was horrible. And I made $4.55 an hour.
>
> During the parades, I've seen many characters in ninety-degree heat vomit in their costumes and faint on the floats and were never taken off the float. There's so much going on during a parade that people are not going to notice if Dopey is doing this [*slumps*] and he's not waving. . . . I've never seen them take a character off a float.

In one instance described to me, Chip of Chip 'n Dale fame passed out while mounted to the top of a float by a post that ran up one leg of the costume and into the head. Although this was intended as a pre-

2

3

4

5

6

7

caution to keep him from falling off when the float jerked or hit a bump, the visual effect was crucifixion: Chip held up by a post for public exhibition, head hanging to one side, out cold.

Examining the Reading

Finding Meaning

1. Explain the difference between being "on property" and being "on stage" in Disney World.
2. What is the "cardinal rule" at Disney World?
3. What happens at Disney World if a character is seen in costume but without the head on?
4. What are these employees expected to do if they feel ill while in costume?
5. Why do so many of the characters faint during a parade?

Understanding Technique

1. Identify and evaluate the essay's thesis. How well is it supported?
2. Describe the tone of the essay's introduction and final paragraph. Are they similar or different? Why?

Thinking Critically

1. What does the author mean by "this is a place where workers, workplace, and labor are referred to as cast, theater, and performance"?
2. Why do you think the Disney spokesperson refused to talk to the author about the people inside the character costumes?
3. From reading this article, what image do you think Disney World is trying to present to its visitors?
4. Do you think that the rules at Disney World are fair or unfair? Explain.
5. Considering the working conditions, why do you think people want to work at Disney World?

Writing About the Reading

A Journal Entry

Imagine you are working as Mickey Mouse at Disney World. Write a journal entry about your day's experiences.

A Paragraph

1. Write a paragraph describing one of your jobs. Include your duties, the working conditions, and how the management treated you.
2. Would you like to work at Disney World? Write a paragraph explaining why or why not.

An Essay

1. Write an essay about the differences between the public's image of Disney World and the experiences of its employees.
2. Write a letter to the president of the Disney World Corporation about the working conditions and what you think should be done about them.

A Creative Activity

Imagine that, on a hot summer day at Disney World, Donald Duck felt sick. He removed his head in a public area and sat down to rest. Write about this scene and the reactions of the Disney World visitors, coworkers, and the Disney executives.

Mojado Like Me

▶ Joseph Tovares

For people born in America, it is often easy to forget about the roots of their ethnic heritage. This reading, first published in Hispanic *magazine, defines one man's cultural roots and describes how he got in touch with his past.*

Reading Strategy

While or after you read, highlight words and phrases that describe Tovares's life as a television producer. Use a different color to highlight descriptions of Mexican farm laborers.

Vocabulary Preview

permeates (3) spreads throughout
infiltrate (5) to enter into gradually
albeit (6) although
pejorative (7) negative; meant to belittle
condescending (8) snobby; superior; uppity
exacerbated (11) made worse; intensified
menial (11) low status; unskilled; tedious
odyssey (11) travels; quest
segued (18) proceeded without pause from one scene or
         musical number to another
cathartic (18) providing relief of feelings that had been
         hidden

*T*he Mambo Kings. That's what we jokingly called ourselves as we 1
drove across California shooting an undercover story for ABC's *Prime Time Live.* We were three college-educated, U.S.-born Latinos, but for this story we dressed as farm workers, spoke Spanish and broken English, and tried hard to look poor. There was Steve Blanco, a half Cuban American, half Puerto Rican from Miami and an ace freelance sound recordist; Gerardo Rueda, a first-generation Mexican American as well as a first-rate shooter and sound recordist; and me, a documentary producer, a Tejano/Chicano with roots in Texas stretching back to pre-Alamo days who just happens to be Jewish. As we traveled across the state in our beat-up Ford pick-up, drawing nervous stares from shop

owners and accusatory glances from policemen, I learned something about who I am and remembered much about who I used to be.

Back home in San Antonio and Miami, we led the good life. We worked for the networks, made good money, dressed well, and drove nice cars. We were living out our parents' dreams—the dreams of immigrants who longed for a better future for their children. . . .

But over the years, like most television veterans, I had picked up some bad habits. There is an "us and them" attitude that permeates our business. We're on the inside and everyone else is on the outside. Objectivity often forces journalists to put up walls, and Latino journalists are no different. A wall had developed between myself and almost everyone else, including other Chicanos. I somehow saw myself as different. After all, I was a freelance professional and I worked steadily. No one guaranteed me work; I worked because I was good and because I had paid my dues.

After much hard work, I had achieved a measure of success that I felt I had earned. I had been through what most professionals of color go through in this country. As a student I had put up with all the nonsense from white teachers, from first grade through graduate school. I had put up with all the snide remarks from coworkers who had never worked with a "Mexican." All that was behind me now. I didn't have to put up with anybody. In my mind I was a success. I had accomplished much more than I was supposed to. But with that success came the wall that divided me from my people and from my past.

I got the call from *PrimeTime Live* on a Sunday, and a few days later the job was set. Gerardo and I set out from San Antonio and Steve Blanco flew in from Miami a few days later. Susan Barnett, the producer, and Claudia Swift, the associate producer, had done their homework. Our job was to infiltrate work groups made up of Mexican workers, then determine their legal status and whether or not they were being exploited. Unconfirmed sources indicated that the workers were being illegally charged for transportation and tools. It was the old "company store" routine. In the end, the workers owed the boss money. If that wasn't bad enough, many workers were often forced to live in subhuman conditions deep inside our national forests. We suspected all of this was occurring under the watchful eye of the U.S. Forest Service, which awarded the contracts for reforestation. The scenario had the two most essential elements for a good story: clearly identifiable victims and bad guys.

We began our new, albeit temporary, life in old faded work pants, well worn flannel shirts, and dusty work boots. Susan and Claudia provided us with the proper vehicle—a 1979 Ford truck that had been in so many accidents it was now composed mostly of Bondo.

At first the job reminded me of *Black Like Me,* a sixties book by   7
John Howard Griffin in which a white man foolishly thinks he can understand what it's like to be a black man in America by temporarily
changing his skin color. A friend would later kid me about my adventure, referring to it as *"Mojado* Like Me." *Mojado* is a pejorative term,
the Spanish equivalent of "wetback." But I didn't need to change my
skin color; nor was I venturing into completely new territory.

We entered the town of Lindsay, California, anxiously looking for   8
work. We walked the streets, chatting with everyone we could. On
street corners, in restaurants, and in bars, we searched out employment in the *sierra,* the mountains. We only spoke Spanish—not the
Spanish we learned in school but the language of the *campesinos.* By
the end of the first day we knew we were "passing." We knew by the
help we received from real farm workers and others we approached for
information on jobs. Waitresses, barkeeps, and people on the streets
would all refer us to contractors. But we also knew we were "passing"
by the stares we received. Cops, shopkeepers, businesspeople would
look at us with suspicion and speak to us in condescending tones. I had
forgotten what that felt like, and it took me back to Michigan, to
1969. . . .

It had been almost 25 years since that summer in Michigan. That   9
was the last time I worked the fields. . . .

A lot had changed in 25 years. I had gone from *campesino*[1] child to   10
East Coast–educated, hip (or so I thought) Latino. But like a lot of
Latino professionals, there had developed a great distance between
who I had once been and who I had become. I never forgot where I
came from, but the memory had become fuzzier with time.

I had forgotten how much baggage poverty carries. Being without   11
money is only part of the story. There is a side to poverty, exacerbated
by race, that is much more difficult to understand. It is subtle yet op-
pressive. It is communicated by stares, gestures, and tone. Unless
you've been there, you can't possibly understand. I had tried very hard
to leave those feelings of inferiority far behind. I had graduated from
high school, won a scholarship to college, and obtained a fellowship at
graduate school. I thought I had come a long way. Yet, as I walked the
streets looking for menial work, I realized that after all these years I
had been only one change of clothes away from my past. A past I had
tried to bury long ago.

---

[1]field worker; peasant

The competition for jobs was stiff. There was a surplus of labor   12
around, and it was hard to pin down the *contratistas*[2] as to when they
would get their contracts. We dogged one guy for days, hanging
around his storefront office until he finally agreed to add us to his work
crew. The entire time we were wired for video and sound, wondering if
our mannerisms and movements would give us away and wondering
what would happen if we were found out. . . . Landing the job was a
cause for some celebration—not only did we get work, we got it on
tape. But the scope of the accomplishment was diminished by the severe reality of the work we were going to have to perform.

The work in the California mountains was more than hard—it was   13
brutal. We left camp at six in the morning and returned around seven
at night. The official term for the job is "manual release" but the other
workers, all of whom were from Mexico and undocumented, simply
called it *"limpieza,"* or "cleaning." In "manual release," workers move
along in a line, and with hoes, shears, and brute force, clear thick
brush from around recently planted pine trees. Those little seedlings
had value; in many ways they were much more valuable than we were.
Lots of money went into planting those little trees, and we were there
to protect them. The thick brush we were taking out had been robbing
the pine trees of valuable nutrients and had to be removed. But it was
no easy matter. Some bushes were bigger than we were and virtually
impossible to completely take out. I hadn't worked that hard in a long
time. There I was, my hands cut and scratched, my body completely
covered in dirt, trying to chip away at thicket after thicket. We had no
idea how much we would wind up being paid or when; no idea when
we would eat lunch, no idea if we would get a break. Under the watchful eye of our *patron,* a fellow Chicano, we worked. At his request, several men sang old Mexican songs. The National Forest had been
transformed into a hacienda.

The plan was for us to complete fourteen acres that first day of   14
work, but we only finished six. Midway through the afternoon the boss
gave us a pep talk. "The quicker we finish, the more money you make,"
he said. But the work was too much. The Mambo Kings were the first
to quit. We got the pictures we needed and left.

Over the course of several days, we wandered among various work   15
camps, taking more pictures and gathering information. Living in
tents and working twelve hours a day proved too much of a strain for
many of the laborers. Fresh workers were brought in to replace those

---

[2]contractors who hire workers

who left. We were told that during a period of seven weeks more than 100 men had come and gone from the crew. . . .

All day we would crawl to reach the trunks of the large and thorny 16 bushes—constantly on the lookout for dangerous snakes. We were allowed fifteen minutes for lunch and given a ten-minute break in the late afternoon. . . .

Our job with ABC News lasted three weeks, but the memory will be 17 with me forever. I can still remember the pain of the distrustful stares, the agony of watching men being treated like animals, and the anger of seeing Chicano contractors exploit Mexican workers. The lessons from those three weeks were startling. It didn't matter how different I thought I was from these men who hail from places like Oaxaca and Michoacan. To virtually all the people I met, I was one of them. The walls that I had built turned out to be made of paper, and they quickly crumbled.

Barely a month after the odyssey began, I was back home attend- 18 ing my twentieth high school reunion. There were doctors, lawyers, accountants, and businessmen—a dozen Hispanic success stories. Drinking and dancing at the San Antonio country club, we represented the new Chicano middle class. Part of me felt very much at home there, and the feeling troubled me. As I tried to make sense of my conflict, I glanced down and touched a small scar on my left hand. The scar had been left there by a careless boy trying to work as a man 25 years ago in Michigan. Day dreaming and machetes don't mix. Effortlessly the band segued from a rock tune to a Mexican polka, and the Chicanos shifted into barrio gear and slid across the dance floor with ease. As my wife and I danced, I realized that it is impossible to leave one life behind and simply begin another. Our lives are built on a series of experiences and, like it or not, even the difficult ones count.

So what started out as a good job with lots of overtime potential 19 turned into a cathartic event that changed my life. I had tried for years to bury unpleasant memories, to deny they even existed. My career had made it easy to do. But during those weeks in California I was forced into a deep reexamination of myself. The experience made me confront ugly realities about how this society treats a hidden underclass. Most important, it made me realize how easy it is for many of us who have escaped to simply forget.

Examining the Reading

Finding Meaning

1. What was Joseph Tovares's assignment for *PrimeTime Live*?
2. Before starting on this assignment, what was the author's attitude toward his ethnic background?
3. Why was this article entitled *"Mojado* Like Me"?
4. How did the television crew know that they were successfully passing as Mexican farm workers?
5. What experiences during the three-week undercover assignment had the longest lasting effect on the author?

Understanding Technique

1. Analyze the meaning and effectiveness of the title.
2. In the introduction, the author summarizes the adventure his entire essay describes. Evaluate this technique. In what other ways might Tovares have begun the essay?

Thinking Critically

1. How did the author's career as a journalist affect his interactions with other people?
2. What did the author mean when he said, "I realized that after all these years I had been only one change of clothes away from my past."
3. Why do you think Tovares said that the tree seedlings "in many ways . . . were much more valuable than we were"?
4. Why do you think the Chicano contractors treated the Mexican workers so badly?
5. Why was the author troubled that he felt at home among the other middle class Chicanos at his high school reunion?

Writing About the Reading

A Journal Entry

Write a journal entry describing your family's ethnic, racial, or national background and what it means to you.

A Paragraph

1. Write a paragraph about some of the ways you think the author's life may have changed after this assignment.

2. Write a paragraph describing the most difficult or most challenging job you ever had or task you ever completed.

An Essay

1. Have you ever had an experience that significantly changed your self-image? Write an essay describing this experience and how it affected you.
2. There is an old saying that, to understand someone from a different background accurately, it is necessary to "walk a mile in their shoes," that is, to live the same way they do, for a time. Write an essay explaining why you agree or disagree with this statement.

A Creative Activity

Imagine that Joseph Tovares wrote a letter to one of his former teachers or to the Mexican workers described in this article. What do you think the letter would say?

Sexual Harassment

▶ **Joseph A. DeVito**
Textbook Excerpt

This selection, taken from a communications textbook titled
Messages, *explores the nature of sexual harassment, how to*
avoid sending harassing messages, and what to do when you
think you are being sexually harassed.

Reading Strategy

As you read, write an outline of the selection. Include these
headings: Definitions of Sexual Harassment, Avoiding Sexual
Harassment, and Dealing with Sexual Harassment.

Vocabulary Preview

intimidating (3) threatening; frightening
constitute (4) become; equal
explicitly (4) openly; perfectly clear
implicitly (4) not directly stated but taken for granted
assumption (8) basic idea; starting point
assertively (9) firmly and confidently
unheeded (9) not listened to; unnoticed
corroboration (9) supporting information
channels (9) pathways for information and authority

Sexual harassment is not a single act but rather a series of commu-   1
nicative acts that come to characterize a relationship; so, it is useful to
place sexual harassment in the context of interpersonal conflict.

Source: "Sexual Harrassment" pp. 316–317 from *Messages: Building Interpersonal Communication Skills* 3rd. ed. by Joseph A. DeVito. Copyright © 1996 by HarperCollins College Publishers. Reprinted by permission of Addison-Wesley Educational Publishers,
Inc.

What Is Sexual Harassment?

Ellen Bravo and Ellen Cassedy (1992) define sexual harassment as "bothering someone in a sexual way. The harasser offers sexual attention to someone who didn't ask for it and doesn't welcome it. The unwelcome behavior might or might not involve touching. It could just as well be spoken words, graphics, gestures, or even looks (not any look—but the kind of leer or stare that says, 'I want to undress you')."

Attorneys note that legally "sexual harassment is any unwelcome sexual advance or conduct on the job that creates an intimidating, hostile, or offensive working environment" (Petrocelli & Repa, 1992).

The Equal Employment Opportunity Commission (EEOC) has its own definition: "Unwelcome sexual advances, requests for sexual favors and another verbal or physical conduct of a sexual nature constitute sexual harassment when (1) submission to such conduct is made either explicitly or implicitly a term or condition of an individual's employment, (2) submission to or rejection of such conduct by an individual is used as the basis for employment decisions affecting such individual, or (3) such conduct has the purpose or effect of unreasonably interfering with an individual's work performance or creating an intimidating, hostile, or offensive working environment" (Friedman, Boumil, & Taylor, 1992).

In a . . . Harris Poll (*New York Times*, June 2, 1993) of sexual harassment in junior and senior high school, 56 percent of the boys and 75 percent of the girls said that they were the target of some form of sexual harassment consisting of sexually explicit comments, jokes, or gestures. Forty-two percent of the boys and 66 percent of the girls said they were the victims of sexual touching, grabbing, or pinching. The major behaviors reported by the victims included: sexual comments or looks; touching, grabbing, and pinching; intentionally brushing up against the person; spreading sexual rumors about the person; pulling at the person's clothing; showing or giving sexual materials; and writing sexual messages in public areas.

The students noted that among the effects of such sexual harassment were not wanting to go to school, reluctance to talk in class, finding it difficult to pay attention or to study, getting lower grades, and even considering changing schools.

In order to discover whether behavior constitutes sexual harassment, Memory VanHyning (1993) suggests you ask these four questions to help you assess your own situation objectively rather than emotionally:

- Is it real? Does this behavior have the meaning it seems to have?
- Is it job-related? Does it have something to do with or will it influence the way you do your job?
- Did you reject this behavior? Did you make your rejection of these messages clear to the other person?
- Have these types of messages persisted? Is there a pattern, a consistency to these messages?

Avoiding Sexual Harassment Behaviors

Three suggestions for avoiding behaviors that might be considered as   8
sexual harassment will help to further clarify the concept and to prevent its occurrence (Bravo & Cassedy, 1992):

- Begin with the assumption that others at work are not interested in your sexual advances, sexual stories and jokes, or sexual gestures.
- Listen and watch for negative reactions to any sexually related discussion.
- Avoid saying or doing what you think would/might prove offensive to your parent, partner, or child should they be working with someone who engages in such behavior.

What to Do About Sexual Harassment

What should you do if you feel you are being sexually harassed and you   9
feel you should do something about it? Here are a few suggestions recommended by workers in the field (Petrocelli & Repa, 1992; Bravo & Cassedy, 1992; Rubenstein, 1993):

1. Talk to the harasser. Tell this person, assertively, that you do not welcome this behavior and that you find it offensive. Simply informing Fred that his sexual jokes are not appreciated and are seen as offensive may be sufficient to make him stop this joke-telling. Unfortunately, in some instances such criticism goes unheeded and the offensive behavior continues.
2. Collect some evidence, perhaps corroboration from others who have experienced similar harassment at the hands of the same individual, perhaps a log of such offensive behaviors.
3. Use appropriate channels within the organization. Most organizations have established channels to deal with such grievances. This step will in most cases eliminate any further harassment. In the event that it doesn't you may consider going further.
4. File a complaint with some organization or government agency or perhaps take legal action.

5. Don't blame yourself. Like many who are abused, there is a tendency to blame yourself, to feel that you are somehow responsible for being harassed. You aren't, but you may need to secure emotional support from friends or perhaps from trained professionals.

Examining the Reading

Finding Meaning

1. In your own words, restate the definition of sexual harassment given by Ellen Bravo and Ellen Cassedy.
2. How does the Equal Employment Opportunity Commission's definition of sexual harassment differ from the legal definition?
3. What are some of the possible effects of sexual harassment on students?
4. If you think someone is sexually harassing you, what should you do first?
5. If this doesn't work, what should you do next?

Understanding Technique

1. Discuss the effectiveness of headings, bulleted lists, and numbered lists. In what types of writing are they appropriate?
2. Because this reading is an excerpt from a textbook chapter, it lacks a conclusion. Would a conclusion to this excerpt be helpful? Why or why not? If so, what should it include?

Thinking Critically

1. Why do you think the authors give several different definitions of sexual harassment?

References: Ellen Bravo and Ellen Cassedy, *The 9 to 5 Guide to Combating Sexual Harassment* [New York: Wiley, 1992]; William Petrocelli and Barbara Kate Repa, *Sexual Harassment on the Job* [Berkeley: Nolo Press, 1992]; Joel Friedman, Marcia Mobilia Boumil and Barbara Ewert Taylor, *Sexual Harassment: What it Is, What it Isn't, What it Does to You and What You Can Do About it* [Deerfield Beach, FL: Health Communications, 1992]; Memory VanHyning, *Crossed Signals: How to Say NO to Sexual Harassment* [Los Angeles: Infotrend Press, 1993]; Michael Rubenstein, *How to Combat Sexual Harassment at Work: A Guide to Implementing the European Commission Code of Practice* [Luxembourg: Office for Official Publications of the European Community, 1993].

2. Why is sexual harassment an issue for the Equal Employment Opportunity Commission?
3. Could spreading sexual rumors about someone in middle school be considered sexual harassment? Why or why not? Explain.
4. Why do you think it is often difficult to prove that an individual is guilty of sexual harassment?
5. Do you think the issue of sexual harassment has gone too far? Explain.

Writing About the Reading

A Journal Entry

Write a journal entry about what you would consider an offensive working environment or about your own experiences with sexual harassment.

A Paragraph

In one paragraph, explain how you would fight sexual harassment.

An Essay

1. In the past, many of the behaviors described in this essay would not be considered sexual harassment. Write an essay explaining why you think public and legal opinion about it has changed in recent years.
2. Write an essay explaining why sexual harassment is a problem in the workplace and what managers can do to help eliminate it.

A Creative Activity

Imagine that you are a manager and one of your employees has just reported an incident of sexual harassment to you. What would you do?

A Seafood Survey

▶ **Robert Wood**
Student Essay

Robert Wood, a student at Niagara County Community College,
humorously describes his work experiences at the fish depart-
ment of a local supermarket. You will be surprised by the ques-
tions his customers ask him and how he responds.

*O*verall, I would have to say I have a very unique part-time job. I   1
work in the seafood department at Wegmans supermarket, and since I
deal with customers all day long, I get a wide range of questions and
requests from people of all ages. Sometimes the questions come so fast
that it feels like I am responding to a seafood survey!

When I first started at Wegmans I really didn't know very much   2
about seafood, only what I had tried in the past. At first I was kind of
nervous when customers would ask me question after question about
seafood and I didn't have the answers. Now, after two years on the job,
I think I know a great deal about seafood, and more than I want to
know about customers and how to handle them.

Most of the time, customers' questions are just the routine ones.   3
They might want to know how long the fish should be cooked or what
recipes are best for a particular type of fish. Routine, polite answers are
all that are required. But once in a great while I get some really out of the
ordinary questions or requests and they require diplomatic handling.

Once a customer asked me for a lobster. We have those live in a big   4
tank, so you have to go in with these special tongs and get them out.
But they had just brought in a lot of lobsters that day, and they were all
packed on top of each other. So, the lady picked out the one she wanted
which, of course, was on the bottom of the pile. The tongs kept slip-
ping, and each time I would go to grab the lobster she wanted, he'd get
away. Finally, I got a good hold on him and dragged him up to the top,
and he was struggling. I didn't think anything of it because they always
do that, but the lady was watching him the whole time and I guess she
felt sorry for him or something because she told me to put him back!
Naturally, I asked her why, and she said that after seeing him fight for
his life, she couldn't take him home and cook him. It was as if she

thought he would be on her conscience. She went over to the meat department instead and bought a steak.

Another thing about lobsters is that once people see them crawling   5
around alive in that tank, they think all the other fish on the ice is frozen and maybe not really fish. One customer asked me once, "How fresh are those fish—really?" He stressed the word *really* like he didn't believe they were all that fresh. I told him they were, and he tried to tell me that to be really fresh, they should be swimming around in a tank of their own! I explained to him, politely of course, that if Wegmans had a tank for each fish, there wouldn't be room for anything else. He said he thought he'd rather go down to the river and catch his own. That way he'd know it was fresh.

One of the weirdest requests I ever had was made when we han-   6
dled "whole fish" at my store, and we would scale, clean, and fillet each fish to order. One day, an old lady wanted to purchase some whole yellow pike. She selected her fish and I weighed it up and asked what she would like done to it. She said that she would like it scaled, gutted, and the head and fins removed—so far a normal order. But then she said she wanted me to dig out the eyes for her and wrap them separately. I thought to myself, "What does she want with a yellow pike's eyes?" I finished processing the fish and marked the package with the eyes in it so she could find it when she got home. After I handed her order to her, I had to ask her why she needed the eyes. She replied that she used the eyes in a recipe for a delicious soup! I didn't ask her what it tastes like.

Every once in awhile you get those questions or customers that   7
make your day. There was a young boy who came to the seafood department every Saturday when I would be working, to look at the fish on display. He was about eight years old, was very bright, and was interested in fish. He always asked questions about where particular fish came from and what they ate. One time, he asked me if he could have a clam for his aquarium at home. Of course I gave him one to take home. The next Saturday, he came back and asked me what clams eat for food because he thought his clam was hungry. I was surprised that the clam was still alive. When I told him this, he said he thought it was still alive, but it never moved or opened up. He said he had taken good care of it. He had even cleaned it up and removed some meat that was stuck in its shell. I tried not to laugh as I explained to him that the meat part was the clam's body and that was why it wasn't moving. He replied, "Well, it tasted pretty good, anyway."

One of the funniest things that ever happened, though, was when a   8
girl about my age came up to me with a shopping cart that had about 10 cans of tuna fish in it. She told me she wanted to impress her new boyfriend by cooking outdoors for him, and he didn't eat meat. She asked me what was the easiest way to grill tuna. I thought she was

pulling my leg, so I told her she could open all those cans and empty them onto the barbecue or she could just buy one big one. That's how I said it, "one big one." And she looked at me like I was crazy! Then she looked at all the cans of tuna fish in her cart and said, "You mean I can buy, like, one really, really big can of tuna fish?" Then I realized she didn't have a clue, so I pointed to the whole tuna lying there on the ice next to the flounder, and she got really wide-eyed and said, "Oh, you mean there's an actual fish called a tuna? I thought they only came in a can." I couldn't help laughing. Fortunately, she laughed too, or I could've lost my job.

During the time I worked at Wegmans, I have learned many important skills. In addition to the skills required for processing and selling seafood, this job has taught me important "people" skills. I have learned that if you keep an open mind and maintain your sense of humor, you can succeed not only at the seafood market but also at anything in your life.

Examining the Essay

1. Evaluate the essay's title.
2. Wood relates stories about customers to support his thesis. What other types of details might he have used?
3. Evaluate Wood's use of transitions to connect his ideas.

Writing an Essay

1. Write an essay describing strange or peculiar people you have met, tasks that you have been asked to perform, or questions or requests that you have encountered on the job.
2. Wood asserts that he has learned a great deal about customers and how to handle them. Write an essay discussing what you have learned from a job that you hold now or have held.

Making Connections ──────────────

1. Both "The Family Farm" and "*Mojado* Like Me" are concerned, in part, with family or cultural roots. Write an essay comparing Masumoto's attitudes toward his family with those of Tovares toward his Tejano/Chicano roots.

2. "Disney's Head Trips" and "A Seafood Survey" discuss employment in a large business. Write an essay comparing Wood's working conditions with that of the Disney employees.

3. Write an essay explaining what Sabra Chartrand ("Working Students Need to Look for Career Experience") would think of Robert Wood's part-time job ("A Seafood Survey").

Chapter 4

Cultures That Shape
Our Lives

PEOPLE IN THE UNITED STATES represent a wide variety of cultural backgrounds. Culture refers to the values and ways of doing things that a group of people share. Except for the Native Americans, our ancestors all came from somewhere else—Africa, China, Eastern or Western Europe, South America, Vietnam, and so on. Although Americans are an ethnically diverse bunch, they share some common concerns, goals, and values. Regardless of our cultural heritage, we all value our

121

families; we value our friendships; we seek self-worth and self-esteem; we seek freedom, opportunity, and knowledge.

Subcultures exist within a culture. They are groups that share some common identity. From the shared identity, shared customs and behaviors develop. A good example is the college student subculture. All members of this group attend college (their shared identity), and many act and dress in similar ways (many carry backpacks, wear jeans, etc.). Other subcultures include religious sects, sports players, and musicians.

Learning about others' cultures and subcultures can give life and meaning to our shared concerns and values. As we discover how different cultures celebrate a holiday, for example, the significance of our own celebrations becomes more important and more clear. Or as we study birth and death rituals of various groups, our own traditions become more meaningful, and feelings toward those experiences surface, making us richer, more self-aware people. Cultural awareness shapes our lives by expanding our self-awareness.

The readings in this chapter are about subcultures, ethnic and otherwise, and how they define who we are. For example, you will read a description of the birth and burial rituals of the Tewa tribe ("Through Tewa Eyes"). But many times, these cultural "definitions" are limiting and lead to painful experiences that we would prefer to avoid. This is the topic of "Fifth Chinese Daughter," in which a young woman attempts to break away from cultural traditions; "The Misunderstood Arab," which describes the prejudicial treatment of an Arab man married to an American woman; "Primary Colors," which describes how an interracial child fits in society; and "Black *and* Latino," which relates a young man's experience of being both black and Puerto Rican. Subcultures do not always have to be racial or ethnic divisions, as you will see in a homeless man's account of how he searches for food ("Dumpster Diving") and how some deaf people wish to maintain a separate subculture ("Silenced Voices: Deaf Cultures and 'Hearing' Families").

Brainstorming About Culture

Class Activity: Each group of students should brainstorm to create lists of all the cultures and subcultures of which any group member has any inside knowledge or experience.

Primary Colors

▶ **Kim McLarin**

In this essay from The New York Times Magazine, *a mother writes about how society has trouble seeing the connection between her and her lighter-skinned, daughter.*

Reading Strategy

As you read, highlight words and phrases that reveal the author's attitude toward her daughter.

Vocabulary Preview

retrospect (5) looking back
eccentricities (5) oddities; exceptions
umber (6) brownish
abduction (9) kidnapping
disconcerting (10) unsettling; upsetting
condemnation (13) strong criticism or disapproval
allegiances (13) loyalties
denounce (13) condemn; criticize openly
align (14) identify; join

A few weeks after my daughter was born, I took her to a new pediatrician for an exam. The doctor took one look at Samantha and exclaimed: "Wow! She's so light!" I explained that my husband is white, but it didn't seem to help. The doctor commented on Sam's skin color so often that I finally asked what was on her mind." 1

"I'm thinking albino," she said. 2

The doctor, who is white, claimed she had seen the offspring of many interracial couples, but never a child this fair. "They're usually a darker, coffee-with-cream color. Some of them are this light at birth, but by 72 hours you can tell they have a black parent." 3

To prove her point, she held her arm next to Samantha's stomach. "I mean, this could be my child!" 4

It's funny now, in retrospect. But at the time, with my hormones still raging from childbirth, the incident sent me into a panic. Any fool could see that Samantha wasn't an albino—she had black hair and dark blue eyes. It must be a trick. The doctor, who had left the room, 5 probably suspected me of kidnapping this "white" child and was out-side calling the police. By the time she returned I was ready to fight.

Fortunately, her partner dismissed the albino theory, and we es-   6
caped and found a new pediatrician, one who knows a little more about genetic eccentricities. But the incident stayed with me because, in the months since, other white people have assumed Samantha is not my child. This is curious to me, this inability to connect across skin tones, especially since Samantha has my full lips and broad nose. I'll admit that I myself didn't expect Sam to be quite so pale, so much closer to her father's Nordic coloring than my own umber tones. My husband is a blue-eyed strawberry blond; I figured that my genes would take his genes in the first round.

Wrong.   7

Needless to say, I love Sam just as she is. She is amazingly, heart-   8
breakingly beautiful to me in the way that babies are to their parents. She sweeps me away with her mischievous grin and her belly laugh, with the coy way she tilts her head after flinging the cup from her high-chair. When we are alone and I look at Samantha, I see Samantha, not the color of her skin.

And yet. I admit that I wouldn't mind if she were darker, dark   9
enough so that white people would know she was mine and black people wouldn't give her a hard time. I know a black guy who, while crossing into Canada, was suspected of having kidnapped his fair-skinned son. So far no one has accused me of child abduction, but I have been mistaken for Samantha's nanny. It has happened so often that I've considered going into business as a nanny spy. I could sit in the park and take notes on your child-care worker. Better than hiding a video camera in the living room.

In a way it's disconcerting, my being mistaken for a nanny. Be-   10
cause, to be blunt, I don't like seeing black women caring for white children. It may be because I grew up in the South, where black women once had no choice but to leave their own children and suckle the offspring of others. The weight of that past, the whiff of a power imbalance, still stains such pairings for me. That's unfair, I know, to the professional, hard-working (mostly Caribbean) black nannies of New York. But there you are.

On the flip side, I think being darker wouldn't hurt Samantha with   11
black people, either. A few weeks ago, in my beauty shop, I overheard a woman trashing a friend for "slathering" his light-skinned children with sunscreen during the summer.

"Maybe he doesn't want them getting skin cancer," suggested the   12
listener. But my girl was having none of that.

"He doesn't want them getting black!" she said, as full of righteous   13
condemnation as only a black woman in a beauty shop can be. Now,

maybe the woman was right about her friend's motivation. Or maybe she was 100 percent wrong. Maybe because she herself is the color of butterscotch she felt she had to declare her allegiances loudly, had to place herself prominently high on the unofficial black scale and denounce anyone caught not doing the same. Either way, I know it means grief for Sam.

I think that as time goes on my daughter will probably align with black people anyway, regardless of the relative fairness of her skin. My husband is fine with that, as long as it doesn't mean denying him or his family.

The bottom line is that society has a deep need to categorize people, to classify and, yes, to stereotype. Race is still the easiest, most convenient way of doing so. That race tells you, in the end, little or nothing about a person is beside the point. We still feel safer believing that we can sum up one another at a glance.

Examining the Reading

Finding Meaning

1. When McLarin took Samantha to her pediatrician, how did the doctor respond?
2. Why did this incident cause the author to "panic"?
3. Why did McLarin find a new pediatrician?
4. What does the author's husband look like?
5. How does the author feel about black women caring for white children who are not their own?

Understanding Technique

1. Identify McLarin's thesis and evaluate its placement.
2. How does McLarin reveal the attitude of various groups within our society toward her daughter?

Thinking Critically

1. What does the author mean by an "inability to connect across skin tones" (paragraph 6)?
2. Describe the tone of this essay.
3. What do you think was the author's purpose in writing this essay?
4. Why does the author say, "I think being darker wouldn't hurt Samantha."
5. What does the author most worry about for her daughter?

Writing About the Reading

A Journal Entry

Write a journal entry about an event or situation in which you felt that you stood out from other people around you.

A Paragraph

1. Write a paragraph explaining what you notice first when you meet a person for the first time.
2. Write a paragraph about how it feels to be different in any sense of the word.

An Essay

1. Do you agree with the author that society needs to categorize, classify, and stereotype people? Write an essay defending or rejecting this idea.
2. Write an essay explaining how your first impression of another person proved to be incorrect.

A Creative Activity

Imagine yourself in the author's situation. If you were part of an interracial couple, what concerns might you have for your child? What could you do to protect your child?

Black *and* Latino

> ▶ **Roberto Santiago**

Am I black or am I Latino? This is the question that troubled Santiago throughout his childhood as a member of two ethnic groups. Read this essay, first published in Essence *magazine, to discover how he resolved this issue.*

Reading Strategy

To strengthen your comprehension of this essay, highlight statements by Santiago that reveal his attitude toward his biracial heritage.

Vocabulary Preview

perplexes (1) confuses
heritages (1) inherited backgrounds
parody (4) ridiculous imitation
eons (6) long periods of time
conquests (6) subjugations; forced colonizations
predominant (6) most important
determinant (6) deciding
slur (8) disrespectful remark
solace (9) comfort
pegged (11) marked; identified
iconoclast (11) someone who overthrows a traditional idea or
           image

"*T*here is no way that you can be black and Puerto Rican at the 1
same time." What? Despite the many times I've heard this over the years, that statement still perplexes me. I *am* both and always have been. My color is a blend of my mother's rich, dark skin tone and my father's white complexion. As they were both Puerto Rican, I spoke Spanish before English, but I am totally bilingual. My life has been shaped by my black and Latino heritages, and despite other people's confusion, I don't feel I have to choose one or the other. To do so would be to deny a part of myself.

There has not been a moment in my life when I did not know that 2
I looked black—and I never thought that others did not see it, too. But growing up in East Harlem, I was also aware that I did not "act black," according to the African-American boys on the block.

My lighter-skinned Puerto Rican friends were less of a help in this 3
department. "You're not black," they would whine, shaking their
heads. "You're a *boriqua* [slang for Puerto Rican], you ain't no *moreno*
[black]." If that was true, why did my mirror defy the rules of logic?
And most of all, why did I feel that there was some serious unknown
force trying to make me choose sides?

Acting black. Looking black. Being a real black. This debate among 4
us is almost a parody. The fact is that I am black, so why do I need to
prove it?

The island of Puerto Rico is only a stone's throw away from Haiti, 5
and, no fooling, if you climb a palm tree, you can see Jamaica bobbing
on the Atlantic. The slave trade ran through the Caribbean basin, and
virtually all Puerto Rican citizens have some African blood in their
veins. My grandparents on my mother's side were the classic *negro
como carbón* (black as carbon) people, but despite the fact that they
were as dark as can be, they are officially not considered black.

There is an explanation for this, but not one that makes much 6
sense, or difference, to a working-class kid from Harlem. Puerto Ricans identify themselves as Hispanics—part of a worldwide race that
originated from eons of white Spanish conquests—a mixture of white,
African, and *Indio* blood, which, categorically, is apart from black. In
other words, the culture is the predominant and determinant factor.
But there are frustrations in being caught in a duo-culture, where your
skin color does not necessarily dictate what you are. When I read Piri
Thomas's searing autobiography, *Down These Mean Streets*, in my early
teens, I saw that he couldn't figure out other people's attitudes toward
his blackness, either.

My first encounter with this attitude about the race thing rode on 7
horseback. I had just turned six years old and ran toward the bridle
path in Central Park as I saw two horses about to trot past. "Yea! Hor-
sie! Yea!" I yelled. Then I noticed one figure on horseback. She was
white, and she shouted, "Shut up, you f—g nigger! Shut up!" She
pulled back on the reins and twisted the horse in my direction. I can
still feel the spray of gravel that the horse kicked at my chest. And suddenly she was gone. I looked back, and, in the distance, saw my parents playing Whiffle Ball with my sister. They seemed miles away.

They still don't know about this incident. But I told my Aunt Aure- 8
lia almost immediately. She explained what the words meant and why
they were said. Ever since then I have been able to express my anger
appropriately through words or action in similar situations. Self-
preservation, ego, and pride forbid men from ever ignoring, much less
forgetting, a slur.

Aunt Aurelia became, unintentionally, my source for answers I 9
needed about color and race. I never sought her out. She just seemed

to appear at my home during the points in my childhood when I most needed her for solace. "Puerto Ricans are different from American blacks," she told me once. "There is no racism between what you call white and black. Nobody even considers the marriages interracial." She then pointed out the difference in color between my father and mother. "You never noticed that," she said, "because you were not raised with that hang-up."

Aunt Aurelia passed away before I could follow up on her observation. But she had made an important point. It's why I never liked the attitude that says I should be exclusive to one race.   10

My behavior toward this race thing pegged me as an iconoclast of sorts. Children from mixed marriages, from my experience, also share this attitude. If I have to bear the label of iconoclast because the world wants people to be in set categories and I don't want to, then I will.   11

A month before Aunt Aurelia died, she saw I was a little down about the whole race thing, and she said, "Roberto, don't worry. Even if—no matter what you do—black people in this country don't, you can always depend on white people to treat you like a black."   12

Examining the Reading

Finding Meaning

1. What problems did Santiago face during childhood?
2. According to the author, what other race (besides white and African) do all Puerto Rican citizens have in their blood?
3. What explanation does the author give for his maternal grandparents being "black as carbon" and yet being "officially not considered black"?
4. Describe the author's first encounter with prejudice.
5. According to his aunt, why had the author never noticed the difference in color between his mother and his father?

Understanding Technique

Santiago opens his essay with a question. Discuss the effectiveness of this strategy as a means of starting the essay.

Thinking Critically

1. Is there a tendency in our society to label or compartmentalize people? Why do you think people do this, and what are its positive and negative effects?
2. When the author had his first encounter with prejudice, why do you think he chose to tell his aunt but not his parents?

3. What part did the author's aunt play in shaping his life—particularly with regard to ideas about race?
4. What does the last sentence of the reading reveal about discrimination in our country?

Writing About the Reading

A Journal Entry

Write a journal entry describing what you know about your ethnic origins. Are they important to you?

A Paragraph

1. Santiago experiences conflict about his ethnic origins. Write a paragraph describing a conflict, ethnic or otherwise, that you have experienced. Explain how you resolved it.
2. Santiago read an autobiography of a man who shared his confusion about race. Have you ever read a book or watched a movie or television program that dealt with a problem you were experiencing? Write a paragraph explaining whether seeing others deal with a problem helps you cope with it.

An Essay

1. Santiago felt that people wanted him to be either black or Puerto Rican; they wanted him to choose sides. Many times in our lives, we are asked or forced to take sides. Write an essay discussing a situation in which you were asked or forced to take sides or to take a stand on an issue.
2. Santiago asks, "I am black, so why do I need to prove it?" Often, in our culture, we are called upon to prove who or what we are. Write an essay describing a situation in which you were called upon to prove yourself.
3. Imagine that you are black raised in a white family or white raised in a black family. Write an essay discussing the problems you would face.

A Creative Activity

Suppose Santiago, in adulthood, were to meet the woman on the horse. What do you think he would say to her?

Fifth Chinese Daughter

▶ Jade Snow Wong

Traditional Chinese families hold to a culture in which children must obey their parents and seek permission for what they do. In this essay, the author describes her breaking from this cultural tradition. This essay was taken from a book titled The Immigrant Experience.

Reading Strategy

Highlight words, phrases, and descriptions that reveal how Wong's parents felt about her actions.

Vocabulary Preview

impulsively (1) without thinking or planning
incredulous (5) not believing
unfilial (5) against family
revered (5) admired and respected
denounced (5) spoke out against
ingrate (5) ungrateful person
whims (5) sudden, fanciful ideas
proclamation (6) announcement
innuendoes (7) subtle or indirect negative comments
underscored (7) made the point more clear
devastated (8) stunned; overwhelmed
conceding (9) acknowledging; admitting

One afternoon on a Saturday, which was normally occupied with   1
my housework job, I was unexpectedly released by my employer, who was departing for a country weekend. It was a rare joy to have free time and I wanted to enjoy myself for a change. There had been a Chinese-American boy who shared some classes with me. Sometimes we had found each other walking to the same 8:00 A.M. class. He was not a special boyfriend, but I had enjoyed talking to him and had confided in him some of my problems. Impulsively, I telephoned him. I

Source: "Fifth Chinese Daughter," from *The Immigrant Experience* by Thomas C. Wheeler. Copyright © 1971 by Doubleday, a division of Bantam Doubleday Dell Publishing Group, Inc. Used by permission of Doubleday, a division of Random House, Inc.

knew I must be breaking rules, and I felt shy and scared. At the same time, I was excited at this newly found forwardness, with nothing more purposeful than to suggest another walk together.

He understood my awkwardness and shared my anticipation. He asked me to "dress up" for my first movie date. My clothes were limited but I changed to look more graceful in silk stockings and found a bright ribbon for my long black hair. Daddy watched, catching my mood, observing the dashing preparations. He asked me where I was going without his permission and with whom.

I refused to answer him. I thought of my rights! I thought he surely would not try to understand. Thereupon Daddy thundered his displeasure and forbade my departure.

I found a new courage as I heard my voice announce calmly that I was no longer a child, and if I could work my way through college, I would choose my own friends. It was my right as a person.

My mother heard the commotion and joined my father to face me; both appeared shocked and incredulous. Daddy at once demanded the source of this unfilial, non-Chinese theory. And when I quoted my college professor, reminding him that he had always felt teachers should be revered, my father denounced that professor as a foreigner who was disregarding the superiority of our Chinese culture, with its sound family strength. My father did not spare me; I was condemned as an ingrate for echoing dishonorable opinions which should only be temporary whims, yet nonetheless inexcusable.

The scene was not yet over. I completed my proclamation to my father, who had never allowed me to learn how to dance, by adding that I was attending a movie, unchaperoned, with a boy I met at college.

My startled father was sure that my reputation would be subject to whispered innuendos. I must be bent on disgracing the family name; I was ruining my future, for surely I would yield to temptation. My mother underscored him by saying that I hadn't any notion of the problems endured by parents of a young girl.

I would not give in. I reminded them that they and I were not in China, that I wasn't going out with just anybody but someone I trusted! Daddy gave a roar that no man could be trusted, but I devastated them in declaring that I wished the freedom to find my own answers.

Both parents were thoroughly angered, scolded me for being shameless, and predicted that I would some day tell them I was wrong. But I dimly perceived that they were conceding defeat and were perplexed at this breakdown of their training. I was too old to beat and too bold to intimidate.

Examining the Reading

Finding Meaning

1. How did Wong's father respond when she refused to tell him where she was going and with whom?
2. What was the argument between father and daughter really about?
3. What rules was Wong breaking?
4. Summarize the father's argument.
5. What was Wong's mother's reaction when she heard the argument between her husband and her daughter?
6. In the end, how did Wong win the argument?

Understanding Technique

1. Although Wong recounts a family dispute, she does not include dialogue. How would her essay have been changed by including it? Suggest places where dialogue could be added.
2. Describe how the essay is organized.
3. Wong's sentence structure is varied and therefore interesting. Cite several examples.

Thinking Critically

1. Why did the author assume that her father would not understand even before she attempted to explain the situation?
2. Why do you think the author's parents were so upset by her need for privacy and independence?
3. In what way was this incident a turning point in the author's life?
4. To what extent and in what ways do you think this incident shaped Wong's future actions in going against cultural traditions?

Writing About the Reading

A Journal Entry

Write a journal entry on how you feel after having a heated argument with a family member or close friend.

A Paragraph

1. Write a paragraph explaining a conflict between you and your parents or an incident in which you disagreed with them about "the way to do things" (cultural traditions).
2. Sometimes it's necessary to do the opposite of what you know your

family or friends want you to do. Write a paragraph describing a time when you felt that way or when you observed someone else doing so.

An Essay

At some point, we have all decided to act against a cultural tradition. Write an essay describing a situation in which you acted against tradition. Explain how other people responded to your decision and how you attempted to resolve any conflicts.

A Creative Activity

Write a paragraph describing what you think happened between Wong and her parents the day after her movie date.

Through Tewa Eyes

▶ Alfonso Ortiz

Different cultures have different ways of marking important life events. This essay describes rituals celebrated by the Tewa tribe. It was originally published in National Geographic *magazine.*

Reading Strategy

As you read, highlight each ceremonial event in a Tewa's life. For each, write an annotation that summarizes its purpose.

Vocabulary Preview

proffered (1) held out; presented
evokes (2) calls to mind
duality (3) twofoldness
moieties (7) halves; parts
deities (11) gods
kiva (11) ceremonial structure
cicada (15) insect whose wings produce high-pitched sounds
admonishes (15) warns; advises

I do not remember the day, of course, but I know what happened. 1
Four days after I was born in the Pueblo Indian village of San Juan in the Rio Grande Valley in New Mexico, the "umbilical cord-cutting mother" and her assistant came to present me to the sun and to give me a name. They took me from the house just as the sun's first rays appeared over the Sangre de Cristo Mountains. The cord-cutting mother proffered me and two perfect ears of corn, one blue and one white, to the six sacred directions. A prayer was said:

> *Here is a child who has been given to us. Let us bring him to manhood. . . . You who are dawn youths and dawn maidens. You who are winter spirits. You who are summer spirits. . . . Take therefore. . . . Give him good fortune, we ask of you.*

Now the name was given. It was not the name at the head of this 2
story. It was my Tewa name, a thing of power. Usually such a name evokes either nature—the mountains or the hills or the season—or a ceremony under way at the time of the birth. By custom such a name is shared only within the community, and with those we know well.

Thus, in the eyes of my Tewa people, I was "brought in out of the darkness," where I had no identity. Thus I became a child of the Tewa. My world is the Tewa world. It is different from your world. . . .

Remember my naming ceremony: There were two women attending, two ears of corn offered with me to the sun. This duality is basic to understanding our behavior.   3

When the Tewa came onto land, the Hunt Chief took an ear of blue corn and handed it to one of the other men and said: "You are to lead and care for all of the people during the summer." To another man he handed an ear of white corn and told him: "You shall lead and care for the people during the winter." This is how the Summer and Winter Chiefs were instituted.   4

The Hunt Chief then divided the people between the two chiefs. As they moved south down the Rio Grande, the Summer People traveled on the west side of the river, the Winter People on the east side.   5

The Summer People lived by agriculture, the Winter People by hunting.   6

From this time, the story tells us, the Tewa have been divided during their lives into moieties—Winter People, Summer People. Still today a Summer Chief guides us seven months of the year, during the agricultural cycle; a Winter Chief during the five months of hunting. There are special rituals, dances, costumes, and colors attached to each moiety. Everything that has symbolic significance to the Tewa is classified in dualities: Games, plants, and diseases are hot or cold, winter or summer. Some persons or things, like healers, are of the middle, mediating between the two. This gives order to our lives.   7

A child is incorporated into his moiety through the water-giving ceremony during his first year. The Winter Chief conducts his rite in October; the Summer Chief in late February or March. The ceremony is held in a sanctuary at the chief's home. There are an altar, a sand painting, and various symbols; the chief and his assistants dress in white buckskin. A final character appears, preceded by the call of a fox, as in the creation story. It is the Hunt Chief.   8

A female assistant holds the child; the moiety chief recites a short prayer and administers a drink of the sacred medicinal water from an abalone shell, thereby welcoming the child into the moiety.   9

The third rite in a child's life—water pouring—comes between the ages of six and ten and is held within the moiety. It marks the transition from the carefree, innocent state of early childhood to the status of adult, one of the Dry Food People. For four days the boys are made to carry a load of firewood they have chopped themselves, and the girls a basket of corn, meal they have ground themselves, to the homes of their sponsors.   10

A sponsor instructs each child in the beliefs and practices of the village. On the fourth night, the deities come to the kiva, and the child   11 may go to watch. Afterward, the sponsor bathes the child, pouring water over him. From this time, the child is given duties judged proper for his sex.

A finishing ritual a few years later brings the girls and boys to 12 adulthood. For the boys it is particularly meaningful, for they now become eligible to assist and participate in the coming of the gods in their moiety's kiva. Thus the bonds of the moiety are further strengthened.

It is at death that the bond of moiety is broken and the solidarity of 13 the whole society emphasized again. This echoes the genesis story, for after the people had divided into two for their journey from the lake, they came together again when they arrived at their destination.

When a Tewa dies, relatives dress the corpse. The moccasins are 14 reversed—for the Tewa believe everything in the afterlife is reversed from this life. There is a Spanish Catholic wake, a Requiem Mass, then the trip to the cemetery. There the priest completes the church's funeral rites: the sprinkling of holy water, a prayer, a handful of dirt thrown into the grave. Then all non-Indians leave.

A bag containing the clothing of the deceased is now placed under 15 his head as a pillow, along with other personal possessions. When the grave is covered, a Tewa official tells the survivors that the deceased has gone to the place "of endless cicada singing," that he will be happy, and he admonishes them not to let the loss divide the home.

During the four days following death, the soul, or Dry Food Who Is 16 No Longer, is believed to wander about in this world in the company of the ancestors. These four days produce a time of unease. There is the fear among relatives that the soul may become lonely and return to take one of them for company. Children are deemed most susceptible. The house itself must not be left unoccupied.

The uneasiness ends on the fourth night, when relatives gather 17 again to perform the releasing rite. There are rituals with tobacco, a piece of charcoal, a series of four lines drawn on the floor. A pottery bowl, used in his naming ceremony long ago and cherished by him all his life, is broken, or "killed." Then a prayer reveals the purpose of the symbols:

> We have muddied the waters for you [the smoke]. We have cast shadows between us [the charcoal]. We have made steep gullies between us [the lines]. Do not, therefore, reach for even a hair on our heads. Rather, help us attain that which we are always seeking: Long life, that our children may grow, abundant game, the raising of crops. . . . Now you must go, for you are now free.

With the soul released, all breathe a sigh of relief. They wash their 18 hands. As each finishes, he says, "May you have life." The others respond, "Let it be so." Everyone now eats.

The Tewa begin and end life as one people; we call the life cycle   19
poeh, or emergence path. As a Tewa elder told me:

"In the beginning we were one. Then we divided into Summer   20
People and Winter People; in the end we came together again as we are
today."

This is the path of our lives.   21

Examining the Reading

Finding Meaning

1. With what Tewa customs is this reading concerned?
2. Explain the importance of duality (twofoldness) in the Tewa culture.
3. What do Tewa names usually stand for?
4. What four rituals occur in a child's life? Explain their significance.
5. Why do the Tewa reverse the moccasins on their deceased relatives?

Understanding Technique

1. Ortiz includes two prayers within the essay. Why are they included? What purpose do they serve?
2. Ortiz uses transitional words and phrases to connect ideas and events. Highlight several that are particularly effective.

Thinking Critically

1. Who do you think the Hunt Chief is?
2. Discuss religious rituals that symbolize the passage from childhood to adulthood.
3. Discuss your beliefs about what happens to the soul after the body dies.
4. The Tewa follow a life cycle called a *poeh*. Do life cycles exist in American culture? If so, describe them.

Writing About the Reading

A Journal Entry

Brainstorm about your reaction to the Tewa practices. Do you wish your culture had more traditions to follow?

A Paragraph

1. Write a paragraph identifying an ethnic or religious ritual in which you participated or that you have observed. Explain its significance.
2. Write a paragraph agreeing or disagreeing with the following statement: Ceremonies or rituals occur at changing points in our lives. Support your paragraph with examples.

An Essay

1. In the Tewa culture, many things are divided into twos. The author explains that "this gives order to our lives." Write an essay discussing what values, beliefs, or traditions give order to your life.
2. Write an essay discussing the function or purpose of rituals or ceremonies. Why does each culture have them? What do they accomplish?

A Creative Activity

After a Tewa dies, the house is guarded so that the deceased may not return to claim the life of a relative. Assume that you are a Tewa child and that you and your parents are staying in your home immediately after the death of a close relative. Write a paragraph describing what you might do and feel when you are alone in your room at night.

Dumpster Diving

▶ Lars Eighner

*In this essay, the author, at the time homeless, describes how he
and others survived by scavenging for food and possessions in
Dumpsters. Through the essay you learn about Eighner's values
and attitudes toward others, as well as his survival techniques.
This essay first appeared in* The Threepenny Review.

Reading Strategy

Highlight factual information that Eighner provides about
Dumpster diving. Annotate your responses to these facts.

Vocabulary Preview

niche (3) position; place in life
pristine (6) pure; unspoiled
utility (7) usefulness
bohemian (8) unconventional (usually with an interest in the
                             arts)
dilettanti (9) amateurs; dabblers
contaminants (10) dirt; germs; unhealthy material
dysentery (12) a temporary intestinal disorder; extreme
                             diarrhea
transience (14) changeability; briefness
envisioning (15) picturing in one's mind
gaudy (16) flashy; showy
bauble (16) small ornament; piece of jewelry
sated (16) satisfied; taken care of
confounded (16) mixed up; confused

I began Dumpster diving about a year before I became homeless.   1

I prefer the term *scavenging*. I have heard people, evidently mean-   2
ing to be polite, use the word *foraging,* but I prefer to reserve that word
for gathering nuts and berries and such, which I also do, according to
the season and opportunity.

I like the frankness of the word *scavenging*. I live from the refuse of   3
others. I am a scavenger. I think it a sound and honorable niche, although if I could I would naturally prefer to live the comfortable consumer life, perhaps—and only perhaps—as a slightly less wasteful
consumer owing to what I have learned as a scavenger.

Except for jeans, all my clothes come from Dumpsters. Boom 4
boxes, candles, bedding, toilet paper, medicine, books, a typewriter, a
virgin male love doll, coins sometimes amounting to many dollars: all
came from Dumpsters. And, yes, I eat from Dumpsters, too.

There is a predictable series of stages that a person goes through in 5
learning to scavenge. At first the new scavenger is filled with disgust
and self-loathing. He is ashamed of being seen.

This stage passes with experience. The scavenger finds a pair of 6
running shoes that fit and look and smell brand-new. He finds a pocket
calculator in perfect working order. He finds pristine ice cream, still
frozen, more than he can eat or keep. He begins to understand: people
do throw away perfectly good stuff, a lot of perfectly good stuff.

At this stage he may become lost and never recover. All the Dump- 7
ster divers I have known come to the point of trying to acquire everything they touch. Why not take it, they reason, it is all free. This is, of
course, hopeless, and most divers come to realize that they must re-
strict themselves to items of relatively immediate utility.

The finding of objects is becoming something of an urban art. 8
Even respectable, employed people will sometimes find something
tempting sticking out of a Dumpster or standing beside one. Quite a
number of people, not all of them of the bohemian type, are willing to
brag that they found this or that piece in the trash.

But eating from Dumpsters is the thing that separates the dilet- 9
tanti from the professionals. Eating safely involves three principles: using the senses and common sense to evaluate the condition of the
found materials; knowing the Dumpsters of a given area and checking
them regularly; and seeking always to answer the question "Why was
this discarded?"

Yet perfectly good food can be found in Dumpsters. Canned goods, 10
for example, turn up fairly often in the Dumpsters I frequent. I also
have few qualms about dry foods such as crackers, cookies, cereal,
chips, and pasta if they are free of visible contaminants and still dry
and crisp. Raw fruits and vegetables with intact skins seem perfectly
safe to me, excluding, of course, the obviously rotten. Many are discarded for minor imperfections that can be pared away.

A typical discard is a half jar of peanut butter—though nonorganic 11
peanut butter does not require refrigeration and is unlikely to spoil in
any reasonable time. One of my favorite finds is yogurt—often discarded, still sealed, when the expiration date has passed—because it
will keep for several days, even in warm weather.

No matter how careful I am I still get dysentery at least once 12
a month, oftener in warm weather. I do not want to paint too ro-
mantic a picture. Dumpster diving has serious drawbacks as a way of
life.

I find from the experience of scavenging two rather deep lessons. 13
The first is to take what I can use and let the rest go. I have come to
think that there is no value in the abstract. A thing I cannot use or
make useful, perhaps by trading, has no value, however fine or rare it
may be.

The second lesson is the transience of material being. I do not sup- 14
pose that ideas are immortal, but certainly they are longer-lived than
material objects.

The things I find in Dumpsters, the love letters and rag dolls of so 15
many lives, remind me of this lesson. Now I hardly pick up a thing
without envisioning the time I will cast it away. This, I think, is a
healthy state of mind. Almost everything I have now has already been
cast out at least once, proving that what I own is valueless to someone.

I find that my desire to grab for the gaudy bauble has been largely 16
sated. I think this is an attitude I share with the very wealthy—we both
know there is plenty more where whatever we have came from. Between us are the rat-race millions who have confounded their selves
with the objects they grasp and who nightly scavenge the cable channels for they know not what.

I am sorry for them. 17

Examining the Reading

Finding Meaning

1. What is Dumpster diving?
2. Why does the author prefer the word *scavenging*?
3. What does the author say is the primary disadvantage of eating out
   of Dumpsters?
4. Summarize the three stages that Dumpster divers go through.
5. What two lessons has the author learned through Dumpster diving?

Understanding Technique

1. Eighner uses topic sentences to structure his paragraphs and help
   identify the main point in his paragraphs. Identify several topic sentences and note their placement.
2. Describe Eighner's tone (his attitude toward his subject).
3. Evaluate the title and its meaning.

Thinking Critically

1. How do you think the average person looks upon a Dumpster diver?
   Why?
2. Can you imagine yourself eating out of a Dumpster? Why or why not?

3. Do you think Lars Eighner would continue to acquire things from Dumpsters if he didn't need to? What in the reading might indicate that he would or would not?
4. What does the author mean by the statement: "I do not suppose that ideas are immortal"?
5. The author says he feels sorry for people who "scavenge the cable channels." Why do you think this is?

Writing About the Reading

A Journal Entry

Think of a homeless person you've seen and write a journal entry describing him or her and what thoughts or feelings you had at the time.

A Paragraph

1. Eighner places little value on personal possessions. As he picks something up, he imagines throwing it out. Think of a personal possession that you could easily do without or one that you could never do without. Write a paragraph explaining why the object is or is not important to you.
2. Imagine that some people in your neighborhood that you didn't know were moving and left their unwanted, but useful belongings on the sidewalk. Write a paragraph describing the kinds of "treasures" you might expect to find.

An Essay

1. The author believes that the usefulness of material possessions is short-lived. He also describes this belief as a "healthy state of mind." Write an essay discussing whether you agree or disagree and why.
2. The number and variety of perfectly good items the author has found in Dumpsters emphasizes the amount of waste in our society. Write an essay explaining how this waste affects us and suggesting alternatives to just throwing out unwanted items.

A Creative Activity

Imagine that you were the author of this essay, finding "love letters and rag dolls of so many lives," as he does. Recall an object or letter and write an essay that re-creates the life of the person who threw it away.

Silenced Voices: Deaf Cultures and "Hearing" Families

▶ **Richard Appelbaum and William J. Chambliss**
Textbook Excerpt

This textbook excerpt, taken from Sociology, *describes one of many groups that have formed their own subculture. These authors take the position that deaf people prefer to share experiences with others who are deaf.*

Reading Strategy

Highlight the topic sentence of each paragraph and the key details that support each topic sentence.

Vocabulary Preview

heritage (2) background
simulated (4) imitated
virtually (4) practically
fraught (4) filled
wary (5) cautious; worried
confront (5) face; challenge
daunting (5) intimidating
confer (6) give; bestow
mainstream (6) integrate
fundamental (7) basic

*T*here are as many as 450,000 Americans who are completely unable   1
to hear; about 250,000 were born deaf. For them, family life poses
unique challenges. As a consequence, many deaf people prefer to practice endogamy, marrying others who are deaf and therefore share a
common experience.

There is a growing movement within the deaf community to   2
redefine the meaning of deafness not as a form of disability, but rather
as a positive culture. A growing number of deaf people see themselves
as similar to any ethnic group, sharing a common language (American

Sign Language, or ASL), possessing a strong sense of cultural identity, and taking pride in their heritage. One survey reported that the overwhelming majority would not even elect to have a free surgical implant that would enable them to hear.

Roslyn Rosen is an example of a person who takes great pride in   3
being deaf. Born of deaf parents and the mother of deaf children, Rosen is the president of the National Association of the Deaf:

> *I'm happy with who I am, and I don't want to be "fixed." Would an Italian-American rather be a WASP [White Anglo-Saxon Protestant]? In our society everybody agrees that whites have an easier time than blacks. But do you think that a black person would undergo operations to be a white?*

The desire for a deaf identity reflects the near impossibility of deaf   4
people ever learning to communicate with "hearing" people (people who are not deaf) through lipreading and simulated speech. People who have never heard a sound find it virtually impossible to utter sounds that most "hearing" people can recognize as words. Lipreading is equally problematic and is fraught with error. Reading, which depends on an understanding of the meaning of spoken words, can prove to be a frustrating experience. Yet for those who "hear" and "speak" ASL, a rich form of communication is possible, and with it comes a strong sense of shared identity.

Many deaf parents are wary when their deaf children get involved   5
in relationships with "hearing" people, preferring that they remain within their own community. Among those who marry, 90 percent choose spouses who are also deaf. Although many deaf people have succeeded in the "hearing" world, the problems that confront them can be daunting. Most will never be able to speak in a way that is likely to be understood by "hearing" people, and most of the "hearing" people they encounter will not know ASL. It is not surprising that when it comes to intimate relations, most deaf people choose to marry others who share their own language and culture.

Although families ordinarily confer their own ethnic status on   6
their children, this is not true for the nine out of ten deaf children who are born to "hearing" parents. Their parents are of one culture; they are of another. This can pose difficult choices for their families. On the one hand, "hearing" parents want the same sorts of things for their deaf children as do any parents: happiness, fulfillment, and successful lives as adults. Many would like their children to mainstream into the "hearing" world as best as possible. Yet they know that this will prove extremely difficult.

On the other hand, the deaf community argues that the deaf chil-   7
dren of "hearing" parents can never fully belong to the "hearing" world, or, for that matter, even to their own "hearing" parents. Many

leaders in the deaf community urge "hearing" parents to send their deaf children to residential schools for the deaf, where they will be fully accepted, learn deaf culture, and be with their own people. Fundamental questions about the meaning of "family" arise when the children and parents largely live in two different cultures.

Examining the Reading

Finding Meaning

1. What is endogamy?
2. According to the article, how do many deaf people wish to define themselves?
3. Why are deaf parents of deaf children wary when their children become involved with hearing people?
4. Why is it almost impossible for people who are deaf to speak?
5. Name one problem with lipreading.

Understanding Technique

1. Identify the authors' tone.
2. What type of evidence do the authors provide to support their thesis?

Thinking Critically

1. Explain what is meant by deaf people desiring a "deaf identity."
2. Discuss the advantages and disadvantages of deaf people learning American Sign Language.
3. Discuss the problems that confront deaf people when they mainstream into a hearing society.
4. What other groups of people have formed their own subculture?

Writing About the Reading

A Journal Entry

Write a journal entry discussing your reaction to the idea that many deaf people do not want to be able to hear.

A Paragraph

1. Suppose you had become deaf through illness or injury. Would you elect to read lips or learn American Sign Language? Write a paragraph explaining your choice.

2. Write a paragraph identifying what you think would be the major challenges in a relationship between a hearing person and a deaf person.

An Essay

1. If you had a child who was born deaf, would you choose a residential school for the deaf or a traditional school? Write an essay explaining your choice.
2. Deaf people develop their own language, which builds group identity. In a sense, groups of hearing people also develop language that establishes their identity. For example, teenagers use slang; medical doctors speak in medical jargon. Choose a group of people and describe the language that identifies them. (*Hint:* You might write about football fans, salespeople, computer hackers, car enthusiasts.)

A Creative Activity

Some deaf people have formed their own culture. Do you think other groups of people with physical illnesses and disabilities (blindness, cancer, muscular dystrophy, etc.) also have a separate culture? Write a paragraph describing the shared problems and concerns of a particular group.

The Misunderstood Arab

▶ **Jennifer Kabalan**
Student Essay

Jennifer Kabalan, who wrote this essay while a college student,
describes stereotypes she has observed as the American wife of
an Arab man. She offers an interesting perspective on both
American and Arab culture.

*F*or nine and a half years I have been the American wife of an Arab   1
man named Andre. He was born and spent the first seven years
of his life in Lebanon. He is the first generation to come to America. His family came to America looking for a better way of life in
hopes of finding the American dream: Peace, prosperity, and equal
opportunity.

When I married my husband, I often confided to my mother my   2
concerns about how I saw people treating him, especially when they
found out he was Lebanese. I often felt that this kind of prejudiced
treatment only happened to blacks. Wow, was I ignorant! Out of the
blue one day, my mother said, "Maybe Andre's treated differently because he looks like a terrorist." I was shocked that she could even think
like that, yet I realized that if my mother saw my husband in this light
(not that she thought he was a terrorist), how many other people
thought this way?

I spoke to my Arab in-laws and my husband, Andre, to try to gain   3
a better understanding of the misconceptions people have about Arabs
and where these prejudicial thoughts come from. The more questions
I asked, the more I found that I also had my own misconceptions and
misunderstandings.

I found that most people see Arabs as "one cluster of people" (like   4
grapes off the same vine). In reality, there are hundreds and thousands
of different individual groups of Arabs that think differently, act differently, speak with different dialects, eat different foods, live in different
provinces, etc. Not all Arabs, for example, live in tents out in the desert
or ride camels. Most people see all Arabs as Moslems who are fanatic
about their religion and resort to violent means of expressing their religious beliefs. In Lebanon, the country is divided into Moslems and
Christians. Moslems and Christians have very different beliefs and

mannerisms. For example, Moslem women have to cover their bodies up, whereas Christian women don't.

I asked some Arabs for their opinions as to the reasons Americans 5 think this way about them. They said that a lot of problems started during the war in 1973 in Lebanon. The media, whether television, radio, or newspapers, all around the United States had painted all Arabs as violent and cold-hearted people. The press and its influence changed American opinion forever. My mother-in-law said, "It's the few bad Arabs who spoil the good names of hundreds of thousands of great men and women in Arab countries." When my in-laws came to the United States in 1970 before the war, they were treated with "respect and kindness despite our many differences and language barriers."

This stigma on being an Arab stems from an unfortunate igno- 6 rance on our part. We all have cultural differences and many prejudiced feelings toward many things and ideas. But we are all people wanting to be understood, wanting to love and to be loved by all. With time and many prayers, we hope to see oneness and peace among all. We hope our love for each other will be the bridge that fills the gap. With determination and better understanding and a lot of hard work, anything is possible to those who believe.

Examining the Essay

1. Evaluate Kabalan's thesis statement.
2. Evaluate Kabalan's use of topic sentences.
3. What additional information do you wish Kabalan had included?

Writing an Essay

1. The family of Kabalan's husband came to America in search of "peace, prosperity, and equal opportunity." What do you think the American dream is? That is, what is it that many Americans value and are striving for? Write an essay explaining what the term *American dream* means to you and assess whether you have attained or will attain it.
2. Some of the Arabs that Kabalan spoke with felt that the media are, in part, responsible for the misconceptions about Arabs. Do you agree that the media affect people's attitudes toward various religious, ethnic, and racial groups? Think of an international incident currently in the news. Write an essay describing how the media are conveying information about the people or countries involved. Could the media coverage lead to misconceptions about a group or groups of people?

3. Kabalan describes stereotypes held about Arabs. What stereotypes are often held about college students? Write an essay describing what many people think about college students. Then explain how this stereotype is or is not correct.

 ## Making Connections

1. Both "The Misunderstood Arab" and "Black *and* Latino" deal with ethnic issues. Suppose the authors could meet and discuss their experiences. What do you think they would talk about?

2. Both "Silenced Voices: Deaf Cultures and 'Hearing' Families" and "Dumpster Diving" deal with sub-cultures, groups with their own identity that create customs and behaviors. Write an essay comparing the two subcultures.

3. Customs and rituals are very important in the Tewa culture ("Through Tewa Eyes"). Do you sense that rit-ual and custom are important in any of the other cul-tures discussed in this unit? Write an essay explaining the importance of ritual and custom in one of these other cultures.

Chapter 5

Others Who Shape Our Lives

OUR LIVES ARE SHAPED by those around us, particularly our family and friends. We have vivid memories of fun-filled days spent with a close friend; we recall someone we could confide in; we treasure intimate moments with a mate or spouse; and we remember close, comforting times with a parent.

As important as friends and family may be, our lives are also shaped by those we do not know personally—a radio disk jockey who wakes us up each morning, a sports star we cheer for at each game, or a character we admire in a novel. Local, state, and national figures—presidents, senators, talk show hosts—may shape our lives through the issues they raise and the actions they take. And then there are the unsung heroes—people who may shape our lives without our directly knowing it or them. A local businessperson who donates food for a community fair, a medical researcher who develops a new vaccine or antibiotic, and people who selflessly volunteer their time by working in a local homeless shelter are examples.

In this chapter, the readings focus on people who have shaped the lives of others. You will read about how people—both friends and strangers, in the family and at work—influence one another, and the positive experiences that result from such influence. Examples can be found in the story of a woman who tries to offer advice to an uncle suffering from heart disease ("Our Wounded Hearts"), how a father's advice had long-lasting effects ("Poppa and the Spruce Tree"), and how Bill Cosby's parents shaped their lives so that they "fit" each other ("The Promised Land"). You will also read about people whose actions affect hundreds, even thousands, of other people, such as the group of teenagers who begin their own company in "Food from the 'Hood" and Bill Gates, the world's richest man, who started his own computer empire ("Bill Gates: Computer Wizard"). In addition, you will read about how others make shopping a difficult task for a blind woman ("Shopping Can Be a Challenge") and consider whether sports heroes should follow the golden rule ("Do unto Others").

Brainstorming About Others

Class Activity: Form groups of three to four students. Each group member should brainstorm a list of at least ten influential or important people in the news over the past week. Group members should compare lists and prepare a final list, which includes names that appeared on two or more individual lists. Groups then can compare lists and, again, identify recurring names.

Shopping Can Be a Challenge

> ▸ **Carol Fleischman**

This essay, published in the Buffalo News, *provides a fresh viewpoint of a common experience—shopping. The writer, who is blind, focuses on how her experience is shaped by those around her.*

Reading Strategy

In this essay, Fleischman reveals her attitude toward the sighted people around her in several different ways. As you read, highlight words, phrases, and sentences that reveal how the writer feels.

Vocabulary Preview

ritual (2) habit; routine
beeline (4) direct route; straight line
imposing (5) impressive; mildly threatening
chastised (19) scolded; criticized
composing (21) calming; controlling
preoccupied (23) busy; distracted
retrieve (23) get and bring back
reminiscent (24) reminding one of
foiled (24) stopped; prevented

*H*ave you ever tried to buy a dress when you can't see? I have, be- 1
cause I'm blind.

At one time, I would shop with friends. This ritual ended after the 2
time I happily brought home a dress a friend had helped me choose,
and my husband, Don, offered a surprising observation: "The fit is
great, but do you like all those huge fish?" The dress went back.

Now I rely on Don and my guide dog, Misty, as my shopping 3
partners.

We enter the store and make a beeline for the dress department. 4
Don usually sees two or three salespeople scatter. The aisles empty as
if a bomber had come on the scene.

Then I realize I'm holding the "live wire." But I'm not judgmental— 5
once I, too, was uneasy around large dogs. Although Misty is better be-
haved than most children, I know a 65-pound German shepherd is
imposing.

On one recent shopping trip, a brave saleswoman finally ap- 6
proached us. "Can I help you?" she said to my husband.

"Yes, I'm looking for a dress," I replied. (After all, I'm the one who 7
will be wearing it.) "Maybe something in red or white."

"RED OR WHITE," she said, speaking very slowly and loudly even 8
though my hearing is fine. I managed not to fall as Misty jumped back
on my feet, frightened by the woman's booming voice.

Don was distracted too. I heard him rustling through hangers on a 9
nearby rack. I called his name softly to get his attention, and another
man answered my call. Bad luck. What were the chances of two Dons
being in earshot?

"This is great!" Don said, holding up a treasure. 10

I swept my hand over the dress to examine it. It had a neckline that 11
plunged to the hemline. "Hmmm," I said. I walk three miles daily with
Misty and stay current with fashion, but I'm positive this costume
would look best on one of the Spice Girls.

Finally, I chose three dresses to try on. 12

Another shopper distracted Misty, even though the harness sign 13
reads: "Please do not pet. I'm working." She said, "Your dog reminds
me of my Max, who I recently put to sleep," so I am sympathetic. We
discussed her loss for 15 minutes. Some therapists don't spend that
much time with grieving clients.

Don was back. He told me the route to travel to the dressing room. 14
I commanded Misty: right, left, right and straight ahead. We wove our
way past several small voices.

"Mom, why is that dog in the store?" 15

"Mom, is that a dog or a wolf?" 16

And my personal favorite: "But that lady's eyes are open." 17

I trust parents to explain: "The lady is giving her guide dog com- 18
mands. Her dog is a helping dog. They're partners." I questioned
whether this positive message had been communicated though, when
I heard an adult say: "Oh, there's one of those blind dogs."

Other people, though well-intentioned, can interfere with my ef- 19
fective use of Misty. Guide dogs are highly trained and very dependable
but occasionally make potentially dangerous mistakes. On my way
through the aisles, Misty bumped me into a pointed rack, requiring my
quick action. I used a firm tone to correct her, and she dived to the
ground like a dying actress. Witnessing this performance, another
shopper chastised me for being cruel.

I was shocked. Misty's pride was hurt, but I needed to point out the error in order to avoid future mistakes. If I did not discipline her, what would prevent Misty from walking me off the curb into traffic? 20

Composing myself, I was delighted by the saleswoman's suggestion: "Can I take you to your dressing room?" I was less delighted when she grabbed me and pushed me ahead while Misty trailed us on a leash. I wriggled out of the woman's hold. Gently pushed her ahead, I lightly held her elbow in sighted-guide technique (called so because the person who sees goes first). 21

"This is better. Please put my hand on the door knob. I'll take it from here," I said. 22

In the room, Misty plopped down and sighed with boredom. I sighed with relief that she was still with me. On one shopping trip, I was so preoccupied with trying on clothes that Misty sneaked out beneath the dressing room's doors. I heard her tags jingling as she left but was half-dressed and couldn't retrieve her. Fortunately, Don was outside the door and snagged her leash. 23

I modeled the dresses for Don and, feeling numb, bought all three. As we left the store, Misty's magnetism, reminiscent of the Pied Piper's, attracted a toddler who draped himself over her. She remained calm, as he tried to ride her. The boy's fun was soon foiled by his frantic mother. 24

When we returned to our car, I gave Misty a treat and lots of praise. A good day's work deserves a good day's pay for both of us. 25

"Shop till you drop" or "retail therapy" could never be my motto. To me, "charge" means going into battle. 26

Examining the Reading

Finding Meaning

1. Summarize Fleischman's attitude toward shopping.
2. Why did the author stop shopping with friends?
3. According to Fleischman, what types of problems do blind people face?
4. What did the author do when Misty bumped her into a pointed display rack? Why?
5. Describe Fleischman's attitude toward those around her. Where in the essay are these attitudes revealed?

Understanding Technique

1. Evaluate the effectiveness of opening this essay by asking and answering a question.
2. Fleischman makes extensive use of dialogue and description to express her ideas. Identify several particularly effective examples of each.
3. How does Fleischman establish a humorous tone?

Thinking Critically

1. Why do you think the saleswoman spoke loudly to the author?
2. Why might some people find the writer's guide dog threatening?
3. According to the article, what can you infer is meant by "sighted-guide technique?"
4. What did the author mean when she said, "To me, 'charge' means going into battle"?
5. From this article, can you conclude that most people understand the partnership between blind people and their dogs? Why?

Writing About the Reading

A Journal Entry

Write a journal entry describing a time in your life when you were unable to carry out everyday activities without help from others. How did you feel about this situation?

A Paragraph

1. Write a paragraph explaining what a parent should teach a child about guide dogs.
2. Write a paragraph describing the disability of a family member, friend, or acquaintance.

An Essay

1. Write an essay explaining a situation in which you felt frustrated by those around you.
2. Write a letter to the salesclerk who assisted Fleischman, informing her about the needs and sensitivities of blind customers and suggesting how she might change her approach.

A Creative Activity

Imagine that Fleischman is deaf rather than blind, and that she has a hearing guide dog. What problems might she experience while shopping or elsewhere?

The Promised Land

▸ Bill Cosby

*In this reading, actor and humorist Bill Cosby tells of the stage of
ultimate marital bliss his parents have reached. This essay is
taken from his book titled* Love and Marriage.

Reading Strategy

This essay is intended to be light and entertaining. As you read
it, highlight or annotate sections that contribute to Cosby's
light, humorous tone.

Vocabulary Preview

residing (1) living
mellowness (1) the state of being toned down (by passage of
 years)
Dalai Lama (1) religious and political Tibetan leader, known
 for being wise and calm
ascended (2) gone up; risen
plane (2) level
rapport (9) relationship marked by harmony
literal (9) actual
planetarium (16) a building for viewing a model of the solar
 system
lotus land (18) a place of extreme contentment
follies (24) silly actions or foolish decisions

> *Grow old along with me!*
> *The best is yet to be.*

When Browning wrote these lines, he wasn't thinking of my mother   1
and father or anyone else in North Philadelphia; but whenever I see my
mother and father together, I know they're residing in a state where I
want to live with Camille, a state of such blessed mellowness that they
make the Dalai Lama seem like a Type A personality.

I will never forget my first awareness that my mother and father   2
had ascended to a matrimonial plane where only God knew what they

were doing—perhaps. We were driving to Philadelphia from Atlantic City, with my father at the wheel, my mother beside him, and me in the back.

"Oh, there's a car from Pittsburgh," said my mother, looking at a license plate in the next lane.   3

"How do you know it's from Pittsburgh?" said my father.   4

"Because I couldn't think of Pennsylvania," she replied.   5

And I waited for my father to respond to this Einsteinian leap into another dimension, but he didn't speak. He simply continued to drive, a supremely contented man.   6

Because he had understood.   7

He had understood that my mother's Pittsburgh was a mythical place, located where the Monongahela entered the twilight zone. My mother also had not been able to think of Afghanistan, but she didn't say that the car was from Kabul. However, *had* she said that the car was from Kabul, my father would have understood it bore Afghans moving to Allentown.   8

For the next twenty minutes, I thought about fifty-three years of marriage and how they had bonded my parents in this remarkable Zen rapport; but then I was suddenly aware that my father had just driven past the exit for Philadelphia. Not the exit for Pennsylvania or for North America, but for Philadelphia, the literal city.   9

"Mom," I said, "didn't Dad just pass the exit we want?"   10

"Yes, he did," she replied.   11

"Well, why don't you *say* something?"   12

"Your father knows what he's doing."   13

Had *I* driven past the proper exit, my wife would have said, *Please pull over and let me out. I'd like to finish this trip by hitching a ride on a chicken truck.*   14

But if Camille and I can just stay together another twenty-five years, then we also will have reached the Twilight Zone, where one of us will do something idiotic and the other one not only will understand it but admire it as well.   15

You turned out the light where I'm reading, I will tell her. *Thank you for the surprise trip to the planetarium.*   16

You left your shoes in the bathtub, she will tell me. *Thank you for giving me two more boats.*   17

One morning a few days after that memorably roundabout trip to Philadelphia, I got another glimpse of the lotus land where my parents dwelled. My father came into the house, took off his hat, put it on a chair, gave some money to my children, and then went back and sat on his hat.   18

"You just sat on your hat," my mother told him.   19

"Of course I did," he replied, and then neither one of them said another word about hat reduction. When the time came to leave, my   20 father picked up the crushed hat and put it on his head, where it sat like a piece of Pop Art. My mother glanced at it, as if to make sure that it would not fall off, and then she took his arm and they walked out the door, ready to be the sweethearts of the Mummers Parade.

However, if *I* ever sat on my hat, Camille would say, *Can't you feel that you're sitting on your hat?*   21

And I would reply, *It's a tradition in my family for a man to sit on his hat. It's one of the little things that my father did for my mother.*   22

Yes, twenty-five years, happy as they have been, are still not enough to have given Camille and me that Ringling Brothers rhythm my mother and father enjoy. But we can hear the circus calling to us.   23

Love, what follies are committed in thy name, said Francis Bacon.   24

So far, most of marriage has been the Ziegfeld Follies for Camille and me. And now we're getting ready to send in the clowns.   25

Examining the Reading

Finding Meaning

1. What is it about his parents' marriage that Cosby finds so endearing?
2. How did Cosby's father respond when his mother said the car was from Pittsburgh?
3. Why didn't Cosby's mother stop his father from driving past the correct exit?
4. How did Cosby's father respond when his mother informed him that he was sitting on his hat?

Understanding Technique

1. Evaluate the effectiveness of opening the essay with a quotation.
2. Describe the essay's organization.

Thinking Critically

1. How has Cosby's parents' marriage shaped the expectations Cosby now has in his own marriage?
2. Explain what Cosby means when he refers to his parents' marriage as having "that Ringling Brothers rhythm."
3. Discuss how Cosby views his own twenty-five years of marriage.
4. Explain Bacon's statement, "Love, what follies are committed in thy name."

Writing About the Reading

A Journal Entry

Write a journal entry about longlasting marriages. Why do some marriages last while others do not?

A Paragraph

1. Our lives are constantly being shaped by others' experiences. Write a paragraph on how a couple you know has influenced a relationship you have had.
2. Every individual has different "requirements" for a spouse. Write a paragraph identifying the requirements you have found essential—or would look for—in a spouse or potential spouse.

An Essay

1. Cosby's parents seemed to have reached a state of complete compatibility and understanding of each other. Have you ever reached that state in a relationship? Write an essay explaining why you have or have not reached it with another person.
2. Write an essay describing a couple you know. Explain the type of relationship they have. Use specific instances, events, or conversations to illustrate your points.
3. Cosby's parents readily accept each other's idiosyncrasies. Think of a person with whom you are close. Write an essay describing how you respond to that person's idiosyncrasies and how he or she reacts to yours.

A Creative Activity

What other crazy, zany, or inconsistent exchanges can you imagine might have occurred between Cosby's parents? Describe several in paragraph form.

Our Wounded Hearts

▶ Allison Bernard

What could you do about a relative whose personal habits are killing him or her? In this reading from Health *magazine, the author relates her experience with an uncle who suffered from heart disease.*

Reading Strategy

As you read, highlight the details that describe the uncle's original condition and those that reveal a change in his lifestyle following his second heart attack.

Vocabulary Preview

malice (3) ill will; evil intent
bypass (4) heart surgery that replaces clogged arteries with
        clear ones
squelched (10) covered up; held back
momentous (11) eventful; important
abundance (12) large amount
bullied (12) forced; pushed
deteriorate (16) worsen; decline

*I*t didn't take a rocket scientist to see the problem. My uncle ate too   1
much, never exercised, threw few but awesome temper tantrums, and
was an on-again, off-again smoker. In fact, more than a decade before,
at the age of 40, he'd had a minor heart attack. After that there was a
lot of talk and activity: This cheese is fat-free, that omelette was made
with egg whites only. Always turkey breast, never lasagna. A new treadmill in front of the television—but little change in his habits.

It drove me nuts. Not necessarily him or his health, but the entire   2
situation. Everyone ate so much at my aunt and uncle's home in Con-
necticut. No one ever left the house, and the television was always on.
When I first came to the East Coast for college, I would visit them on
holidays and realize only on the way home, two or three days later, that
I hadn't gone outdoors the entire time. I found myself suggesting walks
and tentatively volunteering recipes for brown rice. I pointed out articles on nutrition, cooking, starting exercise programs. I wanted to
help; I was aching to help.

"We eat fat-free," my aunt would tell me impatiently. I got the message, though I felt like a bystander watching an accident in slow motion. During these visits my uncle didn't talk much. He watched sports on TV with my male cousins. He was always friendly if distant, not particularly interested in a young woman who didn't understand football. One day when I was visiting him and my aunt at the beach, a friend I'd brought along commented, "Your uncle is a very large person." It was said without malice, and I was about to point out that he was just tall and big-boned when I realized that, yes, he was fat.   3

So it wasn't a major shock when I heard he'd had a second heart attack. Initially everyone was calm. He seemed fine, was in the hospital, resting. Then tests showed that as much as 70 percent of his heart was dead. A bypass would be useless, and the alternatives narrowed to a transplant. Before he could get on the list for a new heart, however, he would have to lose 75 pounds.   4

I was visiting when the doctor gave him the news. My cousin asked about a possible genetic basis for his condition, but the doctor politely dismissed the idea. "Your father is very heavy," he said. "He must eat less and take drugs for his blood pressure." There wasn't much else to do.   5

After the doctor left, my uncle sighed. "I don't want to have to worry about what I eat for the rest of my life," he said.   6

"Tough," I heard my cousin mutter.   7

I followed her out of the hospital room and suggested that maybe he could learn to cook. If he prepared his own food, he would know what he could and couldn't eat. She looked at me as though I were a lunatic. "There is no way my father will ever set foot in the kitchen," she said.   8

I called my aunt a few days later to see how things were going. He was starting his diet, she reported, and she had finally figured out the trick. "Portion size," she said. "We ate fat-free for years when we should have been cutting down on how much we eat."   9

Did I know that? Well, yes, actually, I did. I'd even given her an article I'd written on portion control. I realized my aunt had never read past the first few sentences. I put a smile in my voice, squelched my frustration, and said that I was looking forward to helping at Christmas, only three weeks away.   10

That Christmas was a momentous one. My parents were visiting—having given up hope of my sister and me ever making it out west—and it was the first time the two families were to spend the holidays together. I'd heard my uncle had been losing weight, 15 pounds so far—but he still had 60 to go.   11

When we arrived at the house, my aunt immediately set us to preparing food: my mother to cutting up vegetables, my father to   12 mashing potatoes with whole milk and butter. I wandered in and out of the kitchen, amazed at the abundance of rich, fattening food. I was bullied into sprinkling cups of brown sugar and pouring pints of maple syrup over a small number of yams.

When we sat down to dinner, however, I noticed that my uncle ate   13
well: turkey, a plain potato, steamed green beans. I was impressed, even envious.

Earlier, during the food preparation, we'd had our first real con-   14
versation. He'd talked about his exercising, about the seven-minute stints he did on the treadmill, his determination to lose weight. For once I felt some hope that my prodding was justified, maybe welcome. Then he told me that his father—a sharp quiet man watching TV in the next room—didn't know he was waiting for a heart transplant. "Why worry him?" he said.

Why not: He's his *father,* after all. This sad secrecy, this willingness   15
to keep something as serious as a heart transplant from his own father, stunned me. So did the other things I heard a few weeks later: that my uncle had tried to cut up the Christmas turkey for us to take back to the city and was too weak to do it; that my aunt had thrown a tantrum be-fore we arrived and stalked out of the house; that she was furious with my uncle for letting himself get so sick and with herself for not stop-ping him.

Now we all felt guilty—and angry—at how we'd watched my un-   16
cle's health deteriorate. But was there really anything we could have done?

I called William Castelli, a cardiologist and former director of the   17
legendary Framingham Heart Study, who's responsible for much of what we know about the causes of heart disease, lung cancer, and stroke. Over 30 years he repeatedly interviewed 13,000 participants and gave them advice time and again about eating and smoking—ad-vice that was mostly ignored.

"How did you keep from getting angry?" I asked him.   18

Castelli seemed surprised; anger hadn't occurred to him. "Well, you   19
don't want to be unpleasant. . . . It's a tough problem. You have to create a reality. Most people won't change unless some disaster strikes them.

"But once they see a benefit, even just a slight one, they begin to get   20
a feeling of what they can accomplish," he continued. "Otherwise, all families can do is show love and respect but also remind them what the evidence is, what the route is, and what's at the end of the tunnel."

It hit me just how vain my so-called help had been: Had I really   21
hoped to save my uncle? Had I felt obliged to? Or had I just wanted to be right after seeing my advice ignored for so long? In the thick of it, I couldn't tell. And gradually I pulled back. I'd go on giving feedback, but I stopped expecting it to matter.

Then, to my surprise, my uncle made the transplant list. He danced   22
and glowed at his daughter's wedding and became, for less than a year,
a man full of hope and conversation and life. We talked more during
those few months than we had in previous decades.

But it all came too late. In December he died of a third heart attack   23
while waiting for his transplant. I realized then, perhaps for the first
time, how being right can be a false reward. Being wrong, sometimes,
is so much better.

Examining the Reading

Finding Meaning

1. Describe the lifestyle of Allison Bernard's uncle.
2. Why was Bernard's uncle unable to have bypass surgery?
3. What did the doctor say her uncle should do after he had the second heart attack?
4. How did the author try to help her uncle?
5. According to Dr. Castelli, a cardiologist, what can families do for patients like the author's uncle?

Understanding Technique

1. Describe how this essay is organized.
2. Evaluate Bernard's conclusion. What additional information does it contribute to the essay?

Thinking Critically

1. Why was it so difficult for the author's uncle to change his lifestyle?
2. Why did Bernard say that she "felt like a bystander watching an accident in slow motion" when she visited her uncle?
3. How did the author feel about her uncle keeping his heart transplant a secret from his own father?
4. What did the author mean by "I realized then, perhaps for the first time, how being right can be a false reward"?
5. Is the title "Our Wounded Hearts" appropriate for this essay? Why or why not?

Writing About the Reading

A Journal Entry

Write a journal entry describing your lifestyle. How do you think it affects your health?

A Paragraph

1. Write a paragraph describing the attitudes of Bernard's aunt and cousin toward her uncle. Explain why you think they felt as they did.
2. Choose a friend or relative who is particularly close to you. Write a paragraph explaining why you admire that person.

An Essay

1. Write an essay describing a time you tried to help a friend or family member by offering advice. Did the person follow your advice? If not, explain what you think you should have done differently to help that person.
2. Imagine that you are Allison Bernard. Write a letter she might have written to her uncle after her Thanksgiving visit.

A Creative Activity

Imagine that Bernard's uncle had lived. How do you think he might have felt, thought, and lived his life? Rewrite the ending of this essay as if he had lived.

Poppa and the Spruce Tree

▶ Mario Cuomo

*In this essay Mario Cuomo, former governor of New York, recalls
an experience with his father that serves as an inspiration to
him. It was first published in the* Diaries of Mario M. Cuomo.

Reading Strategy

As you read, underline words, phrases, or statements that reveal Cuomo's attitude toward his father.

Vocabulary Preview

rummaging (2) looking through; searching
accumulate (2) collect; pile up
scale (5) climb
stakes (8) large sticks, usually sharpened, used for support
vengeance (10) great force

*P*oppa taught me a lot about life, especially its hard times. I remem-   1
bered one of his lessons one night when I was ready to quit a political
campaign I was losing, and wrote about it in my diary:

Tired, feeling the many months of struggle, I went up to the den to   2
make some notes. I was looking for a pencil, rummaging through papers in the back of my desk drawer, where things accumulate for years,
when I turned up one of Poppa's old business cards, the ones we made
up for him, that he was so proud of: *Andrea Cuomo, Italian-American
Groceries—Fine Imported Products.* Poppa never had occasion to give
anyone a calling card, but he loved having them.

I couldn't help wondering what Poppa would have said if I told him   3
I was tired or—God forbid—discouraged. Then I thought about how
he dealt with hard circumstances. A thousand pictures flashed through
my mind, but one scene came sharply into view.

We had just moved to Holliswood, New York, from our apartment   4
behind the store. We had our own house for the first time; it had some
land around it, even trees. One, in particular, was a great blue spruce
that must have been 40 feet tall.

Less than a week after we moved in, there was a terrible storm. We ⁵ came home from the store that night to find the spruce pulled almost totally from the ground and flung forward, its mighty nose bent in the asphalt of the street. My brother Frankie and I could climb poles all day; we were great at fire escapes; we could scale fences with barbed wire—but we knew nothing about trees. When we saw our spruce, defeated, its cheek on the canvas, our hearts sank. But not Poppa's.

Maybe he was five feet six if his heels were not worn. Maybe he ⁶ weighed 155 pounds if he had a good meal. Maybe he could see a block away if his glasses were clean. But he was stronger than Frankie and me and Marie and Mamma all together.

We stood in the street looking down at the tree. The rain was ⁷ falling. Then he announced, "O.K., we gonna push 'im up!" "What are you talking about, Poppa? The roots are out of the ground!" "Shut up, we gonna push 'im up, he's gonna grow again." We didn't know what to say to him. You couldn't say no to him. So we followed him into the house and we got what rope there was and we tied the rope around the tip of the tree that lay in the asphalt, and he stood up by the house, with me pulling on the rope and Frankie in the street in the rain, helping to push up the great blue spruce. In no time at all, we had it standing up straight again!

With the rain still falling, Poppa dug away at the place where the ⁸ roots were, making a muddy hole wider and wider as the tree sank lower and lower toward security. Then we shoveled mud over the roots and moved boulders to the base to keep the tree in place. Poppa drove stakes in the ground, tied rope from the trunk to the stakes, and maybe two hours later looked at the spruce, the crippled spruce made straight by ropes, and said, "Don't worry, he's gonna grow again. . . ."

I looked at the card and wanted to cry. If you were to drive past that ⁹ house today, you would see the great, straight blue spruce, maybe 65 feet tall, pointing straight up to the heavens, pretending it never had its nose in the asphalt.

I put Poppa's card back in the drawer, closed it with a vengeance. I ¹⁰ couldn't wait to get back into the campaign.

Examining the Reading

Finding Meaning

1. Describe Cuomo's father's reaction when the forty-foot blue spruce fell during the storm.
2. What actions did Cuomo's family take to get the tree to grow again?
3. What triggered Cuomo's recollection of the spruce tree story?
4. Compare Cuomo's emotional state before and after recalling the story of the spruce tree.

Understanding Technique

1. What is the thesis of the essay? Is it stated or implied (suggested)?
2. Study Cuomo's use of dialogue in paragraph 7. What did it contribute to the essay?

Thinking Critically

1. Why do you think Cuomo's father went to such great lengths to save the tree?
2. Based on the story, what kind of man do you think Cuomo's father was?
3. How did remembering this story about his father and the tree help Cuomo in his campaign?
4. Based on this reading, what do you know about how Cuomo feels about his father?

Writing About the Reading

A Journal Entry

Write an entry describing an event or experience that made you feel terribly discouraged.

A Paragraph

1. Write a paragraph describing a situation in which you felt like giving up. Include the outcome. Did you give up? If so, did you make the right decision? If not, how did you motivate yourself to continue?
2. Cuomo says his father taught him a lot about life, especially its hard times. Write a paragraph describing a hard time you experienced and what you learned from it.

An Essay

1. Write an essay describing something your mother, father, or another important person in your life once did or said that later inspired you.
2. By raising the spruce tree, Cuomo's father accomplished what Cuomo thought to be an impossible task. Write an essay describing an event or situation that you felt was impossible or unlikely but that actually happened. Include why it happened and explain your reaction to it.

A Creative Activity

Suppose Cuomo's father were still alive and Mario called him on the phone to announce that he was quitting his campaign. Write a dialogue re-creating what you think Cuomo's father would have said. Use the following format, if you wish.

Mario: Dad, I've decided to quit the campaign.

Father:

Mario:

Food from the 'Hood

▶ Lester Sloan

This essay describes a student project that eventually became a national enterprise, producing funds for college scholarships. The account originally appeared in Newsweek.

Reading Strategy

As you read, highlight the key details that describe how Food from the 'Hood began and what it has accomplished.

Vocabulary Preview

reclaim (1) take back
mural (1) wall painting
oasis (1) fertile area
buoyed (2) lifted up; inspired
roster (2) list
diversify (2) create more variety; branch out
burgeoning (2) rapidly expanding; blossoming
catapulted (2) hurled; quickly raised up or over
franchise (3) to sell rights to market a product in a different
              area
logo (3) identifying symbol
mentor (3) an experienced person who advises and guides a
              novice
incarcerated (3) imprisoned

*I*t may not be history's biggest victory garden, but don't underesti-   1
mate the size of the victory. Shortly after the Los Angeles riots in 1992,
a group of 40 students at Crenshaw High School and their energetic biology teacher decided to reclaim the weedy quarter-acre plot that had
long been abandoned behind the school's football field. The goal was
simple: to create a community garden that would bring life back to one
of the city's most battered neighborhoods while giving the students
some hands-on science experience. They planted flowers, herbs, lettuce, collard greens, and other vegetables. A colorful mural soon appeared on the back wall, with a brown hand reaching toward a white
one. In the middle of South-Central L.A., an oasis bloomed. The kids

donated some of the produce to needy families in South-Central and sold the rest at local farmers markets. They called their project Food from the 'Hood.

And the ideas kept on sprouting. Buoyed by their success and aided by a growing roster of adult volunteers, the Crenshaw students decided to diversify. They had the herbs, they had the lettuce—what could be a better accompaniment than salad dressing? The Food from the 'Hood members created their own recipe and designed their own label for the brand, called Straight Out 'the Garden. Local business leaders helped with the marketing and manufacturing, and now the dressing is sold, for $2.59 a bottle, in more than 2,000 stores in 23 states. The burgeoning enterprise has catapulted the student farmers into student owners; they expect to earn $50,000 in profits this year, which will go toward funding college scholarships. Ten of the 15 seniors in Food from the 'Hood have been accepted at four-year colleges—a remarkable record for an inner-city public school. "When a kid gets an acceptance letter to college, that's our immediate payoff," says Melinda McMullen, a marketing consultant who worked with teacher Tammy Bird to steer the kids toward produce and profits.

Even more important than the money is the sense of accomplishment that has grown out of Food from the 'Hood. "We showed that a group of inner-city kids can and did make a difference," says freshman Terie Smith, 15. The students run all aspects of the business—from weeding and harvesting to public relations and computer logs. They've received inquiries from across the country about duplicating their business plan, and they may franchise their logo to a group of New

York kids who hope to sell applesauce. Food from the 'Hood members also have set up a mentor system and an SAT preparatory program. "We all try to help each other in everything," says Jaynell Grayson, 17, who will attend Babson College on scholarship next year. Grayson doesn't know who her father is; her mother has been incarcerated most of her life. Food from the 'Hood has been a substitute family for her. "What comes from that garden is inspiration," says McMullen. "From anything—even the riots—amazing things can grow."

Examining the Reading

Finding Meaning

1. What was the goal of the students when they began the gardening project?
2. How did they continue the project after they grew vegetables?
3. How will they spend the $50,000 they expect to earn this year?
4. Explain how the group came to be named "Food from the 'Hood."
5. What activities have the students who began Food from the 'Hood designed to help one other?

Understanding Technique

1. Analyze Sloan's use of topic sentences.
2. What types of details does he use to support his main points?

Thinking Critically

1. Why do you think the biology teacher took a special interest in helping students coordinate Food from the 'Hood?
2. What do you think has been the most important result of Food from the 'Hood?
3. In what sense can the Food from the 'Hood members be considered heroes?
4. What did McMullen mean when she said, "What comes from that garden is inspiration"?

Writing About the Reading

A Journal Entry

Write a journal entry exploring your feelings toward getting involved in community projects. Have you done so? Why or why not?

A Paragraph

1. Both the name of the group and the name of the salad dressing use nonstandard English. Write a paragraph describing situations in which you feel nonstandard English should and should not be used.
2. Write a paragraph explaining what, if anything, you feel the scholarship recipients should give back to the project. (Should they be required to work on the project during the summer, for example?)

An Essay

1. Suppose you were given the opportunity to coordinate a fundraising activity for college scholarships. Write an essay describing what product you would try to sell and how you would market it.
2. Suppose you were required, as part of your graduation requirements, to work in a community or college service program designed to help others. Write an essay describing the kind of project you'd like to get involved with and what you'd hope to accomplish.

A Creative Activity

Suppose Food from the 'Hood continues to expand. What types of foods do you think they might sell next? Write a paragraph describing their expansion. Include the names of the new products, and explain where they will get their ingredients and materials.

Bill Gates:
Computer Wizard

▶ Michael Schaller, Virginia Scharff, and Robert D. Schulzinger
Textbook Excerpt

This reading describes how Bill Gates, the world's richest man, built his Microsoft computer company. Taken from a United States history textbook, Present Tense, *it traces his life from age 12 to 1997. (In the fall of 1997, Microsoft was sued by nineteen states for using illegal means to expand its monopoly on computer-operating systems.)*

Reading Strategy

A time line is a diagram that shows events in the order in which they happened. Draw a time line showing the major events in Gates's life.

Vocabulary Preview

envisioned (1) saw in the mind; imagined
revolutionize (1) change completely
mainstream (1) normal; average
entrepreneurial (1) pertaining to one who turns an idea into a business
insatiable (1) never satisfied; limitless
penchant (2) strong liking; tendency
municipalities (3) governments of cities, towns, or villages
dominated (5) controlled; had taken over
squelch (6) stamp out; do away with
contested (6) called into question; challenged

*I*n the mid-1960s, few Americans envisioned the ways in which computers would later revolutionize American life. Even those who were most familiar with the machines could not foresee the time when millions of American families would assume the necessity of owning, and using daily, a personal computer. Being interested in computers then, recalled William H. Gates III, was "not a mainstream thing. I couldn't imagine spending the rest of my life at it." But by the 1990s, Bill Gates would become America's richest man, an inventor and entrepreneurial genius who built his vast fortune on the world's insatiable appetite for computer technology.

The son of a well-to-do Seattle family, Gates first became fascinated   2
with computers as a child of twelve, in 1967, when he and three friends from the exclusive Lakeside School formed the Lakeside Programming Group. One of his first programs was a class schedule for the school, which he engineered so that he would share classes with all the prettiest girls. The school paid him $4,200 for a summer's work. Soon, the Lakeside students were doing consulting work for the Computer Center Corporation, but Gates's penchant for pulling pranks got him into trouble when he hacked into, and crashed, Control Data Corporation's CYBERNET computer system.

By the time Gates was 14, he was president of his own company,   3
Traf-o-Data. The firm earned $20,000 selling traffic-counting systems to municipalities before its customers even found out that the company was run by high school students. He interrupted a thriving career, however, and enrolled at Harvard University in 1973, planning to become a lawyer.

At Harvard, Gates remained fascinated by the possibilities of com-   4
puter programs, operating systems, and software. In 1975, at the end of his sophomore year, he dropped out, moved to Albuquerque, New Mexico, and with his old Lakeside friend Paul Allen, founded Microsoft. Securing a contract with the Tandy Corporation to develop software for Radio Shack computers, Microsoft grew quickly and moved to Seattle. The company hit the big time when IBM contacted Gates about creating an operating system for a new product, the "personal computer." The result, the MS-DOS operating system, was eventually licensed to more than one hundred companies producing IBM-compatible computers, and by 1981 Microsoft was earning $16 million a year.

Like Thomas Edison, Gates was the rare inventor who mastered   5
the marketplace as well as the laboratory. In the late 1980s, Microsoft introduced its Windows operating system, which allowed users to run IBM-compatible computers with a hand-held "mouse" and on-screen symbols. Windows was as simple to use and "user-friendly" as the operating system pioneered by arch-rival Apple Computer, and IBM "clones" were much less expensive than Apple's famous Macintosh model. Soon Windows dominated the market, and Gates, at the age of 32, became a billionaire.

An intensely competitive man, Gates has often been described as 6 aloof, sarcastic, and abrupt, but also as charming, funny, and able to inspire strong loyalty in his employees. The very model of a nineties corporate executive, he puts in long days and works weekends, and he expects employees who aspire to upward mobility to do the same. Microsoft has also earned a reputation as a cutthroat competitor: the Federal Trade Commission has investigated allegations that the company used its dominant position to squelch competition. But however contested his business practices, Gates undeniably had more to do with bringing the computer revolution into American homes and offices than any other individual.

Examining the Reading

Finding Meaning

1. What was Bill Gates's first professional computer experience?
2. How did Bill Gates get into trouble with a major computer corporation when he was young?
3. When Gates was the president of his first company, what did his company do?
4. Describe the development that made Gates a billionaire.
5. How has Gates influenced his employees?
6. How has Gates been described by others?

Understanding Technique

1. What is the essay's thesis? Which sentence in the conclusion refers to it again?
2. Although the essay is primarily factual, the writer's attitude toward Gates is revealed. Highlight those sections in which the author's attitude is revealed.
3. Highlight the transitions.
4. Evaluate the essay's introduction. How do the writers capture your interest?

Thinking Critically

1. How did Gates's contributions influence the computer world?
2. Why was the development of Windows perceived as a major contribution?
3. In the reading, Bill Gates is compared with Thomas Edison. Do you think this is a fair and reasonable comparison? Why or why not?

4. This reading was taken from a U.S. history textbook. Do you think Bill Gates has already become an important historical figure?
5. From the reading, what can you conclude about Gates's methods of doing business?

Writing About the Reading

A Journal Entry

Bill Gates is first and foremost an inventor. Brainstorm a list of inventions that have influenced your life.

A Paragraph

1. The frequent and extensive use of computers in this country has both a negative and a positive side. Write a paragraph explaining whether you believe the advent of the computer is more positive than negative or the other way around.
2. Since Gates works long days and weekends, he might be described as a workaholic. Are you a workaholic or do you know someone who is? Write a paragraph describing the traits and characteristics of a workaholic.

An Essay

1. Suppose someone was willing to loan you $20,000 to start your own business. Write an essay describing the product, service, or project you would focus on and how you would get started.
2. The introductory paragraph of this article states that computers have revolutionized American life. Write an essay presenting reasons why you think this statement is or is not true.

A Creative Activity

Select a point in this article at which Bill Gates's life could have gone in a different direction if he had made a particular decision differently. Rewrite the remainder of this article as if he had made a different choice at this point.

Do unto Others

▶ **David Polmer**
Student Essay

*In this essay, Polmer explains how his beliefs about sportsman-
ship have changed since childhood. He wrote this while he was a
student at Washington University in St. Louis.*

*R*emember life when you were ten years old? It was simple. Your   1
responsibilities were to obey the rules your mother repeatedly
preached—the foremost being, "Do unto others as you would have others do unto you"—and if you followed these rules, she would declare
you the best child in the world. The rules were basic, and while you
may not have grasped them all as quickly as your mother would have
liked, before too long you had managed to conquer not only the easy
rules, but even some of the tougher ones (including looking both ways
before crossing the street and keeping your elbows off the dinner
table). The one rule that seemed obvious from the second Mom explained it to me was "do unto others." It was catchy, concise and, most
of all, easy to accept. Yet at age ten I learned that not even professional
athletes always adhere to the rule I had considered the easiest of my
mother's to follow.

On one of my first days as a ball boy for the ATP tennis tournament   2
in Washington, D.C., I was assigned to work a doubles match involving
highly ranked Brad Gilbert. What I witnessed that day permanently
changed my perception of Gilbert. After a close line call went against
him, Gilbert turned to the linesman, unleashed a profanity-filled
tirade, then let loose a wad of spit meant only for him. The instant I
witnessed Gilbert's actions, I decided (as only a kid can) that this guy
was not only my least favorite tennis player in the world, but an unde-
sirable person altogether.

Ten years later, a similar incident occurred. It involved the same   3
scenario—an official, umpire John Hirschbeck, making a close call
that does not go in the player's favor. The player, Roberto Alomar of the
Orioles, turns to the umpire and spits in his face. There was, however,
one significant difference for me in the Alomar incident—the athlete
played for a team I have passionately rooted for my entire life, a team
that has not reached postseason play since 1983. Furthermore, I knew

that for the Orioles to have a successful postseason, Alomar would be desperately needed. Because of these factors, I tried to rationalize why Alomar should be exempt from my mother's "do unto others" rule and thereby escape banishment from the play-offs because of his actions.

And I do have my reasons.   4

First, Hirschbeck clearly blew the call at a crucial time during a   5
critical season-ending series. Second, he apparently egged on Alomar after the player had begun to walk back to the dugout. And third, Alomar is a fierce competitor whose job entails competing at the highest level possible every night. (Hirschbeck no doubt approaches his work in the same manner.) Not only did my mother refuse to accept any of my theories, she pointed out that most of them could have held true for Brad Gilbert.

So why was my reaction to the two events so different? Why, after   6
ten years, did I find myself trying to excuse a ballplayer's actions that a decade ago I would have acknowledged instantly as disgraceful for any individual?

Clearly, as long as fans create emotional ties to specific players and   7
teams, there will be some people willing to excuse misconduct involving their favorite players or teams, no matter how offensive their actions may be. When Albert Belle played for the Indians, his insolence usually was tolerated by Cleveland fans; now, it's different. Also, society bombards us with the message that winning must be achieved because the pain of losing is too great to handle. Most ten-year-olds have yet to establish emotional ties to specific players on teams. When a kid sees his team win or lose, he is affected for maybe half an hour.

Yet, as a boy grows up and becomes better acquainted with the ex-   8
pectations of society and the impact of money in pro sports (particularly as it relates to that great end-all, winning), the games he loves lose their purity.

Consider the New York media and Yankees fans who treated   9
twelve-year-old Jeff Maier like a king after his interference altered the outcome of Game 1 of the 1996 AL Championship Series. The next day, Maier was given box seats behind the Yankees' dugout, courtesy of the *New York Post*, and he became the star of every New York early-morning and late-night talk show. All this for a kid who, instead of going to school that day, assisted the Yankees in winning a big game. To every die-hard Yankees fan, Maier's actions were heroic; it was the victory that mattered, not how it was achieved. Thus, the lesson from society is evident. Simply enjoying the game, as you did as a child, isn't enough.

I have become a victim of these twisted rules. As I watch my fa-   10
vorite pro teams, I realize the fun is not in seeing them compete, but in seeing them win. And when I participate in sports, I find little satisfac-

tion in the competition, or the exercise, or the skills I acquire. Winning is the must.

When I reflect on the simple "do unto others" rule my mother in- 11 stilled, I think of how much easier it was to believe in it back then. When you're ten, the rule, like sports itself, is simple. Now that I have grown, society has taught me—for better or worse—that my mother's rule doesn't mix very well with today's sports world.

Unfortunately for Brad Gilbert, I had yet to be brainwashed by 12 society's crazy rules when I was a boy. Now that I am older, and feel somehow trapped into accepting much of society's winning-is-everything mentality, I try as best I can to excuse Roberto Alomar. However, what I have learned most from these two spitting incidents is that regardless of what society plants in my brain, my mother will love me no matter what I choose to believe—although she would surely prefer that her kindness credo be a priority.

Examining the Essay.

1. Identify and evaluate Polmer's thesis.
2. In what ways do Polmer's references to his mother's golden rule strengthen his essay?
3. Evaluate Polmer's introduction and conclusion.
4. Polmer bases his essay on two incidents, that of Brad Gilbert and Roberto Alomar. What other types of evidence would strengthen his thesis?

Writing an Essay

1. Write an essay about a belief or opinion you held as a child and describe how it changed as you grew older. Explain why you think the change occurred.
2. Besides the sports world, can you think of other situations in which winning seems to be the most important thing? Write an essay describing the situation.
3. Write an essay describing what you think are the most important aspects of playing or watching sports.

Making Connections ————————————

1. Compare "Bernard's attitude toward her uncle in "Our Wounded Hearts" with Mario Cuomo's attitude toward his father in "Poppa and the Spruce Tree."

2. Both "The Promised Land" and "Poppa and the Spruce Tree" deal with family members who affect the writers' lives. Write an essay comparing the ways in which the different authors perceive family relationships and how they were affected by them.

3. Both "Bill Gates: Computer Wizard" and "Food from the 'Hood" discuss entrepreneurship. Write an essay comparing the two business ventures.

Chapter 6

Media That Shape
Our Lives

HARDLY A DAY GOES BY when we do not pick up a newspaper, look at a magazine, watch some television, listen to a radio, or spend some time with all four types of media. New forms of media are also developing: laser disks, CD-ROMs, videos, infomercials, closed-circuit and interactive television. Media include all means of communicating information, ideas, or attitudes to an anonymous public audience. And everywhere there are advertisements—on public transportation; in shopping carts, ball parks, hotel rooms, even public rest rooms; on cable shows that air in some high schools; and, increasingly, on nonprofit public broadcasting stations. In fact, we are bombarded by the media, whether we like it or not.

The media have a powerful impact on our beliefs and desires. Through advertising, the media influence what we buy. By choosing to follow certain stories and trends and ignoring others, the media focus our attention on particular topics. Talk shows, television series, and movies affect what we might talk about at the dinner table, dream about, or feel about ourselves and others. For example, the Clinton impeachment trial led to increased public awareness of the private behavior of those holding public office. The readings in this unit explore the impact of the media on the lives of others. Through them you will come to a fuller realization of how the media affect your life.

In this unit you will read about television, including the popularity of Oprah Winfrey and the issues she raises on her talk show ("Oprah Winfrey"). You'll read about the effects of advertising both products and events in "Advertising: Institutionalized Lying" and in "Promoting Lotteries: Is It Right to Encourage Gambling?" You'll also hear from two journalists, one concerned that the media create negative images of black Americans ("A Case of 'Severe Bias'") and another discussing her first professional writing experience ("My First Story"). You will also read about how one form of media, music, affects our lives (Music 'n Moods").

Brainstorming About the Media

Class Activities:

1. Working in pairs, brainstorm a list of all the types of media you have come in contact with in the past twenty-four hours.
2. Brainstorm a list of programs that have influenced or inspired you or led you to a decision or important change.

Oprah Winfrey

▸ Deborah Tannen

In this essay from Time *magazine, Deborah Tannen, a noted authority on human communication, examines Oprah Winfrey's rise to fame and her impact on talk shows and our society.*

Reading Strategy

As you read, highlight factors that account for Winfrey's popularity.

Vocabulary Preview

poised (1) self-confident
insouciant (1) carefree; unconcerned
beacon (2) guiding force
discourse (2) conversation; talk
solace (4) comfort; relief
overt (6) open; obvious
paradox (8) contradiction; puzzle
legacy (8) gift; something left to future generations
permeate (8) spread throughout

*T*he Sudanese-born supermodel Alek Wek stands poised and insouciant as the talk-show host, admiring her classic African features, cradles Wek's cheek and says, "What a difference it would have made to my childhood if I had seen someone who looks like you on television." The host is Oprah Winfrey, and she has been making that difference for millions of viewers, young and old, black and white, for nearly a dozen years. 1

Winfrey stands as a beacon, not only in the worlds of media and entertainment but also in the larger realm of public discourse. At 44, she has a personal fortune estimated at more than half a billion dollars. She owns her own production company, which creates feature films, prime-time TV specials and home videos. An accomplished actress, she won an Academy Award nomination for her role in *The Color Purple,* and this fall with star in her own film production of Toni Morrison's *Beloved.* 2

But it is through her talk show that her influence has been greatest. When Winfrey talks, her viewers—an estimated 14 million daily in the 3

U.S. and millions more in 132 other countries—listen. Any book she chooses for her on-air book club becomes an instant best seller. When she established the "world's largest piggy bank," people all over the country contributed spare change to raise more than $1 million (matched by Oprah) to send disadvantaged kids to college. When she blurted that hearing about the threat of mad-cow disease "just stopped me cold from eating another burger," the perceived threat to the beef industry was enough to trigger a multimillion-dollar lawsuit (which she won).

Born in 1954 to unmarried parents, Winfrey was raised by her grandmother on a farm with no indoor plumbing in Kosciusko, Miss. By age 3 she was reading the Bible and reciting in church. At 6 she moved to her mother's home in Milwaukee, Wis.; later, to her father's in Nashville, Tenn. A lonely child, she found solace in books. When a seventh-grade teacher noticed the young girl reading during lunch, he got her a scholarship to a better school. Winfrey's talent for public performance and spontaneity in answering questions helped her win beauty contests—and get her first taste of public attention.

Crowned Miss Fire Prevention in Nashville at 17, Winfrey visited a local radio station, where she was invited to read copy for a lark—and was hired to read news on the air. Two years later, while a sophomore at Tennessee State University, she was hired as Nashville's first female and first black TV-news anchor. After graduation, she took an anchor position in Baltimore, Md., but lacked the detachment to be a reporter. She cried when a story was sad, laughed when she misread a word. Instead, she was given an early-morning talk show. She had found her medium. In 1984 she moved on to be the host of *A.M. Chicago*, which became *The Oprah Winfrey Show*. It was syndicated in 1986—when Winfrey was 32—and soon overtook *Donahue* as the nation's top-rated talk show.

Women, especially, listen to Winfrey because they feel as if she's a friend. Although Phil Donahue pioneered the format she uses (mike-holding host moves among an audience whose members question guests), his show was mostly what I call "report-talk," which often typifies men's conversation. The overt focus is on information. Winfrey transformed the format into what I call "rapport-talk," the back-and-forth conversation that is the basis of female friendship, with its emphasis on self-revealing intimacies. She turned the focus from experts to ordinary people talking about personal issues. Girls' and women's friendships are often built on trading secrets. Winfrey's power is that she tells her own, divulging that she once ate a package of hot-dog buns drenched in maple syrup, that she had smoked cocaine, even that she had been raped as a child. With Winfrey, the talk show became more immediate, more confessional, more personal. When a guest's story moves her, she cries and spreads her arms for a hug.

When my book *You Just Don't Understand: Women and Men in*   7
Conversation was published, I was lucky enough to appear on both
Donahue and *Oprah*—and to glimpse the difference between them.
Winfrey related my book to her own life: she began by saying that she
had read the book and "saw myself over and over" in it. She then told
one of my examples, adding, "I've done that a thousand times"—and il-
lustrated it by describing herself and Stedman. (Like close friends,
viewers know her "steady beau" by first name.)

Winfrey saw television's power to blend public and private; while it   8
links strangers and conveys information over public airwaves, TV is
most often viewed in the privacy of our homes. Like a family member,
it sits down to meals with us and talks to us in the lonely afternoons.
Grasping this paradox, Oprah exhorts viewers to improve their lives
and the world. She makes people care because she cares. That is Winfrey's genius, and will be her legacy, as the changes she has wrought in
the talk show continue to permeate our culture and shape our lives.

Examining the Reading

Finding Meaning

1. What was Winfrey's childhood like?
2. How did Winfrey first become a public figure?
3. What was the purpose of the "world's largest piggy bank"?
4. According to Tannen, what is the difference between the interview styles of Winfrey and Phil Donahue?
5. What did Winfrey do when she interviewed the author on her television show?

Understanding Technique

1. Identify Tannen's thesis statement.
2. Describe the organization of the essay.
3. The title of the essay identifies its subject, but it does little to capture the readers' interest or suggest its thesis. Suggest several possible alternative titles that might be more effective.

Thinking Critically

1. What did Winfrey mean when she told model Alek Wek, "What a difference it would have made to my childhood if I had seen someone who looks like you on television"?
2. Why was Winfrey sued by the beef industry? Why do you think the author included this incident in the article?
3. Why does the author describe television as a "paradox"?
4. What do you think makes Winfrey so different from others in her business?
5. The author believes that talk shows "shape our lives." Do you agree or disagree with her? Why?

Writing About the Reading

A Journal Entry

Write a journal entry about a book or article you have read or a movie you have seen that was so much like your own life that you saw yourself over and over in it.

A Paragraph

1. Write a paragraph explaining why you think Winfrey has become so influential.

2. Talk shows deal with various issues. Write a paragraph describing an issue that is of major importance to you.

An Essay

1. Write an essay about a public figure (a television personality, musician, politician, author, etc.) who has made a difference in your life. Describe how this person has influenced you and why.
2. Do you agree with Tannen that men and women speak to each other differently? Explain why you agree or disagree and give some examples to back your opinion.

A Creative Activity

Imagine you have been chosen to be interviewed on Winfrey's show. What would you like to discuss with Winfrey?

My First Story

> **Patrice Gaines**

Patrice Gaines, a successful journalist and writer, describes how her career began with a page filled with corrections and criticisms. This essay is taken from Gaines's autobiography, Laughing in the Dark.

Reading Strategy

As you read, highlight words, phrases, and sentences that reveal Gaines's attitude toward her job and toward writing. Write annotations of any personal experiences about jobs or writing that the essays brings to mind.

Vocabulary Preview

muster (2) call forth; gather
fate (2) a force beyond one's control that directs events
excel (2) be better than others
confidant (3) one with whom secrets are shared
fretting (5) worrying

*D*iscovering I was the only black secretary at the paper didn't make   1
me angry, as it would today; it boosted my self-esteem—at least as much as I would allow. Even though I loved to write, I wasn't excited about working for a newspaper; I didn't have any desire to become a newspaper reporter. I wrote short stories and poetry, not journalism. I had written enough poems now to fill a book, which I kept tucked in my underwear drawer. I wrote short stories with a heavy moral message. One story was about three soldiers killed in Vietnam, their bodies destroyed beyond recognition by a grenade. Their remains were shipped in one casket, and the families—Jewish, Baptist, and atheist— had to hold one funeral. One soldier was black. I wrote a poem about the attention paid to pregnant women and the lack of care given the environment. It ended: "Would things have been different if the fathers of this country had been mothers instead?"

I wrote about matters of the heart and I couldn't see yet that journalists did this, too, with more skill and sense of communication than I could yet muster. Still, if there is such a thing as fate, it had acted on my behalf, to put me in a place where when I woke up I would have before me what I had wanted all the time, where, even though I hadn't been in the upper half of my graduating class, I could still learn to be a writer and, perhaps, have a chance to excel.

My new boss, Peter, was a white guy barely a year older than I was. We immediately struck up a comfortable friendship. He was a member of the new, young, white South, those who tried to build the bridge between the Confederate tradition of Jim Crow and the more integrated future of Martin Luther King, Jr. I became Peter's close confidant and assistant, in many ways no different from the scores of secretaries who in the course of their office duties compose personal as well as business letters, serving as human calendars, remembering flights and meetings, birthdays and anniversaries, covering for bosses who sneak off to play golf. Secretaries can be like members of the family, and with most of them being female, they often become the nurturing mother-wife and sister-friend. It was a position that suited me well for many years, and Peter was as near-perfect a boss-mate as possible.

He arranged for me to have my first chance to write for others, a position on the monthly employee newsletter, which I helped write during my extra time. This was a big deal to me. It was as close as I could get to imagining myself as a writer. Becoming a reporter was too big a dream; just writing for the employee newsletter frightened me to near paralysis.

My first story was about pets—talking birds, big snakes, and show dogs. The editor returned my draft covered with red marks, noting misspelled words, slang, wordiness, and whole paragraphs that needed to be rearranged or dropped. Accompanying his critique was a note: "An ego is too big to fit into a typewriter." I understood immediately what he was saying and dropped my initial feelings of embarrassment and disappointment. I stayed awake that night fretting, but by day my normally oversensitive self, who hurt at any hint of not being accepted, wrote with the attitude that every red mark was an opportunity to learn.

I discovered I thought differently when I wrote; I was smarter on paper. I saw where the mistakes were made and I corrected them. It took a while—maybe six months—but eventually there were fewer red ink marks and among the lines of criticism were a few compliments. For me, it was nothing short of magic to string together words in a way that made people notice and care. This was the answer to my prayers, to be able to touch people in a way that I had not been able to with my actions or the words from my mouth.

Examining the Reading

Finding Meaning

1. Given that the author wanted to be a writer, why was she not excited about working on a newspaper?
2. How did Gaines's boss help launch her career as a writer?
3. Describe Gaines's relationship with her boss.
4. Describe the types of stories Gaines enjoyed writing for herself.
5. Describe how Gaines improved her writing skills.

Understanding Technique

1. Describe this essay's organization.
2. Evaluate Gaines's sentence structure. How does she make sentences lively and interesting?

Thinking Critically

1. How did Gaines use the criticisms of her first story as a positive experience?
2. In what sense is journalism about "matters of the heart"?
3. Explain the meaning of the editor's note: "An ego is too big to fit into a typewriter."
4. Why did Gaines keep her book of short stories and poems in her underwear drawer?

Writing About the Reading

A Journal Entry

Write a journal entry describing your attitude toward your writing. Include likes, dislikes, rewards, problems, and so forth.

A Paragraph

1. Did you ever write something that was seriously criticized? Write a paragraph describing whether this was helpful or harmful to you.
2. Gaines enjoyed writing stories with moral messages. She wrote about "matters of the heart." Write a paragraph describing the kinds of writing or topics that are easy for you or that you enjoy.

An Essay

1. Write an essay describing someone's criticism of something other than your writing and explaining whether it was justified and why or why not.
2. Gaines feels that fate acted on her behalf. Has fate ever worked on your behalf or against you? Write an essay describing a situation in which luck or fate seemed to be involved.

A Creative Activity

Write a paragraph describing what you think happened in Gaines's story about the funeral of the three soldiers.

Music 'n Moods

▸ **Carolyn Gard**

Music not only stirs up your emotions, it also can be beneficial. This article from Current Health, *examines the wide-ranging effects of music.*

Reading Strategy

As you read, make a list of the beneficial effects of music and the evidence Gard offers to substantiate each effect.

Vocabulary Preview

evokes (5) brings out; stirs up
instills (6) builds up; leads to
discordant (6) harsh; unpleasant
cardiovascular (9) of the heart and blood vessels
neurological (10) pertaining to the nervous system
cadence (10) beat; rhythm
synchronized (10) timed; joined
verbalize (13) express in words
autistic children (14) mentally disturbed children who have extreme difficulty learning language, playing normally, and interacting with others
Alzheimer's disease (14) a brain disorder that causes memory loss, confusion, and disturbance of speech and movements.
baroque music (15) a form of classical music created in seventeenth- and eighteenth-century Western Europe; composers include Bach, Handel, and Vivaldi
conducive (16) helpful

You've seen *Psycho* many times. You know exactly what's going to happen in the shower scene—but you're still on the edge of your seat. 1

You're watching *Jaws* again. You know exactly when the shark is going to appear—and you're still anxious. 2

Now rewind the movies and turn off the sound. Janet Leigh steps   3
into the shower, but this time she's just another tired tourist getting
ready for bed. Now do the same when watching *Jaws,* and the people
on the boat are simply sightseers out for an afternoon sail.

It's hard to imagine any movies without music, but originally Al-   4
fred Hitchcock didn't want any music in the shower scene in *Psycho*.
After he saw what screeching violins could do, he raised the composer's salary.

Movie music always evokes strong emotions in the audience—   5
from fear and panic to tenderness and love.

The power of music to set the mood in a movie depends on the fact   6
that most people react in the same way to the same music. Low-
pitched, repetitive sounds suggest fear. A single tone that gets louder
and louder instills anxiety. Kettle drums provoke anger, and a shrill
blast of high notes with a discordant blare of bass notes will drive you
to panic.

Why Does Music Affect Our Emotions?

Although researchers know that music can comfort, delight, convince,   7
frighten, or move us, they don't know how it does this.

One theory is that a fetus responds to sounds. Because of this early   8
association, hearing may evoke a more emotional response than
sight. Music also triggers memory, allowing you to remember a past
experience.

According to Don Campbell, the found of the Institute for Music,   9
Health, and Education, music is linked to many measurable changes
in body function. Music can relax and energize, release anger and
mask pain, cause muscles to tense, change skin temperature, and improve circulation and cardiovascular function. Every thought, feeling,
and movement has its own musical qualities. Your pulse and heartbeat
have a rhythm and tempo, your breath has pattern and flow.

Moving to Music

Music may produce a neurological effect that improves motor control.   10
The brain is organized in a complete pattern—your stride length, step
cadence, and posture are all centrally located. When muscle activity is
synchronized to rhythm, it becomes more regular and efficient. When
one part improves, everything improves.

Music can help you get more out of exercise. If you do jumping   11
jacks you may get tired after 100. With music in the background, you
may do 200 jumps before you get tired. The continuous rhythmic patterns in music increase the body's endurance and strength.

Music chosen specifically for exercising uses the natural rhythms   12
of the body. One company offers tapes of computer-generated music

that encourage you to regulate your walking from a 30-minute walk at 110 steps per minute to a race walk of a 10-minute mile at a rate of 170 steps per minute.

Music Communicates

Music lets you express emotions that are difficult to verbalize. Think 13 about the difference between saying the pledge of allegiance and singing the national anthem. Which one is more likely to give you a thrill? For the same reason, high schools and colleges have fight songs to excite the fans at sports events.

The idea of using music to heal goes back to the ideas of Aristotle 14 and Plato. In music therapy, music is the instrument of communication between the therapist and the patient; the patient doesn't need any particular musical skills to benefit. Music helps people come to an understanding of the inner self. Music therapy is extremely valuable in helping disturbed and autistic children, as well as people with Alzheimer's disease.

Making Music Work for You

You've got a final tomorrow—how can music help you study? Don 15 Campbell suggests that you start with 10 minutes of good, energetic dancing to pop music to get your body oxygenized. When you sit down to study, listen to slow baroque music, such as Bach, that has fewer than 60 beats per minute. This speed allows you to focus and concentrate. The best music for study has no words; words distract you by encouraging your brain to sort them out and make sense of them.

New Age music with a slow pulse is conducive to sleep. And music 16 with a fast beat, above 90 beats per minute, will give you energy for getting things done.

A recent study conducted at the University of California at Irvine 17 indicates that listening to the music of Mozart can raise a person's IQ. It seems that Mozart's music speaks directly to the parts of the brain that enhance learning.

On an even more personal level, music can help you become more 18 aware of your inner self and your feelings.

Suppose you're in a major slump—you flunked a test or you ended 19 a relationship. Campbell finds that there is a therapeutic strain in certain music that helps you get in touch with your emotions. He suggests you find five tapes or CDs that make you feel "safe" and calm so you can feel your own emotions. Play the soundtrack from *Out of Africa* or a symphonic piece such as "A Little Night Music" by Mozart, and write or draw how you're feeling. The music helps you relax, allowing the emotion to come out. When you've worked through your sadness, you'll be ready to face the world again.

Examining the Reading

Finding Meaning

1. How do soundtracks affect audience reaction to films?
2. What kind of music evokes each of the following emotions: fear, anxiety, anger, and panic?
3. How can music help people exercise better?
4. What is music therapy?
5. According to this article, what type of music is best to listen to while you study? To help you fall asleep? To raise your IQ?

Understanding Technique

1. The thesis of this essay is suggested in the title, but it is not directly stated anywhere in the essay itself. Discuss whether you feel a thesis statement is needed. If so, write a possible thesis statement for this essay.
2. What types of evidence does Gard offer to support her claim that music affects us?

Thinking Critically

1. Why do you think Alfred Hitchcock gave the soundtrack composer of the movie *Psycho* a raise?
2. Why do you think music therapy might be helpful for autistic children or for Alzheimer's patients?
3. What did the author mean by "music can help you become more aware of your inner self and your feelings"?
4. Do you agree that classical music is the best music to listen to while studying? Why or why not?

Writing About the Reading

A Journal Entry

Write a journal entry about a favorite song or musical piece. Explain why you like it and how it makes you feel.

A Paragraph

1. Choose an activity you like to do while listening to music. Write a paragraph describing the type of music you prefer while doing this activity and how you think the music affects your performance.

2. You probably react differently when you hear a poem read and when you listen to a song. Write a paragraph explaining the difference.

An Essay

1. Write an essay about a movie you saw recently. Describe the soundtrack and explain how the music added to, or detracted from, your enjoyment of the movie. Be sure to use specific examples.
2. Write a letter to your college president, proposing that students should be allowed to listen to music while taking exams. Use the information presented in this article to back your argument.

A Creative Activity

Imagine that you just had a fight with your best friend and you are very upset about it. Name five CDs or individual pieces of music you think would be helpful to listen to at this time. Explain why you chose this music.

Advertising: Institutionalized Lying

▸ Donna Woolfolk Cross

Are advertisements true? Can you believe their claims? This essay explores the issue of false and misleading advertising. It is an excerpt from a book titled Mediaspeak.

Reading Strategy

This reading contains several examples of misleading advertising. Highlight or annotate why each is misleading. Also, highlight or annotate what the mouthwash story is intended to demonstrate.

Vocabulary Preview

inferential (1) implied; arrived at by drawing your own conclusion
rebuked (2) reprimanded
undaunted (2) not discouraged
purport (2) to claim, often falsely
deterred (5) discouraged from acting
eliciting (6) bringing forth
halitosis (6) bad breath
smiting (7) afflicting
ensued (7) resulted
discourse (7) discuss in detail

*T*he fact is that advertising is institutionalized lying. The lies are tolerated—even encouraged—because they serve the needs of the corporate establishment. . . . By now the falsity—either direct or inferential—of most television commercials is a matter of well-documented fact. Most people accept that ads are not true and yet, 1 because they do not understand the methods by which they are influenced, are still taken in. Can *you* detect the deception behind the following statements?

- *"All aspirin is not alike. In tests for quality, Bayer proved superior."*

Most people assume this means that Bayer aspirin has been shown to relieve pain better than other aspirin. In fact the "tests for quality," which were conducted by Bayer and not an independent testing agency, showed that Bayer was superior, in its own manufacturer's opinion, because the tablets were whiter and less breakable than the other aspirins tested. Nevertheless, this claim is so effective that a recent FTC [Federal Trade Commission] survey revealed that forty percent of consumers believe Bayer is the most effective aspirin.

- *"Sominex makes you drowsy so you can sleep."*

Time and again the advertising agencies peddling over-the-counter   2
remedies for insomnia have been rebuked for stating or implying that these products insure a good night's sleep. Undaunted, the nimble admen simply found a new way of making the same claim: The remedies still do not insure a good night's sleep, but they purport to make us drowsy so we *can* sleep. Reading a dull book or watching an uninteresting TV show would probably have the same effect. It is even possible that ads for insomnia cures can put you to sleep sooner than their product will.

- *"Gallo: because the wine remembers."*

If true, this should put a crimp in dinnertime conversations: "Hush dear, not in front of the Hearty Burgundy."

The late August Sebastiani, who scorned selling techniques such as   3
this, would not allow his wines to be advertised on TV, saying, "If you spend enough on advertising, you can get people to drink sauerkraut juice, juice you couldn't get a thirsty hog to drink."

If there is absolutely no need for a particular product, the adman   4
must invent one. He must convince you that your health and happiness will be in jeopardy if you don't buy his product.

Believe it or not, In the Beginning there was no mouthwash.   5
Proper oral hygiene consisted of a thorough brushing with a good toothpaste. Then one day an enterprising stranger rode into town peddling a new product, a liquid made of water, alcohol, and assorted additives that would "freshen your breath." People weren't interested. "What can this stuff do for me that toothpaste can't?" they asked. Not to be deterred, the stranger hired himself an advertising agency.

Soon the television disease-control center was informing people   6
about a new and terrible disease. No one was immune from it: House-

wives and clerics, teenagers, cab drivers, lawyers, new mothers, were being struck down with a devastating malady. Far from eliciting sympathy, a person who contracted this disease was sure to lose his promotion, friends, loved ones, and paper boy. The sufferer himself was always the last to learn, usually from a hastily departing relative, that his affliction was . . . *halitosis.*

Bad breath was smiting the land, the righteous along with the sinners. A great panic might have ensued but for the miraculously timed appearance, at that very moment, of a cure: *mouthwash.* Soon Americans were buying bottles of it by the millions, and many could discourse knowledgeably about the virtues of various brands: "mediciney" versus "sweet," etc. Skeptical about claims for the product, the American Dental Association and the National Academy of Sciences, after several intensive studies, issued a report stating that mouthwash has no lasting effect on bad breath, and that rinsing one's mouth with salt water is just as beneficial as using mouthwash. But medical science delivered its verdict too late. People had been taught to *believe* in mouthwash. The stranger rode out of town a very rich man.

Examining the Reading

Finding Meaning

1. How does Cross define advertising?
2. According to this reading, do most people believe ads are true or false?
3. In the "tests for quality," give one reason why Bayer was considered superior to other aspirin.
4. If the public has no need for a specific product, how do the advertisers "sell" the product?
5. After many studies on mouthwash, what did the medical organizations conclude about it?

Understanding Technique

1. How does Cross make the transition from examples of misleading advertising to a discussion of how advertisers create a so-called need for a product?
2. Evaluate the essay's final paragraph. How does it summarize the essay?

Thinking Critically

1. If the public recognizes that television ads are false, why do they continue to buy the products advertised?

2. Is there such a thing as advertising that is true but misleading? Explain.
3. Discuss how ads for Sominex and other anti-insomnia products may affect our thinking.
4. How does false advertising shape our lives?
5. Identify an example of false advertising not given in the selection and explain why it is false or deceptive.

Writing About the Reading

A Journal Entry

Explore your reaction to advertising by freewriting or brainstorming about ads and whether they can or should be believed, disbelieved, or ignored.

A Paragraph

1. Mouthwash is an example of a product that was sold to the public by advertising agencies. What other products do you think are popular because of the advertising attention they receive? Write a paragraph identifying these products and explaining how advertising makes them popular.
2. Write a paragraph describing the worst commercial you have ever seen. Explain why it was the worst.

An Essay

1. If advertising is false and/or misleading, should our legal system allow it to appear? Write an essay answering this question. Justify your position.
2. Do you ever buy a certain product simply because you liked the commercial? Write an essay on whether commercials influence what you buy. Include examples in your essay.

A Creative Activity

Find an ad that you think is false or misleading and add it to the essay. Write a paragraph explaining what is wrong with the advertisement.

A Case of "Severe Bias"

▶ Patricia Raybon

Patricia Raybon, a journalist and college professor, argues that the media have created a false image of African Americans. This reading first appeared in Newsweek.

Reading Strategy

As you read, list the negative stereotypes of Black Americans that Raybon identifies.

Vocabulary Preview

dysfunctional (3) unable to operate normally
insidious (3) harmful in a sneaky way
blatancy (3) obviousness
deduce (6) logically conclude
myopic (7) short-sighted
disproportionately (8) at a higher rate than among the
                                            general population
besetting (8) constantly afflicting
relegated (9) assigned to; limited to
aberrant (9) deviant; antisocial
pervasive (10) widespread
subtleness (16) lack of obviousness
enterprise (16) willingness to undertake new projects

*T*his is who I am not. I am not a crack addict. I am not a welfare   1
mother. I am not illiterate. I am not a prostitute. I have never been in
jail. My children are not in gangs. My husband doesn't beat me. My
home is not a tenement. None of these things defines who I am, nor do
they describe the other black people I've known and worked with and
loved and befriended over these forty years of my life.

Nor does it describe most of black America, period.   2

Yet in the eyes of the American news media, this is what black   3
America is: poor, criminal, addicted, and dysfunctional. Indeed, media
coverage of black America is so one-sided, so imbalanced that the most
victimized and hurting segment of the black community—a small segment, at best—is presented not as the exception but as the norm. It is
an insidious practice, all the uglier for its blatancy.

In recent months, I have observed a steady offering of media reports on crack babies, gang warfare, violent youth, poverty, and homelessness—and in most cases, the people featured in the photos and stories were black. At the same time, articles that discuss other aspects of American life—from home buying to medicine to technology to nutrition—rarely, if ever, show blacks playing a positive role, or for that matter, any role at all.

Day after day, week after week, this message—that black America is dysfunctional and unwhole—gets transmitted across the American landscape. Sadly, as a result, America never learns the truth about what is actually a wonderful, vibrant, creative community of people.

Most black Americans are *not* poor. Most black teenagers are *not* crack addicts. Most black mothers are *not* on welfare. Indeed, in sheer numbers, more *white* Americans are poor and on welfare than are black. Yet one never would deduce that by watching television or reading American newspapers and magazines.

Why do the American media insist on playing this myopic, inaccurate picture game? In this game, white America is always whole and lovely and healthy while black America is usually sick and pathetic and deficient. Rarely, indeed, is black America ever depicted in the media as functional and self-sufficient. The free press, indeed, as the main interpreter of American culture and American experience, holds the mirror on American reality—so much so that what the media say is *is*, even if it's not that way at all. The media are guilty of a severe bias and the problem screams out for correction. It is worse than simply lazy journalism, which is bad enough; it is inaccurate journalism.

For black Americans like myself, this isn't just an issue of vanity—of wanting to be seen in a good light. Nor is it a matter of closing one's eyes to the very real problems of the urban underclass—which undeniably is disproportionately black. To be sure, problems besetting the black underclass deserve the utmost attention of the media, as well as the understanding and concern of the rest of American society.

But if their problems consistently are presented as the *only* reality for blacks, any other experience known in the black community ceases to have validity, or to be real. In this scenario, millions of blacks are relegated to a sort of twilight zone, where who we are and what we are isn't based on fact but on image and perception. That's what it feels like to be a black American whose lifestyle is outside of the aberrant behavior that the media present as the norm.

For many of us, life is a curious series of encounters with white people who want to know why we are "different" from other blacks—when, in fact, most of us are only "different" from the now common negative images of black life. So pervasive are these images that they aren't just perceived as the norm, they're *accepted* as the norm.

I am reminded, for example, of the controversial Spike Lee film *Do*   11
the Right Thing and the criticism by some movie reviewers that the
film's ghetto neighborhood isn't populated by addicts and drug push-
ers—and thus is not a true depiction.

In fact, millions of black Americans live in neighborhoods where   12
the most common sights are children playing and couples walking
their dogs. In my own inner-city neighborhood in Denver—an area
that the local press consistently describes as "gang territory"—I have
yet to see a recognizable "gang" member or any "gang" activity (drug
dealing or drive-by shootings), nor have I been the victim of "gang
violence."

Yet to students of American culture—in the case of Spike Lee's   13
film, the movie reviewers—a black, inner-city neighborhood can only
be one thing to be real: drug-infested and dysfunctioning. Is this my
ego talking? In part, yes. For the millions of black people like myself—
ordinary, hard-working, law-abiding, tax-paying Americans—the
media's blindness to the fact that we even exist, let alone to our contributions to American society, is a bitter cup to drink. And as self-reliant
as most black Americans are—because we've had to be self-reliant—
even the strongest among us still crave affirmation.

I want that. I want it for my children. I want it for all the beautiful,   14
healthy, funny, smart black Americans I have known and loved over the
years.

And I want it for the rest of America, too.   15

I want America to know us—all of us—for who we really are. To see   16
us in all of our complexity, our subtleness, our artfulness, our enterprise, our specialness, our loveliness, our American-ness. That is the
real portrait of black America—that we're strong people, surviving
people, capable people. That may be the best-kept secret in America. If
so, it's time to let the truth be known.

Examining the Reading

Finding Meaning

1. According to the author, how do the media portray black Americans?
2. Explain how and why the author believes that the media are biased
   when it comes to portraying black Americans.
3. What kind of journalism does the author believe is being practiced
   today?
4. How does the way the media depict black America shape our per-
   ceptions of black Americans?
5. What types of evidence does Raybon offer to indicate that the media are presenting a distorted viewpoint?

Understanding Technique

1. Identify and evaluate Raybon's thesis statement.
2. Raybon begins the essay by explaining who she is not. Evaluate the effectiveness of this opening.

Thinking Critically

1. Do you agree with the author that the negative images of black Americans presented by the media are "accepted as the norm"?
2. Are other ethnic groups misrepresented by the media? If so, which ones?
3. Why might the media choose to misrepresent black Americans?

Writing About the Reading

A Journal Entry

Brainstorm a list of people or groups who are often depicted negatively by the media.

A Paragraph

1. Write a paragraph describing a situation in which someone mistook you or someone you know for someone or something you are not.
2. Select a specific television program and write a paragraph explaining whether or not you think it presents a biased view of any particular group of people.

An Essay

1. Write an essay describing an advertisement that could lead its readers to make unfair assumptions about a particular group of people. Explain the ad and describe the assumptions that might be made.
2. Do you agree with the author that black America is misrepresented by the media? Write an essay defending your viewpoint.

A Creative Activity

Suppose a national commission were formed to recommend actions that would present an accurate portrait of black Americans and that Raybon was appointed to the commission. Write a paragraph describing the recommendations you think Raybon would offer.

Promoting Lotteries: Is It Right to Encourage Gambling?

▶ **William M. Pride and O. C. Ferrell**
Textbook Excerpt

This selection explores the issue of whether states should encourage gambling by operating and promoting lotteries. It is taken from a business textbook, Marketing.

Reading Strategy

Highlight the topic sentence and key supporting details in each paragraph. Pay particular attention to sections that answer the question posed by the title.

Vocabulary Preview

phenomenon (1) occurrence; development
ban (2) prohibit
private sector (3) business entities, as distinct from government
assert (3) state; say definitely
generate (3) create; make
revenues (3) income, source of money
contend (4) insist; argue
adversely (5) negatively
fundamental (5) basic; most important

*L*otteries are not a recent phenomenon in the United States. Holding a lottery financed the settlement of Jamestown, Virginia, in 1612. By the mid-1800s, however, they fell out of favor. In 1894, the last lottery shut down, and lotteries remained illegal until 1964. As states began exploring ways of raising money without raising taxes, lotteries recaptured their appeal and their legal status. Experts predict that by the turn of the century every state but Utah and Nevada will have one.

The odds of being struck by lightning, 1 in 1.9 million, are small, but the odds of winning the top prize in a state lottery, 1 in 12 million, are even smaller. Why then do millions of people line up to spend a hard-earned $22 billion a year on lottery tickets? They take a chance because the fantasy of getting rich quick is so appealing. To make that fantasy seem like reality, state governments spend almost $300 million a year on entertaining and imaginative lottery advertising. Outspending Colgate-Palmolive, Nike, Nissan, and American Express, lotteries rank among the top fifty advertisers in the United States. As lottery advertising becomes big business, however, efforts are mounting to limit or ban it altogether.

Critics complain that most lottery advertising fails to meet the same accuracy and fairness standards required of private sector advertising. They believe it is wrong for states to encourage gambling, not only because it advances a something-for-nothing mentality, but because it is addictive. Although supporters maintain that lottery participation is voluntary, experts insist lotteries are the most habit-forming type of gambling. Pointing to statistics that low-income families spend a larger proportion of their income on tickets than other groups, opponents assert that lotteries burden the poor rather than generate revenues to help them. With billboards such as those in depressed Chicago neighborhoods proclaiming lotteries as "Your Way Out," it is not surprising that many inner-city residents sell their food stamps to buy lottery tickets.

The Kansas lottery's slogan is, "Somebody's always winning," and New Yorkers are told, "All you need is a dollar and a dream." These kinds of promises, contend those against lottery advertising, mislead consumers about their chances of winning. Duke University economists determined that only 12 percent of TV and radio spots for state lotteries accurately report the odds. Finally, ad opponents believe that it is wrong to encourage gambling as a real alternative to saving, education, and hard work. For example, they point to a New York ad in which a mother tells her daughter that she no longer needs to study to get a college scholarship because they are playing the lottery.

At one time, cigarette and alcohol advertisers faced the question, Should advertisers protect people from themselves? Courts eventually answered yes by placing restrictions on advertising of those products. Lottery advertisers now face similar questions. Should governments promote a game in which the vast majority of players lose? Should states sponsor activities that adversely affect lower income people? Some see the Supreme Court's recent ruling preventing a radio station in North Carolina, which has no lottery, from broadcasting ads for the Virginia lottery as a forecast of similar restrictions on lottery advertising. For now, marketers continue to insist that they advertise a legal product in a truthful way and continue to bank on advertising as the fundamental ingredient in lottery promotion.

Examining the Reading

Finding Meaning

1. Why have states instituted lotteries?
2. According to the article, why do people spend money on lotteries?
3. Why do critics of lotteries believe it is wrong for states to encourage gambling?
4. What do the authors mean by this statement: "Critics complain that most lottery advertising fails to meet the same accuracy and fairness standards required of private sector advertising"?
5. How do the odds of winning the lottery compare to the odds of being struck by lightning?

Understanding Technique

1. Does the first paragraph open the essay effectively? Why or why not?
2. In the title and in several places throughout the essay, the authors ask and answer a question. Is this an effective writing strategy? Why or why not?

Thinking Critically

1. Do you believe it is wrong to advertise gambling? Why or why not?
2. Do you believe that gambling itself is right or wrong? Justify your answer.
3. Given the First Amendment right of free speech, do you believe that the lottery commission has the right to run any advertisement that it wants? Why?
4. Do you think the way the lottery commission chooses to advertise the lottery has a negative effect on people?
5. Do the authors believe lotteries should be promoted? How can you tell?

Writing About the Reading

A Journal Entry

Brainstorm about lotteries and their positive or negative impact on the public. Write about who plays them and why these people play them.

A Paragraph

1. The authors pose an interesting question regarding gambling: "Should governments promote a game in which the vast majority of players

lose?" Write a paragraph describing how much control you think the government should have over whether or not people gamble.

2. Imagine you work for an advertising company and your job is to promote lotteries. Write a paragraph explaining how you could accomplish this without encouraging poor people to spend a disproportionate amount of their income on the lottery.

An Essay

1. Write an essay on how winning the lottery might shape your life. Choose a hypothetical amount of money and explain the circumstances of winning. Be sure to include any changes you would make in your life and what they would be—especially whether you would continue your education.

2. Some people believe gambling is evil and should be outlawed completely. Others believe it's a constitutional right. Write an essay explaining which you believe. Be sure to support your point of view.

A Creative Activity

Suppose you are the author of this article and you feel you need to add some examples of how real people can be hurt by lotteries. You decide to do this by describing the experience of one person or a family with one or more of the "evils" mentioned in paragraph 3. Write a paragraph that could be added to the reading.

Reporting the Facts

▶ **Marissol Rodriguez**
Student Essay

In this essay, Rodriguez, who is a college student, explains her change of heart about becoming a television news reporter.

I used to think I wanted to be a reporter on the evening news. I   1
would look at each reporter with such admiration. They got to go out
and interview interesting people all day and they got paid for it. They
are the people who always get to go to the fun community events for
free—like the County Fair—and eat cotton candy all day long. They get
to go tobogganing in the park during winter and swimming at the local beach in the summer because they have to be where the action is so
they can interview people. Recently, however, I have learned that a reporter's life is not all fun activities; in fact, it involves some fairly unpleasant tasks.

One of the most awful things television news reporters have to do   2
is interview people at the worst times in their lives, like when there's a
natural disaster. For example, if there's a hurricane, the first people out
there to talk to the victims are not the ones who can help them, but the
media. They do this because they have to report the news. But how
many times can you interview someone who's just lost his or her home
because of a flood or tornado or a fire without letting it upset you?

I never thought about this until my best friend's father was brutally   3
murdered. I went over to see if there was anything I could do to help
and as I was walking up the driveway, a reporter from a local TV station was there sticking a microphone in my face and asking me a lot of
questions. Not only that, but he actually asked me to bring out my
friend so he could ask HER questions about her father and the murder.
I asked him to leave.

Later, I realized he hadn't meant to be nasty or anything. He was   4
just doing his job, trying to "report the facts." Unfortunately, reporting
the facts in that case meant causing unnecessary emotional pain to my
friend and her family. Who wants to talk to a stranger about something
as horrible as her father being murdered? This didn't seem to bother

the reporter, but I know it would bother me to have to interview people in these situations.

This raises the question of just how far should the media be allowed to go before they are invading other people's privacy. I'm not sure I know the answer to that. But I don't think reporters should be sticking cameras in the faces of grieving victims. There must be some other way to "report the facts" without causing people harm, especially when these people are in such a vulnerable state. I don't know what that way is, but I know that reporters' jobs are harder than I once thought they were. I finally realized that I really don't want to be a television news reporter anymore.

Examining the Essay

1. Identify Rodriguez's thesis statement.
2. Evaluate the essay's title. Suggest several alternatives.
3. What other types of information or evidence would strengthen the essay?
4. Evaluate Rodriguez's sentence structure. Are her sentences varied and interesting? Give several examples to support your answer.

Writing an Essay

1. Write an essay describing a particular news reporter you watch on a television news program. What traits or characteristics of that person do you admire? Which do you find annoying or offensive?
2. Write a letter to the president of a local television station suggesting that the station be more sensitive toward crime victims and their families. Cite examples from recent news reports to make your case.
3. Write an essay suggesting guidelines that should be used by reporters at accident and crime scenes. Among your guidelines you should include what film footage should and should not be shot, who should be interviewed, and whether the consent of victims and their families should be required.

Making Connections ————————————

1. Drawing upon the information presented in the readings by Tannen, "Oprah Winfrey," and Cross, "Advertising: Institutionalized Lying," as well as your own knowledge about talk shows and advertising, answer the following question: In what sense do both television talk shows and advertising influence the public?

2. "Advertising: Institutionalized Lying," and "Oprah Winfrey" discuss aspects of television viewing. Write an essay describing what attitudes or viewpoints the authors (Cross and Tannen) hold in common.

3. Raybon ("A Case of 'Severe Bias'") and Gaines ("My First Story") are both black female journalists. In what ways are their viewpoints the same, and in what ways are they different? Write an essay comparing the perspectives of the two women.

Chapter 7

Technology That Shapes Our Lives

HOW MANY TOOLS, MACHINES, OR APPLIANCES have you used already today? Your list might include a clock radio, Walkman, coffeemaker, hair dryer, toaster, lock and key, computer, and car or bus. Most of us are so used to these inventions that we don't give them a second thought, but in fact all of these items are the result of study and research. Research has also produced such daily conveniences as no-iron clothing, Post-it notes, and orange juice from concentrate. The use of scientific research to create products or services is called *technology*.

In many cases, technology directly controls our lives. For instance, if your car does not start or the bus breaks down, you may miss classes. If your brakes malfunction, your life could be in danger. If a storm causes an electrical failure, your home may be without heat, light, or cooking facilities. People's lives may have been saved by medical technology, their hearts having stopped but been restarted by a machine.

In other situations, technology influences or shapes the quality of our lives. Without technology, we would not have many conveniences we take for granted: elevators, automatic teller machines, microwave ovens, and so forth. Technology affects our communication through radio and telephones; our diet with convenience and low-fat foods; our comfort with furnaces, air conditioners, and plumbing systems; our health with vaccines, genetic engineering, and drugs; and our jobs with computers, copiers, and fax machines. In fact, it is difficult to think of any aspect of daily life that remains untouched by technology.

In this chapter, the reading selections explore the effects of technology and examine specific instances in which technology has made an impact. The first reading presents one author's listing of the seven most valuable inventions ("The Seven Sustainable Wonders of the World"). Other readings discuss the contributions that computer technology has made or will make to science, such as the issues surrounding artificial insemination, surrogate motherhood, and in vitro fertilization ("When Is a Parent a Parent?"); research that suggests swimming with dolphins may improve human health ("Dr. Dolphin"). Another reading discusses the way people respond to technology without being aware of it ("Virtual Love"). And yet another reading discusses the variety of inventions possible in the future ("Inventing the Future"). You'll read further about the influence of computer technology, both positive, such as computers that can simulate reality for disabled persons ("Stepping Through a Computer Screen, Disabled Veterans Savor Freedom"), and negative, as reflected in "Technology Is a Racket."

Brainstorming About Technology

Class Activities:

1. Working in groups, brainstorm a list of inventions that were developed or that came into widespread use during your lifetime.
2. Working in groups, make a list of inventions that you would eliminate to improve the quality of life.

The Seven Sustainable Wonders of the World

▸ Alan Thein Durning

Simple little things can make a big difference in one's life. In this reading, the writer casts his vote for the seven key inventions—most of them quite simple—that make the biggest difference in our lives. This reading first appeared in the Utne Reader *in 1994.*

Reading Strategy

Read the heading that introduces each invention. Before you read the section that follows it, predict why the writer feels the invention is important.

Vocabulary Preview

sustainable (title) capable of being used continually
thermodynamically (2) having to do with use of heat energy
climes (4) climates
flotsam and jetsam (8) debris or wreckage and discards
scourge (12) affliction

I've never seen any of the Seven Wonders of the World, and to tell you the truth I wouldn't really want to. To me, the real wonders are all the little things—little things that work, especially when they do it without hurting the earth. Here's my list of simple things that, though we take them for granted, are absolute wonders. These implements solve every-day problems so elegantly that everyone in the world to-day—and everyone who is likely to live in it in the next century—could make use of them without Mother Nature's being any the worse for wear.

1. The Bicycle

The most thermodynamically efficient transportation device ever created and the most widely used private vehicle in the world, the bicycle lets you travel three times as far on a plateful of calories as you could walking. And they're 53 times more energy efficient—comparing food calories with gasoline calories—than the typical car. Not to mention the fact that they don't pollute the air, lead to oil spills (and oil wars), change the climate, send cities sprawling over the countryside, lock up half of urban space in roads and parking lots, or kill a quarter million people in traffic accidents each year.

The world doesn't yet have enough bikes for everybody to ride, but it's getting there quickly: Best estimates put the world's expanding fleet of two-wheelers at 850 million—double the number of autos. We Americans have no excuses on this count: We have more bikes per person than China, where they are the principal vehicle. We just don't ride them much.

2. The Ceiling Fan
Appropriate technology's answer to air conditioning, ceiling fans cool tens of millions of people in Asia and Africa. A fan over your bed brings relief in sweltering climes, as I've had plenty of time to reflect on during episodes of digestive turmoil in cheap tropical hotels.

Air conditioning, found in two-thirds of U.S. homes, is a juice hog and the bane of the stratospheric ozone layer because of its CFC coolants. Ceiling fans, on the other hand, are simple, durable, and repairable and take little energy to run.

3. The Clothesline
A few years ago, I read about an engineering laboratory that claimed it had all but perfected a microwave clothes dryer. The dryer, the story went, would get the moisture out of the wash with one-third the energy of a conventional unit and cause less wear and tear on the fabric.

I don't know if they ever got it on the market, but it struck me at the time that if simple wonders had a PR agent, there might have been a news story instead about the perfection of a solar clothes dryer. It takes few materials to manufacture, is safe for kids, requires absolutely no electricity or fuel, and even gets people outdoors where they can talk to their neighbors.

4. The Telephone
The greatest innovation in human communications since Gutenberg's printing press, telephone systems are the only entry on my wonders list invented in this century, and—hype of the information age notwithstanding—I'll wager that they never lose ground to other communications technologies. Unlike fax machines, personal computers and computer networks, televisions, VCRs and camcorders, CD-ROMs, and all the other flotsam and jetsam of the information age, telephones are a simple extension of the most time-tested means of human communication: speech.

5. The Public Library
Public libraries are the most democratic institutions yet invented. Think of it! Equal access to information for any citizen who comes inside. A lifetime of learning, all free. Libraries foster community, too, by

bringing people of different classes, races, and ages together in that endangered form of human habitat: noncommercial public space.

Although conceived without any ecological intention whatsoever,   10
libraries are waste reduction at its best. Each library saves a forestful of trees by making thousands of personal copies of books and periodicals unnecessary. All that paper savings means huge reductions in energy use and water and air pollution, too. In principle, the library concept could be applied to other things—cameras and camcorders, tapes and CDs, cleaning equipment and extra dining chairs—further reducing the number of things our society needs without reducing people's access to them. The town of Takoma Park, Maryland, for example, has a tool library where people can check out a lawn mower, a ratchet set, or a sledgehammer.

6. The Interdepartmental Envelope

I don't know what they're really called: those old-fashioned slotted   11
manila envelopes bound with a string and covered with lines for routing papers to one person after another. Whatever they're called, they put modern recycling to shame.

7. The Condom

It's a remarkable little device: highly effective, inexpensive, and   12
portable. A few purist Greens might complain about disposability and excess packaging, but these objections are trivial considering the work the condom has to do—battling the scourge of AIDS and stabilizing the human population at a level the earth can comfortably support.

Examining the Reading

Finding Meaning

1. Why is the bicycle more efficient than the automobile?
2. In what ways are ceiling fans better than air conditioners?
3. Explain the statement, "Public libraries are the most democratic institutions yet invented."
4. In what ways do libraries "foster community"?

Understanding Technique

1. Evaluate the effectiveness of using a numbered list to organize the essay. Consider both the advantages and the disadvantages
2. This essay lacks a conclusion. Suggest possible ways the writer could have concluded this essay.

Thinking Critically

1. Do you agree with the author that each library "saves a forestful of trees"?
2. What other kinds of libraries can you think of that the author didn't mention?
3. Do you agree with the author that the telephone is a better invention than, for example, a computer or a fax machine? Why or why not?

Writing About the Reading

A Journal Entry

Brainstorm about the author's choice of "wonders." Which ones do you agree with? Which do you disagree with? What others would you include?

A Paragraph

1. Write a paragraph explaining which of the wonders identified by the author you would rank as most important. Justify your choice.
2. Write a paragraph identifying what you believe is the best invention, old or new, other than those listed by the author. Justify your choice.

An Essay

1. Write an essay titled "Three *More* Sustainable Wonders of the World." Use Durning's organization as a model for your own essay.
2. Write an essay comparing your choices for the above assignment with Durning's choices. How did your choices differ? Would you substitute any of Durning's "wonders" for your own? Would you replace any of his with yours? Which ones, and why?

A Creative Activity

This reading identifies the most important inventions of the world. Suppose it had been titled "The Seven *Least* Sustainable Wonders of the World" and had discussed the most useless, silliest, or most wasteful inventions or gadgets ever invented. What do you think it might have included? Write an essay explaining your choices.

Stepping Through a Computer Screen, Disabled Veterans Savor Freedom

▶ **N. R. Kleinfield**

Virtual reality, a new computer technology, will probably affect all of our lives in the future. Journalist N. R. Kleinfield wrote this New York Times *article about what virtual reality is and how it is being used to help disabled veterans.*

Reading Strategy

As you read, highlight or annotate specific uses of virtual reality for those with physical disabilities.

Vocabulary Preview

savor (title) taste; enjoy
paraplegic (1) one who is paralyzed from the waist down
quadriplegic (2) one who is paralyzed from the neck down
full-fledged (5) fully developed; complete
provocative (6) exciting; stimulating
tantalizing (9) arousing desire; tempting
muscular dystrophy (11) a disease in which some muscles
                              lose the ability to function
troves (13) hoards
buoyant (17) cheerful
mobility (18) ability to move

*T*he other day, Angelo Degree single-handedly lifted a couch and ef-   1
fortlessly hauled it into another room. He moved around a lamp, a
crate. He snatched hold of a man and ran outside with him. Ever since
he was shot in the head and spine while being robbed in 1981, Mr. Degree has been a paraplegic. His legs are a wheelchair. One day he is
hoping to play football. Tackle.

The man who plans to suit him up is William Meredith, who is not   2
a doctor with a miracle cure but a recording engineer with a black bag
flush with interactive computer technology. His subjects are the para-

plegics and quadriplegics in the spinal cord injury ward at the Bronx Veterans Affairs Medical Center.

For some 10 years Mr. Meredith has done volunteer work for the Veterans Bedside Network, a 46-year-old organization made up largely of show-business people who try to rally the spirits of sick veterans, engaging them in plays and song-and-dance routines.

"But I always felt there was one group who we weren't able to reach that well, and those were the quadriplegics and paraplegics," Mr. Meredith explained. "And so I thought about virtual reality."

Virtual reality, for those unfamiliar with the outer envelope of technology, enables people to feel, through interactive computers, as though they are inside a three-dimensional electronic image. In full-fledged systems, they can actually sense that they are moving and feel virtual reality objects. To participate, all that is required is a working mind.

The more Mr. Meredith, 52, chewed over the notion, the more provocative it became. "These visions ran through my mind," he said. "These people could fly, which they can't. They could walk, which they can't. They could play sports, which they can't."

After winning over officials at the Bronx Veterans Medical Center and getting a $5,000 equipment budget from the Veterans Bedside Network, Mr. Meredith was in business. In mid-October he got his idea off the ground.

Every Tuesday and Thursday afternoon, he lugs three laptop computers to the Bronx hospital. He is an Air Force man himself, and teaches virtual reality at various schools as well as uses it in his recording work for films. He usually travels to the hospital with Michael Storch, who recently joined Veterans Bedside Network and is studying to enter the virtual reality field. They report to the first-floor spinal cord injury unit, where there are about 50 patients, and set up their equipment in the physical rehabilitation room.

From 2 P.M. to 4:30 P.M., wheelchairs roll up to their corner and patients enter the tantalizing world of virtual reality.

The patients use goggles in which they see a three-dimensional image and a glove that is wired to the computer in a way that, when they move their hand, they seem to grasp and move things on the computer screen. Mr. Meredith has yet to incorporate equipment that enables patients to feel and smell the virtual world they enter, though he hopes to do so soon.

It seemed only a matter of time for this to happen. Virtual reality is being used by therapists to help treat children who have suffered child abuse. It is being used to teach sufferers of muscular dystrophy how to operate a wheelchair. It is being used to help people overcome a fear of heights. They are ushered onto a virtual reality ledge, many stories in the sky. Go on, they are told. Look down.

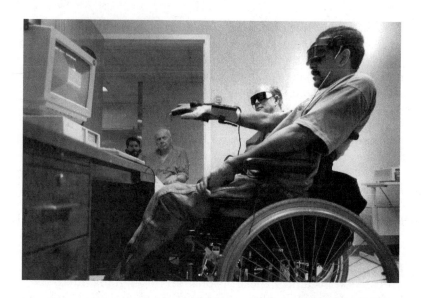

At this early stage in the program, Mr. Meredith is able to offer only   12
limited options to the patients. There are several virtual reality games,
including Heretic, which involves wandering through creepy dungeons
and staving off demons and menacing creatures. There is a program
that allows patients to redecorate a house by moving furniture around
through the use of a Power Glove. There is a chess game, which has
proved especially popular. And Mr. Meredith has designed his own virtual reality baseball game, where patients see the field from whichever
position they assume.

In addition, Mr. Meredith brings along various computer programs   13
that are not virtual reality but enable patients to look up vast troves of
information on the computers. One man has been researching the
places where he made bomber runs during World War II.

The other day, Mr. Degree, 39, finished rearranging the virtual re-   14
ality house and moved on to Heretic. He was reasonably accomplished. He destroyed quite a few knights and flying beasts before
mistakenly grabbing a gas bomb.

"You better work on your recognition," Mr. Meredith chided him.   15

"Next time, I'll give it to them real good," he promised.   16

Mr. Degree was buoyant about the program. "You know why a lot   17
of veterans are in and out of hospitals?" he asked. "Stress. If they want
to have any dreams, they have to get them from a bottle. Here, you can
have dreams without the bottle. All I can do is look here and see a lot
of potential. An angel with a lot of wings."

Mike Abelson, the chief of recreation services for the hospital, is   18
equally enthusiastic. "For these guys, it opens up a whole new world,"
he said. "Physical barriers don't matter. Mobility barriers don't exist."

Mr. Meredith has elaborate ambitions. Many veterans relish their trips to the Intrepid Sea-Air-Space Museum aboard the aircraft carrier permanently moored on West 46th Street. Spinal cord patients usually don't go. Mr. Meredith is having a virtual reality tour of the Intrepid designed so patients can experience it from their beds. He hopes it will be ready by July.

"Ultimately, I want to have interactive sports," Mr. Meredith said. "I'd like to link up several hospitals and have leagues and everything. They'll play baseball, football, whatever they want. They'll be able to feel every hit."

Some patients have employed the computers to assist them in prosaic concerns. "One guy was having problems with the grass on his lawn on Staten Island," Mr. Meredith said, "and so he looked up in one of the data bases in the computer ways of dealing with Bluegrass diseases. I believe he found his answer."

Whatever use they make of the technology, the patients find their bedimmed lives galvanized.

Wilfred Garcia, 55, was keen to gain knowledge. "I've been looking up where I was stationed in Berlin in 1958," he said. "Brings back the memories. I'm into biography. I looked up Christopher Columbus. I looked up Marco Polo. He was born in the same city as Columbus. I looked up Clark Gable. Man, what an actor."

In 1986, Mr. Garcia had an allergic reaction to a tuna sandwich while he was driving on the New York Thruway. He blacked out and his car crashed down an embankment. He was left an "incomplete paraplegic," meaning he can stand up and walk short distances on crutches, but has no balance.

Now he immersed himself in chess. He was a novice. The computer demolished him. "I might look into boxing on this," he said. "I used to box. At the age of 16, I was going to join the Golden Gloves but my mother wouldn't let me."

With limited resources and equipment, Mr. Meredith has been confined to offering his program to those able to come to the rehabilitation room. His goal is to take systems to patient bedsides, which, after all, is what Veterans Bedside Network is supposed to be about.

There are patients itchy to see that happen. Osvaldo Arias, 35, paralyzed from the neck down since being shot in the back by unseen assailants in the Bronx in 1978, was lying in his room at the Veterans hospital. Recovering from surgery, he could not get to the rehabilitation room.

"When you spend a lot of time in bed, you can go crazy," he said. "Right now, I can't get out of bed. I'm bored. You watch TV for a while, then you get tired of it. I try to write letters. An idle mind is the devil's workshop. I want to see that system in here. It's meant for those who can't get out of bed to keep them from going stir crazy."

Examining the Reading

Finding Meaning

1. What is the specific purpose of the Veterans Bedside Network?
2. Describe the equipment used with virtual reality.
3. Name two activities in the world of virtual reality that Meredith has not yet incorporated.
4. Identify two ways in which therapists have used virtual reality.
5. How and why is virtual reality especially useful to patients with spinal cord injuries?

Understanding Technique

1. How does Kleinfield make the essay lively and interesting?
2. Evaluate the introduction and conclusion. Why are they effective?

Thinking Critically

1. Other than the examples cited in the article, name one way in which virtual reality can help people.
2. If you had a complete virtual reality system, how would you use it?
3. What did Degree mean when he said, "Here, you can have dreams without the bottle"?
4. What do you think the single most important use of virtual reality will be in the future?

Writing About the Reading

A Journal Entry

Make a list of virtual reality events—real or imagined—that you would like to participate in.

A Paragraph

1. Suppose you became a paraplegic. Write a paragraph describing in detail three virtual reality activities you would enjoy.
2. Write a paragraph defining virtual reality for someone who has never heard of it.

An Essay

1. Write an essay explaining the process by which a virtual reality system could be used to lessen or eliminate a particular fear.

2. Many tasks are difficult to learn without hands-on experience (driving a car, using a computer, and so forth). In the future, virtual reality may take the place of hands-on training in many fields. Assume it is the year 2025. Write an essay predicting how training for a particular job, occupation, or profession might be different than it is now.

A Creative Activity

Assume that interactive sports using virtual reality became possible. Add a paragraph to the reading explaining the benefits and describing the veterans' reactions to playing interactive sports.

Virtual Love

‣ Susan Lee

Could you love a virtual pet as much as a real one? This selection, taken from Forbes *magazine, considers the way people respond to technology without being aware of it.*

Reading Strategy

As you read, highlight phrases and sentences that reveal Lee's attitude toward virtual pets, computers, and technology.

Vocabulary Preview

virtual (1) nearly real
bereavement (2) sorrow or grief over the loss of a loved one
empowerment (2) being in charge
incessant (5) constant; never ending
suppress (8) hold back
ascribe (9) attach; apply
stereotyping (9) oversimplifying; labeling
obtains (10) applies; is usual
confront (11) face, often in a demanding or hostile way

*T*amagotchi—in case you've just returned from Planet Debbie—is   1
the ultrahot toy, a quite fetching virtual pet that lives on a liquid-crystal
display screen in a plastic egg. And I do mean pet—Tamagotchi requires close attention. Owners have to feed and play with it, adminis-
ter medicine when it gets sick, clean up after it, and turn off the screen
when it sleeps. And, just like a hamster or goldfish, Tamagotchi dies.
Nobody knows for sure its natural life span (maybe 30 days), but if neglected or mistreated, Tamagotchi dies within hours.

Virtual pets. Virtual love. About a month after Tamagotchi hit the   2
U.S. market, there were reports of stricken owners mourning the
deaths of their pets. Tamagotchi bereavement counselors appeared on

---

the Internet. Psychologists debated whether the "feeling of empower-ment" given by caring for Tamagotchi outweighed the "sense of loss" when it died.

Good grief! I thought. It's just a toy.   3

Well, I bought one. I watched it hatch into a dear little face and   4
named it Claudia. The first day was tons of fun. Claudia beeped when she was hungry, played a little tune when I spent quality time with her, smiled when I cleaned up her cyberpoop, and went to sleep quietly at night.

Days two to four were an increasing challenge, however. By day   5
five her (incessant) beeping was making me nuts. I gave her to my hus-band, who, as expected, played baseball games with her for several hours but forgot to feed her. She died on day six. I was devastated. I shook her little egg, calling her name. I blamed her for being too de-manding. I blamed myself for being lazy. I felt bad and sad.

Am I warped?   6

Not according to Stanford professors Byron Reeves and Clifford   7
Nass, whose book, *The Media Equation,* describes how people respond to technology. "Since technical media display enough characteristics that are identical to humans, people treat them like humans," says Reeves. "We just follow the rules of social interaction—like recogniz-ing someone's face. It's difficult to suppress these responses."

Come to think of it, computers do have human characteristics. You   8
ask them to delete something and they do. Even programs with text-only displays use words that suggest a human response—like that an-noying pop-up box: "Do you really want to delete?"

Indeed, people assume their computers have genders. Worse, they   9
ascribe stupid biases, like gender stereotyping, to their computers. Reeves and Nass discovered that if people were given a computer tuto-rial in technical matters that used a woman's voice, they were less likely to be impressed with its teaching than if the same material were presented in a man's voice. Switch the topic to love and relationships, however, and people thought the girl computer did a better job than the boy computer. (Yikes! What kind of dunderheads were these people? "You'd be surprised," says Reeves. "They were exactly the sort who deny they engage in gender stereotyping.")

People even treat computers with the tact that obtains in human-   10
to-human contact. If a computer asks you how it's doing during a tu-torial, you will most likely respond favorably. But when a second computer asks you, Hey! How did the first computer do?—you will be more critical and honest.

Why? According to Reeves, we don't want to confront computers—   11
or hurt their feelings. (I began to feel less warped. Which is more

ridiculous: Mourning the loss of sweet little Claudia or trying to spare the feelings of that dumb girl computer who couldn't teach her way out of a paper bag?)

I recently had a conversation with Chung-Jen Tan, the senior manager of IBM's Deep Blue team. He chuckled at the idea that the chess-playing machine had a gender, saying that the team refers to it by its number—RS/6000 SP—not Deep Blue. "Computers are just machines," he said. "They don't get headaches and don't suffer when they lose—as their human programmers do. Computers are objects or tools. They aren't humans."

"Well, Dr. Tan—meet Tamagotchi.

Examining the Reading

Finding Meaning

1. What is a Tamagotchi?
2. What happens if a Tamagotchi is neglected or mistreated?
3. How did the author feel when her Tamagotchi died?
4. Why do professors Reeves and Nass say that it isn't odd for people to grieve over the death of a Tamagotchi?
5. According to this selection, in what ways do people treat computers as if they were human beings?

Understanding Technique

1. What evidence does Lee include to explore the topic of virtual love?
2. How would you describe the writer's tone? Do you feel it is appropriate for her subject and for a general audience?

Thinking Critically

1. The author uses the term "virtual love." Do you think there can be such a thing as virtual love? Why or why not?
2. What does the author mean when she states that people "ascribe stupid biases, like gender stereotyping, to their computers"?
3. Reeves and Nass discovered that people respond more positively to a male computer voice presenting a technical topic, but they are more impressed with a female voice when the topic is love and relationships. Do you agree with this finding? Explain why.
4. In the article, the author states, "According to Reeves, we don't want to confront computers—or hurt their feelings." Do you agree or disagree? What is the basis for your judgment?
5. Based on the article, do you think the author believes computers have feelings? What indicates that she does or doesn't believe this?

Writing About the Reading

A Journal Entry

Write a journal entry about an attachment you had to a pet or a toy. How did you feel about it? Why do you think you felt that way?

A Paragraph

1. Write a paragraph describing a situation in which you have observed a person treating a computer like a human being.
2. Write a paragraph describing your experience with gender stereotyping of *humans*.

An Essay

1. Write an essay explaining whether you think it is a good or bad idea for young children to have virtual pets. Include the reasons why you believe the way you do.
2. A popular theme in science fiction stories and movies involves the idea of androids, or humanlike robots, being mistaken for humans. This raises the question of whether there is a difference between highly evolved robots and human beings. Write an essay defending or rejecting the idea that it might be possible to create robots that are human.

A Creative Activity

Several unusual toys, such as pet rocks, dolls that came with adoption papers, and more recently furbies, became "crazes" and made their inventors millionaires. Imagine a toy you might invent. What would it be and why do you think children would like it?

Inventing the Future

▸ Thomas J. Frey and Darby L. Frey

In this essay from The Futurist, *the authors discuss several technological advances that are expected to become realities in the future.*

Reading Strategy

After you finish reading this essay, prepare a vertical, two-column list. In the first column, list the future inventions that were discussed. In the second column, list the primary use for each invention.

Vocabulary Preview

profound (1) deep; intense
emerge (1) come out; happen
interjecting (5) including; adding
pundit (5) critic; commentator
leverage (6) advance; take advantage of
dormant (7) inactive; closed down
algorithms (9) step-by-step procedures
formulations (11) ideas; plans
mammalian (11) like warm-blooded animals
spherical (14) having the shape of a globe
itineraries (14) travel plans; routes

At the DaVinci Institute, our goal is to forecast future inventions, many of which will have a profound effect on our lives. We do not make value judgments as to whether or not these technologies should be pursued. Our belief is that these unborn technologies will emerge someday with or without our blessing. We believe it is in society's best interest to thoroughly understand the concepts and be forewarned of the changes that lie ahead. 1

High-Impact Inventions

Here are snapshots of a few highly probable inventions that our research tells us are likely to have a profound effect on the future: 2

Personality services for computers. The day is coming when we will be able to hold an intelligent conversation with our computer. But 3 the novelty of a talking computer will quickly give way to the need for a more complicated humanlike interaction. This need will give birth to a new industry: computers equipped with personality services.

Most people will subscribe to more than one online personality service, adding a new dimension to the human–computer interface. If, for example, you were to subscribe to a David Letterman personality service, suddenly your computer voice would start sounding like David Letterman, interjecting jokes and wild comments. If your choice was a political pundit personality such as Rush Limbaugh or Geraldine Ferraro, you would be able to hold a stimulating conversation about current political topics. If you wanted to ask your computer about the news of the day, you could subscribe to a Tom Brokaw or Peter Jennings personality.

Personality services will be an interesting market to watch as celebrities leverage their name recognition even further and relative newcomers offer unique personality services at bargain prices.

Controlling the brain.   When a person's liver stops working, does it stop because the liver gives out or because the person's brain tells it to stop? This question is currently being debated by theorists in the medical community. We suspect that the answer lies somewhere in the feedback loop of impulses between the brain and the liver.

Many medical researchers believe that the brain has an override capability that can keep an organ functioning in spite of a "shut-down" order. Possibly this brain function could become subject to conscious human control. One can speculate about possible ways to upload the brain's version of a batch file or lines of code to force the brain to override a shut-down signal and restart a dormant body function.

In the past, controlling the brain has always been accomplished through the use of drugs. Chemicals introduced into the body produced a chemical reaction to create the desired effect. In the future, this could be accomplished with medical algorithms, which means sending direct impulses to the brain to trigger the necessary override changes to a given body function. The advantage of algorithms over drugs is that there are no chemical side effects.

Uses for medical algorithms could include curing physical maladies such as color blindness or hearing loss, controlling appetite or desire for sweets, controlling addictions or illicit drug use, and improving stamina, memory, or reaction time.

Meat grown from plants.   Researchers continue trying to develop hybrid plants to serve as meat substitutes, but a more direct breakthrough could soon yield pork, chicken, and beef plants.

In Boulder, Colorado, a company called Somatogen is in a competitive race to produce the first FDA-approved artificial blood product. Plants grown using this blood as the primary source of nutrition (instead of water) could begin to exhibit a mammalian type of growth. There may also be other bio-cloning formulations that will accomplish the same thing. And there is definitely a ready market for plant-grown beef among vegetarians and cardiac patients.

Overlooked Ideas

There are also a number of significant technologies already invented   12
but generally overlooked. Some concepts are already being developed; others may be tied up in legal or funding battles. Here are two ideas that are within the scope of current technology and have the potential to reshape the thinking in several industries:

Spherical-shaped computer display.   Computers come in different   13
colors and sizes, but all computer displays are limited to the same basic shape: the rectangular screen. This configuration hasn't substantially changed since Philo Farnsworth's invention of the television was commercialized in the 1950s. Some would say that operating a computer program with our present monitors is like trying to watch a baseball game through a knothole.

A spherical display will have unique applications for computer   14
users who need to observe the surface of the earth or some other planet. Travel agents will easily plan and display complicated international itineraries by means of a true-shaped image of the earth. Meteorologists will broadcast a real-time global view of weather patterns that will appear on a globe sitting on your desk.

Computers that read aloud.   Systems already exist for visually   15
tracking eye movement; at the same time, talking computers are making inroads. It won't be long before we have a device that combines these technologies in order to pronounce words as a reader reads them. Such devices will have tremendous value in teaching students to read and to understand foreign languages. They will also create a multisensory learning experience for anyone reading a book, vastly improving levels of information retention.

Examining the Reading

Finding Meaning

1. What are the goals of the DaVinci Institute?
2. What are some of the DaVinci Institute's predictions for future computers?
3. How might the brain be controlled without the use of drugs?
4. List several medical applications of brain control.
5. What would be the advantages of meat grown from plants?

Understanding Technique

1. This essay lacks a conclusion. Write a conclusion that could be added to the essay.
2. How do the authors make future inventions clear and understandable to readers who lack a background in technology?

Thinking Critically

1. How do you think medical algorithms can be used to treat alcoholism?
2. What other uses might be developed for artificial blood?
3. How is the technology described in the "Computers That Read Aloud" section different from systems that already exist, such as computers that recognize and pronounce text for blind people?
4. What do the authors mean when they say, "operating a computer program with our present monitors is like trying to watch a baseball game through a knothole"? How will spherical displays be an improvement?
5. What additional information about one or more of these future inventions do you wish the authors had included?

Writing About the Reading

A Journal Entry

Imagine that you are a college student fifty years in the future. Write a journal entry describing a typical day at school.

A Paragraph

1. The authors describe how the brain might be controlled to treat certain physical problems. Write a paragraph describing another way this type of technology might be used.
2. Technology advances rapidly. Write a paragraph describing an example of a major technological change you have experienced since your childhood.

An Essay

1. As computers become more and more humanlike in the future, how do you think relationships between people will be affected? Write an essay describing some possible changes.

2. Write an essay describing a technological advance you would like to see in your lifetime. Explain how this invention would benefit humanity.

A Creative Activity

Suppose you could subscribe to a computer personality service. Who would you choose for your computer's personality? Write the dialogue of a conversation you might have with your computer.

Dr. Dolphin

▶ Richard Blow

Scientific research often leads to life-saving discoveries. This reading explores the fascinating use of dolphins as therapy for humans. Blow's essay appeared in a recent issue of Mother Jones *magazine.*

Reading Strategy

When you have finished reading, list the potential benefits of swimming with dolphins. Then write a brief explanation of how these benefits occur.

Vocabulary Preview

cadre (2) tightly knit group
proponents (3) supporters
black holes (4) regions of space-time from which nothing can escape
visionaries (4) people who develop ideas that seem unlikely but prove true
simulate (5) imitate
obviating (5) doing away with
prototype (6) original model; first of its kind
ambient (6) surrounding; encircling
sonar (19) method of locating objects using sound waves
echolocate (19) use sounds that are reflected back to determine the direction and location of objects
resonates (20) echoes; vibrates
bolster (23) support; make stronger

David Cole knows that people consider him a little odd. Cole spends much of his free time swimming with dolphins, and he has enough perspective to realize that this makes him, by most people's standards, eccentric. He doesn't mind.

Cole, a 28-year-old computer scientist, lives about half an hour south of Los Angeles. With excitable gray eyes and long brown hair in ringlets, he looks a little like a youthful Michael Bolton. Cole works for a computer hardware manufacturer, but in his spare time he heads the

AquaThought Foundation, a cadre of computer wizards, doctors, and naturalists researching "dolphin-assisted therapy."

For about two decades, physical therapists and psychologists have argued that swimming with dolphins can help the sick and handicapped. Dolphin-assisted therapy seems to accelerate the vocal and physical development of autistic and mentally retarded children, for example. Some researchers claim that dolphin swims also boost the human immune system. Most proponents of the therapy say it helps patients' psychological well-being; the dolphins distract them from their suffering.   3

But Cole doesn't buy this conventional wisdom. He rejects the idea that dolphins make humans feel better simply by making them happy. That's what clowns are for. Cole believes that swimming with dolphins can have a profound *physiological* effect on humans. The health of your immune system, the state of your brain, the makeup of your cells—these things, Cole believes, can be radically altered by dolphins.   4

To the layperson, all this might sound a little nutty. (Acquaintances who knew I was working on this article kept making "Flipper" jokes.) But then, black holes and cloning and artificial intelligence seemed nutty, too—except to the people who believed in them, and who turned one day from daydreamers into visionaries.   5

Cole asks me to try Cyberfin, a "virtual reality interaction" he invented to simulate swimming with dolphins. Eventually he hopes to make Cyberfin realistic enough to substitute for the real thing, helping humans who can't afford a dolphin swim and obviating the need for captive dolphins.   6

Cole has fashioned his prototype from a converted flotation tank in his garage. Three-D goggles strapped around my head, I lie down on a water mattress inside the tank. Directly overhead is a television monitor; ambient, surreal music pulses from speakers. I feel a little silly, like I'm about to fight the Red Baron, but I try to keep an open mind.   7

The screen lights up, and suddenly I'm floating in a pool. Two dolphins cavort in the water, zipping by one side of me, a stream of bubbles in their wake. Their whirs and clicks surround me. As I watch, my skepticism fades into curiosity and wonder. One of them swims directly up to my face, and instinctively I shake my head, thinking I'm about to be bumped. Then, with a flip of its tail, the dolphin disappears.   8

Ordinarily, I would never admit this. But I find myself hoping that it will come back soon.   9

Cole grew up in Winter Park, Fla., not far from NASA. After graduating from the University of Central Florida in 1988, he founded a software company called Studiotronics. A year later, Cole hooked up with a   10 group that was conducting dolphin-assisted therapy with cancer patients. They told Cole that the dolphins seemed to have a profound effect on the mental states of their patients; Cole offered to perform neurological tests to see what was going on.

"At first I thought our equipment was not working," Cole remembers. "We were using a fairly conventional statistical evaluation of EEG—'This is your brain, this is your brain on dolphins.' The level of change was like nothing I'd ever seen."   11

Essentially, Cole found a far greater harmony between the left and right sides of the brain after a subject swam with dolphins—a crude suggestion that the brain is functioning more efficiently than normal.   12

When Cole studied the medical literature to try to explain this phenomenon, he couldn't find anything. So in 1991 Cole sold Studiotronics to a Japanese company called Chinon, moved to California, and founded AquaThought with a colleague. Though he now works for Chinon, the company gives him all the time he needs to pursue his dolphin research. To facilitate that research, he and a colleague invented a device called MindSet. Looking like a bathing cap with electrodes attached to it, MindSet translates brain waves into real-time images; the fluctuating brain waves are projected onto a computer screen, and the resulting picture bears some resemblance to a lava lamp. The pair created the device because they couldn't afford a $75,000 EEG.   13

Three years after founding AquaThought, Cole thinks he has figured out why dolphins have beneficial effects on humans. He warns, however, that a lot of people aren't going to believe what he has to say.   14

Cole isn't the first freethinker to be obsessed with dolphins. He's a disciple of futurist writer and scientist John Lilly, who in 1975 founded the Human/Dolphin Foundation to explore the possibility of interspecies communication. (Lilly himself believed he was following in the footsteps of Aristotle, who had an interest in dolphins.) The dolphins he was studying, Lilly wrote in his 1978 work "Communication between Man and Dolphin," "would do anything to convince the humans that they were sentient and capable."   15

The field of dolphin-assisted therapy was probably started by Dr. Betsy Smith, an educational anthropologist at Florida International University. In 1971 Smith, who was researching dolphin-human interaction, let her mentally retarded brother wade into the water with two adolescent dolphins. "They were pretty rough dolphins," Smith remembers. But not with her brother. "The dolphins were around him, still, gentle, rubbing on him." Somehow, they knew he was different.   16

There are now 150 dolphin-assisted therapy researchers worldwide, and there seems little doubt that dolphin swims can help   17 humans with disabilities such as Down's syndrome, autism, depression, attention deficit disorder, muscular dystrophy, and spinal cord injuries. Mentally retarded children who swam with dolphins, for example, "learned their lessons two to 10 times faster than in a normal classroom setting," says Chris Harre of the Dolphin Research Center in Grassy Key, Fla.

18   Other researchers have found that swimming with dolphins boosts the production of infection-fighting T cells. The generally accepted theory is that swimming with dolphins increases relaxation, which helps stimulate the immune system.

19   Such vague psychological explanations drive Cole crazy; he calls them "horseshit," though he's not a very good swearer. Cole doesn't deny that relaxation helps T cell production. ("I could send you to Tahiti for a week, and your T cell count would probably go up," he says.) But Cole believes that relaxation can't explain the changes in brain waves and blood chemistry in humans who've swum with dolphins.

20   Cole thinks these changes are caused by dolphins' sonar, which they use to scan the water around them. The sonar is incredibly precise; dolphins can "echolocate" a shark half a mile away in the ocean and determine whether its stomach is full or empty—and, consequently, whether it might be feeding.

21   "The dolphins produce an intense amount of echolocation energy," Cole says. "It resonates in your bones. You can feel it pass through you and travel up your spine."

22   Cole's theory is too complicated to do justice here, but it goes basically like this: A dolphin's sonar can cause a phenomenon called cavitation, a ripping apart of molecules. (You see it in everyday life when, for example, you throw the throttle of a speedboat all the way down, but the boat doesn't move; for that second, the propeller is cavitating the water.)

23   "It's very possible that dolphins are causing cavitation inside soft tissue in the body," Cole says. "And if they did that with cellular membranes which are the boundaries between cells, they could completely change biomolecules." That could mean stimulating the production of T cells or the release of endorphins, hormones that prompt deep relaxation.

24   Someday, Cole says, scientists may be able to replicate dolphin sonar and use it in a precise, targeted way to bolster the immune system. But for now, he says, "the dolphin is a part of the experience."

25   In the cloudy water, I hear the dolphins before I see them: whirs, clicks, and buzzes fill the water.

26   To find out what it's really like to swim with dolphins, I have come to Dolphins Plus in Key Largo. It's a family-run place, surpris-

ingly small, a suburban house that borders a canal with several large holding pens fenced off. (The dolphins can swim in the canal, but they always return to the pens.) Half an hour in the water costs $75, but before we can take the plunge we are given some guidelines. We are asked not to touch the dolphins; if they want to, they will touch us. We should swim with our hands at our sides, and avoid swimming directly at or behind the dolphins, which they might interpret as hostile. Dolphins generally like children best, women after that, and men last.

27   Equipped with flippers, mask, and snorkel, I slide off the dock. I can see only a few yards in the murky water. I am so nervous that I worry I won't be able to breathe through the snorkel, but my breath eventually settles into a steady rattle.

28   Quickly come the dolphin noises, seeming to feel me out. Still, I see nothing. Suddenly, there is a flash of white and gray to my side; a few moments later, a dolphin passes below me. It looks even larger in the water than it does on the surface.

29   The next time one passes, I dive down. As instructed, I try to make eye contact; for a few seconds the dolphin and I are swimming eye to eye, looking at and—I would swear to it—thinking about each other. These are not just cute, lovable puppy eyes; there's an intelligence here.

30   More dolphins swim by me, moving too fast for me to keep up. As they swim, huge yet graceful in the water, I am acutely aware of my human clumsiness, and grateful that these animals are letting me swim with them. I can't resist the temptation to wave slowly, hoping that they'll understand the gesture. (This is not so bad: One woman sang "Happy birthday, dear dolphin" through her snorkel for her entire half hour.)

31   The dolphins swim so close that I'm convinced I'll bump into them, but somehow they always keep an inch, two, three, between us. The temptation to touch them is great, yet resistable. Corny as it sounds, I want them to like me. To touch them would be like coughing at the opera.

32   At one point I am swimming with a mother and calf; the mother makes eye contact with me, and suddenly I feel it: the zap of the dolphin echolocating me, almost like an electric shock. This, I decide later, is what telepathy must feel like: You hear a sound in your head, but it didn't get there through your ears. It startles me, and I stop swimming. The dolphin opens her mouth, seeming to smile, and she and her calf dart away.

33   When I get out of the water after 30 fleeting minutes, I feel an incredible calm. I wonder if there is a purely psychological explanation—the magic of the experience affecting me. But it feels deeper than that. Somehow, my body feels different. At this moment, I think David Cole is right.

A woman who was swimming with me sits down. She puts her face   34
in her hands and begins sobbing quietly. "I thought I would be all
right," she says to a companion. I never do find out what she means.

Not everyone likes the idea that swimming with dolphins helps hu-   35
mans. Animal rights groups are concerned that such a theory could
lead to an explosion in the number of captured dolphins. "We don't feel
it's right," says Jenny Woods of People for the Ethical Treatment of Animals. "The animal has to be caged for the program to work."

Cole and other dolphin researchers share this concern. Betsy   36
Smith, for example, has given up swimming with captive dolphins and
now only swims with dolphins in the wild. (One concern of Smith's is
that echolocation is less common among captive dolphins. When I tell
her that I was echolocated, she says the dolphin must have found
something about me interesting. "That's flattering," I remark. "Not
necessarily," she says. "It may have been a tumor.")

For his part, Cole is trying hard to perfect Cyberfin, so people can   37
virtually swim with dolphins.

Smith and Cole may be racing against time. As more and more   38
people hear of dolphins' therapeutic effects, the desire to exploit the
animals for a quick buck will spread.

But to Cole, this is not a reason to stop working with dolphins. He   39
wants to establish a permanent dolphin research facility, something
that doesn't exist right now. "We're not looking for a magic bullet," Cole
says. "We're looking for ways of interfering with the progression of disease. It's virgin territory."

And if it means that people think he's a little odd—well, David Cole   40
can live with that.

Examining the Reading

Finding Meaning

1. What does the term *dolphin-assisted therapy* mean?
2. To what do most professionals attribute the positive effects of
   dolphin-assisted therapy?
3. According to Cole, how do dolphins make people feel better?
4. According to researcher Dr. Betsy Smith, dolphins may be able to
   help people with what disabilities?
5. Cole believes that swimming with dolphins has physiological effects
   on humans. After the author swims with dolphins, what does he
   conclude about the effect? What effects have occurred in others?
6. What is Cyberfin?

Understanding Technique

1. Evaluate Blow's sentence structure. How does he use it to add variety and interest to the essay?
2. The middle portion of the essay is written in the first person (I, me), while the first and last sections are written in the third person (he, Cole, etc.). Usually a writer uses one point of view consistently throughout the essay. What is the effect of not doing so?

Thinking Critically

1. Discuss why animal rights groups don't like the idea of people swimming with dolphins (or don't like Cole's research).
2. What is Cole's real (or long-range) goal in conducting his research?
3. What does the author mean when he says this about swimming with dolphins: "To touch [dolphins] would be like coughing at the opera."
4. What does the article imply about the effect of relaxation on the immune system? Explain your answer.

Writing About the Reading

A Journal Entry

Generate a list of questions you would like to ask David Cole about dolphins and their behavior.

A Paragraph

1. Imagine that you get paid to invent products and services that would help people who have physical or mental disabilities. Write a paragraph describing what you would like to invent and how it would be beneficial to people.
2. Write a paragraph explaining how you think Cole would react to a proposed federal law that would ban all animal research.

An Essay

1. The author makes a point of reminding the reader that certain scientific theories that originally seemed "nutty" ended up being factual. He cites black holes, cloning, and artificial intelligence as examples. Did you or a family member ever have an idea that other people thought was "nutty" but that turned out to be reasonable? Write a story that explains your idea and the reaction it received.

2. Assume that further research discovers that swimming with dolphins can cure certain types of cancers. What types of problems do you see? What types of rules and regulations would be needed? Write an essay exploring potential problems.

A Creative Activity

Assume that you are an animal rights activist who is opposed to the use of dolphins for research and therapy. Write a letter to Blow outlining your objections.

When Is a Parent a Parent?

▶ **Danuta Bukatko and Marvin W. Daehler**
Textbook Excerpt

When technology is used in the human reproductive process, some difficult issues may be raised. This reading from a textbook, Child Development, *explores these issues.*

Reading Strategy

List medical procedures that can be performed to enable humans to reproduce. Define each and summarize the legal, social, or medical controversy each raises.

Vocabulary Preview

notions (1) ideas
tangle (1) confused mess
anonymous (2) unknown
prospective (2) future
ovulation (2) the release of eggs from an ovary
conceived (2) come into being
rural (3) country
inadvertently (3) unintentionally
gestational period (4) time of pregnancy
relinquish (5) give up
controversies (6) issues; disputes

Recent advances in the field of genetics and reproductive technol-   1
ogy have revolutionized human conception and childbearing along with our traditional notions about definitions of parenthood. Couples at risk for bearing children with a genetic disease or those among the one in six estimated to be unable to have children now can explore many options, in addition to adoption, in their efforts to become parents. Each new alternative brings hope to many couples but raises a tangle of ethical and legal issues as well.

If a male carries a genetic disorder or is infertile, couples may elect   2
artificial insemination by donor. In this procedure, a donor, usually

anonymous and often selected because of his similarity in physical and other characteristics to a prospective father, contributes sperm that are then artificially provided to the mother when ovulation occurs. Some six thousand to ten thousand children are thought to be conceived by this means every year in the United States.

There is little information about how donors are chosen and screened or how they subsequently feel about being the possible biological father to an unknown number of children. Donors in rural areas have voiced concerns that their known children might inadvertently marry and bear offspring with unknown half-siblings. In addition, whereas adopted children are often informed that they have been adopted, children born via artificial insemination are seldom aware that their legal and biological fathers are not the same person. Even if they are told, however, these children would typically be unable to obtain further information since the approximately thirty sperm banks currently operating in the United States rarely make their records public.

If a female is the carrier of a genetic disease or is infertile, options include *surrogate motherhood* and *in vitro fertilization*. Surrogate motherhood has sometimes been termed the "renting" of another woman's womb, but this concept is a bit misleading in many cases since the surrogate mother often donates an egg for prenatal development as well as her womb. The surrogate is thus the biological mother as well as bearer of the child who has been conceived by artificial insemination using the prospective father's sperm. For in vitro fertilization, eggs are removed from a woman's ovaries, fertilized in a laboratory dish with the prospective father's sperm, then transferred to another woman's uterus. In this situation, biological and social mother may be one and the same except during the gestational period when a surrogate mother's womb is used. Alternatively, a woman who cannot conceive normally might undergo in vitro fertilization and carry her own or another woman's fertilized egg during her pregnancy.

Legal, medical, and social controversy swirl around both surrogate motherhood and in vitro fertilization. Legal debates center on who is the rightful father or mother. In one highly publicized case in the United States involving Baby M, a woman was impregnated by artificial insemination by a man whose wife was afflicted by multiple sclerosis. According to a contract, the surrogate mother was to receive $10,000 for carrying the child. At birth, she would then surrender the child to the couple for adoption. After delivery, however, she refused to relinquish custody of the child. Who should be the legal parent? In the Baby M case, the court ruled against the surrogate mother. In another recent case in California, the court ruled that a baby conceived from a woman's egg and her husband's sperm via in vitro fertilization and carried to term by another woman should be reared by the genetic couple rather than the surrogate mother. Yet the debate surrounding these and similar cases continues as judicial systems try to resolve who is the legal parent: the genetic, the gestational, or the caregiving or social mother.

Other controversies surround the costly medical procedures and complicated ethical and social issues associated with in vitro fertilization and surrogate motherhood. For example, perhaps as many as two hundred clinics in the United States and many more in other countries, often operating as commercial businesses, provide in vitro fertilization services. But perhaps less than 20 percent of their attempts result in live births. Should medical insurance pay the high costs associated with these attempts? Will these new technologies lead to increased pressures to use genetic engineering to ensure only healthy offspring?   6

The desire to have their own children is a powerful motive for most couples. New advances in reproductive technology will help many to reach that goal, yet they cause dilemmas that many nations have not fully resolved.   7

Examining the Reading

Finding Meaning

1. Suppose a couple chooses artificial insemination by donor. How is the donor selected?
2. What is meant by surrogate motherhood?
3. How is surrogate motherhood different from in vitro fertilization?
4. What is the difference between the genetic mother and the gestational mother?
5. How can this type of advanced technology cause a legal problem?
6. Are there other problems associated with these new reproductive procedures? What are they?

Understanding Technique

1. Identify and highlight the authors' thesis.
2. Describe the authors' tone (how they feel about their subject).
3. Evaluate the essay's title. How does it reflect the essay's content?

Thinking Critically

1. The authors of the article suggest that, in the case of surrogate motherhood, there is a question regarding who is the legal parent.

In your opinion, who should be the legal parent—the genetic, the gestational, or the caregiving mother?
2. In the case of artificial insemination by donor, there are medical and ethical concerns regarding whether the child should be told how he or she was conceived and by whom. What do you think the child should be told, if anything?
3. The reading states that donors are often anonymous and that "sperm banks . . . rarely make their records public." Do you think sperm banks that provide such services should be required by law to reveal this information to the couple? Why or why not?
4. In the case of Baby M, do you think the court should have ruled for or against the surrogate mother?
5. Because of the legal, medical, and ethical ways in which reproductive technologies affect the child, do you think such technologies should be practiced? Justify your answer.

Writing About the Reading

A Journal Entry

Write an entry describing how you would feel if you discovered you were conceived by artificial insemination from an anonymous donor.

A Paragraph

1. Write a paragraph explaining the legal complications of surrogate motherhood.
2. Imagine that you or your wife was to be a surrogate mother. Would you be able to give up the child you or your wife carried for nine months? Write a paragraph explaining your feelings.

An Essay

1. Imagine that you are married, you desire a child, and you or your spouse is infertile. Which reproductive technology would you try first and why? Write an essay explaining your decision.
2. In the case of in vitro fertilization, who do you think should have legal guardianship over the child—the biological parents or the surrogate parents? Write an essay explaining your answer.

A Creative Activity

Paragraph 6 raises the question of whether medical insurance should pay the high costs associated with reproductive technology. Write an essay exploring the pros and cons of this issue.

Technology Is a Racket

▶ **Marianne J. Collins**
Student Essay

In the following essay, Collins, a first-year college student, complains about the intrusion of modern technology and expresses her desire to live in a quieter world.

I don't know about anyone else, but I'm "all noised out." This is due 1
to the fact that every time I turn around, some so-called advanced form of technology is beeping or ringing or sing-songing some noise I never asked to hear. I want to go back in time. This may seem like an odd idea for a teenaged college student to propose, but I want to go back to my parents' era, an apparently noiseless period that young people of my generation can only dream about. This was a time when people had more time to think and create because they weren't busily blocking out the sounds of their world with Discmans, Walkmans, and Watchmans. This was a time when technology had not yet designed such antisocial devices.

Perhaps you are wondering why I consider such modern gadgets to 2
be antisocial, so let me explain. Each of these "mans," silent though it may seem, has two problems. First, their users become totally immersed in the music, eliminating any possibility of meaningful social interaction with humans. Second, they are not always silent, since the people who wear them generally have them turned up so loud that everyone nearby can hear them, too. The same is true of computers. Every time I work on a paper in the college's computer center, I am bombarded with some shrill or otherwise uproarious sing-song noise coming from another computer near me. I am subjected to this because the student sitting at that computer tapped into some program playing an electronically jazzed up version of "happy birthday to you," usually in triplicate. This has a purely antisocial effect on every student in the room. By the time the tune finally ends, every student in the center is glaring at the offender, who merely sits with shoulders shrugged and palms upturned in a gesture of helplessness, which is the trademark of the technologically puzzled.

And it doesn't end there. I am reminded of this every time I enter a 3
department store and have my concentration promptly interrupted by

some annoyingly repetitive signals declaring that a salesclerk is needed or wanted or somehow unaccounted for, that is, *if* I am permitted to enter the store in the first place. I say this in reference to those occasions, and there have been more than a few, when I have been carrying in my purse an item from home or somewhere else entirely, that sets off that dreaded buzzer that stores now employ for the sake of trapping would-be thieves. When the management sees that I'm not even in the store yet, I am allowed to enter, but not before I have suffered the hate-filled glance of every single patron who understandably mistakes me for a shoplifter. This may sound like a humorous experience but, trust me, it is not. It *is* a humiliating experience that is caused by modern technology gone wrong.

I want to live in a world that doesn't beep or buzz or bother me   4
with nonessentials. I want to walk into a store in Buffalo on a wintry Sunday without hearing a football game blaring on the radio. After all, this is why I shop on Sunday: to get away from the broadcasting of the Buffalo Bills' football game. I want to wait while the mechanic changes the tires on my car without being subjected to some sappy soap opera blasting on the television set in the waiting room. I want to attend a class just once without being disturbed by a student's cell phone ringing. I want to jog on the indoor track of the college gym in the morning and not be deafened by the sound of people's pagers going off constantly.

In short, I want peace and quiet. I am not talking here about the   5
"peace" my mom and dad say they searched for in the 60s. I'm talking about the kind of peace that can only come from living in a world where private thoughts are respected more than external stimulation. It's not that I want to be alone or isolated from the world; it's just that I'd like to live in the world quietly some of the time. I'd like to go about my business calmly and gently, without the racket connected with all this technology that has turned a previously quiet world into a hubbub of auditory chaos.

Examining the Essay

1. Is Collins's title effective? List several other possible titles.
2. Does Collins use topic sentences to structure her paragraphs? Highlight each.
3. List at least five transitions that Collins uses to connect ideas within the essay.
4. What are Collins's strengths as a writer? Where do you see evidence of these strengths?

Writing an Essay

1. In this essay, Collins complains about noise pollution. Write an essay discussing whether you feel visual pollution is a problem in our society. You might consider billboards, political campaign posters, and other sources of visual pollution.
2. Write an essay explaining what steps can be taken to control the amount of noise pollution in our lives.
3. Collins observes that using certain technological devices such as Walkmans is antisocial. Write an essay describing additional ways that people discourage others from talking or interacting with them.

 ## Making Connections

1. "Stepping Through a Computer Screen, Disabled Veterans Savor Freedom" and "Virtual Love" are both concerned with the use of computers. Write an essay comparing the ways in which computers are used in each reading.

2. Reconsider the following articles: "Dr. Dolphin," "Inventing the Future," and "When Is a Parent a Parent?" In each article, the author discusses new or future directions for the application of technology. Write an essay explaining how feasible you feel each new use of technology to be. Make projections about which applications will be in widespread use in twenty-five years and which will not.

3. Can there be too much technology? Consider the messages of "The Seven Sustainable Wonders of the World," "Inventing the Future," and "Technology Is a Racket."

Glossary

analyze To examine carefully and closely, to determine why something has happened or can be expected to happen.

annotate To write notes or comments in response or reaction to what you read.

argument A set of ideas that states a position (or claim) and offers reasons and evidence in support of that position.

biased One-sided; prejudiced.

brainstorming A method of developing ideas by writing a list of everything that comes to mind about the topic.

chronological sequence A method of organizing ideas according to the order in which they happen.

compare To discover how two or more persons or things are alike and how they differ.

conclusion The ending of an essay that draws it to a close and often reemphasizes the thesis statement; a decision, judgment or opinion reached by reasoning.

describe To provide a picture or account of something in words.

details Specific information that explains a topic sentence; particulars.

develop To make bigger, fuller, or more complete by providing greater detail.

dialogue Conversation between two or more people.

discuss To consider many aspects of a topic; to talk over.

evaluate To consider the worth, value, or importance of something.

evidence Facts that show why something is true or not true; proof.

highlight To mark important information using a wide-tipped pen.

illustrate To make clear or to explain using stories, examples, comparisons, etc.

implied thesis A thesis that is suggested but not directly stated in the essay.

imply (implied) To suggest, but not to state directly; to mean without saying so.

introduction The opening of an essay that identifies the topic and often presents the thesis statement. It may also interest the reader.

justify To demonstrate that something is correct or right; to give reasons for or to defend.

opinion A belief; what one thinks about something.

organization The arrangement or sequence of ideas in a paragraph or essay.

point of view The perspective from which a story is told; the relationship between the narrator of the story and the story itself.

sentence structure The arrangement or order of the parts of a sentence.

structure (n). Arrangement or order of ideas.

subject (n). A general or broad topic.

summarize To express only the main points.

technique The method, skill, or system a writer uses to compose and express ideas.

theme A statement a piece of literature seems to be making about its subject.

thesis statement The main point of an essay; a sentence that identifies and explains what an essay will be about.

tone The attitude of the author toward the subject matter (examples: serious, apologetic, humorous, angry).

topic sentence A sentence that states the main idea of a paragraph; the one idea that all the details in a paragraph explain.

transitions Words or phrases that connects ideas within a paragraph or essay.

Index for Authors and Titles

Credits

Chapter 1   LAURA CUNNINGHAM   "The Chosen One" by Laura Cunningham. Copyright 1994 by Laura Cunningham. Reprinted by permission of William Morris Agency, Inc. on behalf of the Author; ERIC ZICKLIN Excerpt from "Mod Jobs: Strange and Twisted Paths to Contentment and Prosperity" by Eric Zicklin from *Rolling Stone*, October 20, 1994. By Straight Arrow Publishers Company, L.P. 1994. All Rights Reserved. Reprinted by Permission; PAUL CHANCE   Source: Paul Chance, "I'm OK; You're a Bit Odd," *Psychology Today*, July/August 1988. Reprinted with permission from *Psychology Today Magazine*, copyright 1992 (Sussex Publishers, Inc.); JENNIFER S. DICKMAN   Used with permision from Jennifer S. Dickman, *Nursing95* 25 (2): 26, Springhouse Corporation; ANNA QUINDLEN   From *Thinking Out Loud* by Anna Quindlen. Copyright 1993 by Anna Quindlen. Reprinted by permission of Random House, Inc.; SAUL KASSIN   Source: From Kassin, Saul *Psychology*, 1/e. Copyright 1995 by Houghton Mifflin Company. Used with permission.

Chapter 2   MARTA SALINAS   Marta Salinas, "The Scholarship Jacket" from *Nosotras: Latina Literature Today* (1986), edited by Maria del Carmen Boza, Beverly Silva, and Carmen Valle. Copyright 1986 by Bilingual Press/Editorial Belingue, Arizona State University, Tempe, AZ. Reprinted by permission; MICHAEL DATCHER   "Under the Overpass" by Michael Datcher from Image, December 1994, p.64; SIU WAI ANDERSON   From *Making Face, Making Soul/Haciendo Caras: Creative and Critical Perspectives by Feminists of Color*, 1990 by Gloria Anzaldua; IAN FRAZIER   Ian Frazier; "To Mr. Winslow," from *The New Yorker*; Nov. 29, 1993, p. 166. Reprinted with permission of the author; JONATHAN ROSEN   "Breaking Glass" by Jonathan Rosen, *New York Times Magazine*, November 18, 1996. Reprinted by permission of the author; CAROL BERKIN, CHRISTOPHER L. MILLER, ROBERT W. CHERNY, AND JAMES L. GORMLY   Source: From Berkin, Carol, Christopher L. Miller, Robert W. Cherny, and James L. Gormly, *Making America: A History of the United States*, 1/e. Copyright 1995 by Houghton Mifflin Company. Used with permission.

Chapter 3   DANIEL LEVINE   Reprinted with permission from the January 1998 Reader's Digest. Copyright 1998 by The Reader's Digest Assn., Inc.; SABRA CHARTRAND   "Working Students Need to Look for Career Experience" by Sabra Chartrand, *The New York Times*, September 14, 1997. Copyright 1997 by The New York Times. Reprinted by permission; DAVID MAS MASUMOTO   "The Family Farm" adapted from *Epitaph for a Peach* by David Mas Masumoto. Copyright 1995 by David Mas Masumoto. Reprinted by permission of HarperCollins Publishers, Inc.; JANE KEUNZ   From *South Atlantic Quarterly*, Vol. 92, No. 1 (Winter 1993) as "It's a Small World After All: Disney and the Pleasures of Identification."

256